# CLEFT PALATE
## THE NATURE AND REMEDIATION OF COMMUNICATION PROBLEMS

EDITED BY

## JACKIE STENGELHOFEN DipCST, DTST, MEd, MCST

Director of Studies, School of Speech Therapy, Department of Health Sciences, Birmingham Polytechnic.
Tutor in Speech and Language Pathology, Department of Children's Dentistry and Orthodontics,
The Dental School, University of Birmingham

**W**

Whurr Publishers
London

© 1993 Whurr Publishers Ltd
19b Compton Terrace, London N1 2UN, England

First published by Churchill Livingstone 1989
All right acquired by Whurr Publishers Ltd 1993

**British Library Cataloguing in Publication Data**
A catalogue record for this book is available from the
British Library.

ISBN 1-897635-05-2
(previously published by Churchill Livingstone under
ISBN 0-443-03869-4)

Typeset by Longman Singapore Publishers (Pte) Ltd
Printed and bound in the UK by Athenaeum Press Ltd,
Newcastle upon Tyne

*To the many children with cleft palate, their parents and professional colleagues with whom I have had the privilege to work: in particular to Don Foster for his support and encouragement in many aspects of my work.*

# Preface

The field of speech and language pathology is wide and draws on insights from medical and behavioural sciences. There are difficulties in addressing a topic such as cleft palate, which although identifiable as a clinical entity, demands the knowledge and skills from a number of disciplines to provide appropriate management. In some of the literature on cleft palate there has been a tendency to focus on the biological, medical and surgical aspects of the problems. Medicine has a major role to play, for example in ENT, radiographic, surgical and orthodontic provision. However, in the management of the communication problems associated with this condition, knowledge and procedures from other fields need to be drawn on, for example insights provided by the linguistic sciences make a major contribution to the description of speech and language problems, thus forming an essential base on which intervention procedures can be developed.

In a book of this nature, dealing with a complex problem which is managed by a range of professionals, it is difficult to identify the boundaries of interest and concern. I have chosen to make the main focus of the book the identification of the nature, the assessment and remediation of communication problems. It is not possible to cover in depth such areas as details of embryological development, normal anatomy and physiology, accounts of primary and secondary surgical procedures and orthodontic intervention, nor indeed is it necessary, as these have already been extensively covered in many excellent texts: of note is the volume by Edwards and Watson (1980). The present volume is placed in the total context of management. It will refer to procedures not undertaken by the speech and language specialist as a backcloth to speech and language management rather than as main themes. Reference to various procedures are integrated into the case studies included in most chapters.

The majority of contributors to this volume are speech therapists who have extensive clinical experience with individuals with cleft palate. Most work within 'cleft palate teams' and are therefore fully committed to team work in this field. Nonetheless, they are aware that not all clinicians have the opportunity to be part of a team identified in this way. The 'standard' case load of a general speech therapy practitioner is likely to contain only a few cleft palate cases and even fewer cases with developmental or acquired velopharyngeal incompetence from other causes. Thus general speech therapy practitioners frequently feel a great lack of confidence in working in this field. Then, instead of examining the high level generic knowledge and skills already within their competence, they tend to think that they have very little to offer. This volume has been prepared particularly for general speech therapy practitioners and for students of speech and language and linguistic sciences. It should, nonetheless, be of

v

interest and accessible to the cleft palate team—medical, dental, behavioural and family—by demonstrating how other management provisions are an essential foundation for achieving the common goal of acceptable communication for the individual.

Our understanding of the nature and remediation of speech problems is greatly enhanced by knowledge from physiological and instrumental phonetics. A contribution from a specialist in instrumental articulatory phonetics is therefore included. The chapter from the parents serves to remind us all that knowledge and skills offered by professionals can only be used effectively if the family context is taken fully into account in our work with children.

Although the volume focusses mainly on the developmental disorders across a wide age range, the principles of evaluation and remediation are equally applicable to problems of an acquired nature, e.g. progressive neurological disorders and trauma such as maxillectomy.

Successful remediation needs to be based on a thorough understanding of the nature of the original medical condition and how this may lead to problems of communication (Ch. 1), followed by a detailed account of both the subjective and objective evaluation of problems found. Chapter 3, therefore, shows how contributions from all areas of knowledge and skill can be brought together to provide a detailed and scientifically supported analysis of the individual's communication, enabling team planning of procedures tailor-made to individual clients' needs. Procedures such as anemometry, nasendoscopy and speech radiography are fully explained. Management of the infant and toddler is discussed (Ch. 2) on the basis that appropriate early intervention is more likely to ensure adequate communication at least by school entry. This chapter is of interest to all concerned with the welfare of pre-school children. The detailed speech analysis included will be of interest to colleagues in applied linguistics.

Later chapters focus on choice of management approaches and remedial procedures in the routine treatment of articulatory problems (Ch. 4). The use of appliances and training aids in the treatment of speech problems is outlined in Chapter 5. These procedures have particular relevance for the older child, teenager and adult. The chapter is of particular interest to dental colleagues. Chapter 6 shows how the remediation of long-standing entrenched articulatory difficulties, so often a major challenge to clinicians, may be helped by the use of instrumental procedures such as palatography, a chapter which will interest colleagues from articulatory and instrumental phonetics. Although this chapter describes the use of palatography, it also demonstrates how a thorough understanding of the dynamics of the vocal tract and the influence of this on linguo-palatal contacts may lead the clinician to a different focus of remediation. The principles explored are also highly applicable to the work of the speech therapist who does not have access to costly instrumental procedures.

It is worth noting that although general speech examples given in the text and specific phonetic and phonological data in the case studies are taken from English speakers, the principles involved are equally applicable to speakers of any language. The application of these principles can, no doubt, be understood easily in the description and remediation of phonatory and resonatory problems. However, problems at the articulatory level, concerned with how the individual deals with the production of plosives, fricatives, affricates, etc., rest on principles explored in this volume; procedures of analysis and remediation based on such principles can therefore be applied in any language.

The majority of chapters include case studies. These are intended to demonstrate to the practitioner how principles, derived from general theory, can be applied to the particular problems of individual cases. We therefore hope that what is included in this volume will help clinicians to a greater level of confidence in their own practice.

'Learning a theory-of-action so as to become competent in professional practice does not consist of learning to recite a theory: the theory-of-action has not been learned in the most important sense unless it can be put into practice.' (Argyris and Schon 1979, p. 12)

Birmingham, 1989                                    J. S.

## REFERENCES

Argyris C, Schön D 1974 Theory in practice: increasing professional effectiveness. Jossey Bass, San Francisco

Edwards M, Watson A C H 1980, Advances in the management of cleft palate. Churchill Livingstone, Edinburgh

# Acknowledgements

I can remember when, as a student, I purchased Muriel Morley's *Cleft Palate and Speech*, the first volume of which was published by E. S. Livingstone in 1945. Since then there have been six further editions. This is a definitive work still referred to by clinicians and students. At the time of my purchase I did not envisage my future editorial role. I am privileged to continue the tradition of publications in this field. This would not have been possible without the other authors' contributions and support from many colleagues.

I wish to acknowledge the King's Fund for permission to use phonetic representation as described in their Project Paper No. 38, Phonetic Representation of Disordered Speech. (Working Party Report edited by Pam Grunwell 1983, The King's Fund, London).

Sincere thanks are also due to many students at the Birmingham Polytechnic who generously gave constructive comments on early draft chapters, as well as several colleagues for giving their time to provide detailed comments on my own contributions. In particular I wish to thank Val Dinning, Rosemary Hayhow and Bill Wells. Thanks are also due to Don Foster for photographic material, and the Clinical Photography Department at the Birmingham Dental Hospital, and the Educational Development Unit at the Birmingham Polytechnic in the preparation of illustrations.

Thanks are also due to the group of parents who provided many insights included in Chapter 7.

My special thanks to Pam Graham who in the last months provided so much cheerful, unruffled and excellent word processing.

Individual contributors have included further acknowledgements at the end of their own chapters.

J. S.

# Contributors

**Liz Albery** BSc MCST

Chief Speech Therapist, Frenchay Hospital, Bristol

**W. J. Hardcastle** MA DipPhon PhD

Department of Linguistics, University of Reading, Reading

**Christine F. Huskie** DipCST MCST

Chief Speech Therapist, West of Scotland Regional Plastic Surgery Unit, Canniesburn Hospital, Glasgow

**Rosemarie Morgan Barry** BA DipCST MCST

Lecturer in Speech Sciences, The National Hospitals, College of Speech Sciences, University College, London

**Marion Nunn** DipCST MCST

Chief Speech Therapist, The Radcliffe Infirmary, Oxford

**Peter Phillips**

Parent; Past Chairman of Local Cleft Lip and Palate Association Group, West Midlands

**Jane Russell** DipCST MCST

Chief Speech Therapist, The Children's Hospital, Birmingham

**Gill M. Stuffins** DipCST MCST

District Speech Therapist, Dudley Health Authority; Consultant Speech Therapist, Regional Plastic and Jaw Surgery Unit, Wordsley Hospital, Stourbridge, West Midlands

**Jackie Stengelhofen** DipCST DTST MEd MCST

Director of Studies, School of Speech Therapy, Department of Health Sciences, Birmingham Polytechnic, Birmingham

# Contents

**1.** The nature and causes of communication problems in cleft palate   *J. Stengelhofen*   1

**2** Early intervention   *J. Russell*   31

**3** Assessment of speech and language status: subjective
and objective approaches to appraisal of vocal tract structure and function   *C. F. Huskie*   64

**4** Approaches to the treatment of speech problems   *L. Albery*   97

**5** The use of appliances in the treatment of speech problems in cleft palate   *G. M. Stuffins*   111

**6** Instrumental articulatory phonetics in assessment and remediation: case studies with the
electropalatograph   *W. Hardcastle   R. Morgan Barry   M. Nunn*   136

**7** Towards partnership with parents   *P. Phillips   J. Stengelhofen*   165

Index   187

*Congenital clefts of lip and palate*
  *Sub-mucous cleft*

*Other congenital problems affecting velopharyngeal functions*
  *Congenital supra-bulbar paresis*
  *Palatopharyngeal disproportion*
  *Velopharyngeal problems after adenoidectomy*

*The potential for a communication disorder*
  *Speech as an adaptive behaviour*
  *Producing speech sounds*
    *Manner of articulation*
    *Place of articulation*
    *Secondary articulations*

*Factors affecting the development of communication in the cleft palate individual*
  *The timing of surgery*
  *Hearing*
  *The status of the vocal tract*
    *Oro-nasal fistulae*
    *Dental and occlusal problems*
    *Oral sensation and perception*
  *Social factors and the communication context*
  *Intellectual factors*

*Problems in oral communication*
  *Intelligibility*
  *Phonatory and resonatory problems*
    *Phonatory disorders*
    *Resonatory disorders*
    *Nasal emission*
  *Phonetic problems*
  *Phonological problems*
  *Language problems*

*General communication and interaction*

# 1

# The nature and causes of communication problems in cleft palate

*J. Stengelhofen*

This chapter provides the reader with an introductory account of the nature of anomalies of the vocal tract found in cleft lip and palate and some other conditions where the velopharyngeal mechanism is involved. The first section of the chapter describes the features of cleft lip and palate indicating the possible effects on speech. The second section describes other congenital anomalies which affect velopharyngeal function. The third section explores. how children with congenital abnormalities of the vocal tract may be at risk for the development of communication. A wide range of influencing factors is considered, including the timing of surgery, the status of the repaired mechanism, dental and occlusal problems, the role of oral sensation and perception as well as the very important social and psychological factors which influence the development of communication.

## CONGENITAL CLEFTS OF LIP AND PALATE

Congenital cleft of lip and palate may manifest itself in various forms. The mildest form of cleft lip presents as a slight scarring or notching of the vermilion border of the upper

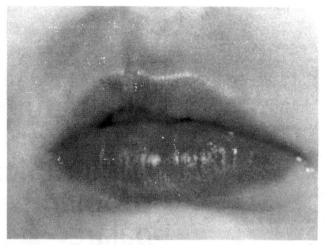

**Fig 1.1** Notching of the vermilion border of the upper lip, natural scar, no surgery

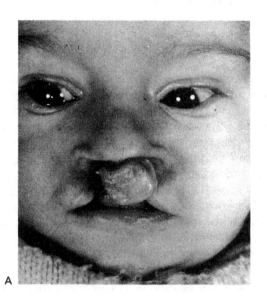

A

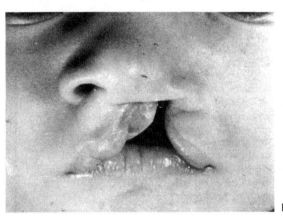

B

**Fig 1.2** (A) Bilateral cleft of lip and alveolus, with forward pre-maxilla. (B) Unilateral cleft of lip and alveolus

lip (Fig. 1.1) while in the severest there is a complete bilateral cleft of lip and alveolus (Fig. 1.2A). If an isolated cleft of lip soft tissue only is involved, the cleft may extend through the fleshy vermilion border of the lip, up through the prolabium towards the nostril, or including the nostril (Fig. 1.2B). This degree of cleft is unlikely to cause a speech problem although an adverse reaction to a difference in appearance may lead to self-consciousness and sometimes difficulties in the development of interpersonal skills. Clefts of lip may be unilateral or bilateral. In more severe clefts of lip the alveolus and dental arch may both be involved. In severe cases clefts in this region may lead to phonetic difficulties in speech. Post-surgery there may be poor sensory feedback in the region of the cleft, particularly in the alveolar ridge, which may result in imprecise articulatory placement. Second dentition may be absent or displaced in the cleft area and may create a space for the tongue to

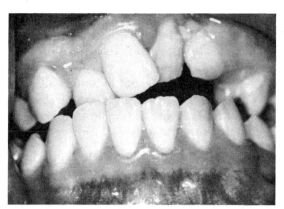

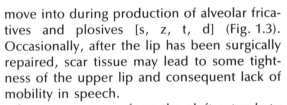

Fig 1.3 Space for tongue to move into in area of alveolar cleft

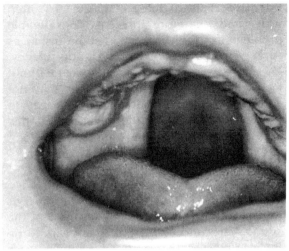

Fig 1.4 Isolated cleft of palate

move into during production of alveolar fricatives and plosives [s, z, t, d] (Fig. 1.3). Occasionally, after the lip has been surgically repaired, scar tissue may lead to some tightness of the upper lip and consequent lack of mobility in speech.

In a more severe form the cleft extends to involve both the hard and soft palate, unilaterally or bilaterally; such defects make major surgical demands. Long-term communication disorders are likely but not inevitable; infants presenting with severe and easily identifiable deformities do not always develop with disorders of communication. In addition to the original deformity many factors affect the development of adequate and acceptable communication, including the timing and outcome of surgery, the presence or absence of other handicapping conditions, the child's intellectual potential and thus his ability to adapt to adverse factors, and the family support available. Most children with cleft lip and palate develop acceptable communication after surgery. Speech therapists and other team members are therefore left with the management of those cases, possibly around 40%, who have long-standing problems leading to deficits in their communication skills. In the U.K. there are an estimated 15 000 cases needing help annually (Enderby & Philipp 1986).

In some instances isolated cleft of the palate

occurs. This is the only type of cleft occurring more commonly in females (Fig. 1.4). It may involve all the soft and hard palate, extending as far forward as the incisive foramen, or may involve only part of the soft palate. The mildest form is a notched or bifid uvula (Fig. 1.5); this may not present any symptomatology either in speech or vegetative functions. Advances in diagnostic procedures, (such as nasendoscopy described in Ch. 3) indicate that the function of the musculus uvulae, which forms the uvula, may be of greater significance in speech than previously understood (Pigott 1969, Shprintzen 1979).

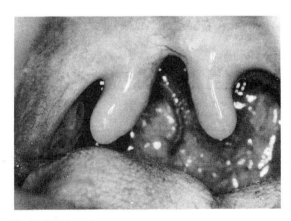

Fig 1.5 Bifid uvula

Extensive clefts of the soft palate are often wide and therefore present considerable problems for the surgeon. In some instances surgery may not be possible during infancy. Therefore, when clefts of palate occur without facial disfigurements, although they may not appear severe, they may nonetheless lead to problems requiring long term surgical, dental and speech management.

### Sub-mucous cleft

This type of cleft occurs below the mucous membrane of the palate; this means that the surface structure of the palate appears to be intact. However, there may be defects of both the muscles and bony structures below the surface (Weatherley-White et al 1972). It is important that the speech clinician bears in mind the possibility of sub-mucous clefting, which may have been undetected in infancy but may become apparent when speech begins to develop. The case history may reveal feeding and nasal regurgitation problems.

On surface examination the palate may appear normal, but on further investigation it may reveal:

1. A bony notch in the hard palate; this may not be seen but can be felt along the posterior border of the hard palate.
2. An opaque line medially in the soft palate, known as the zona pellucida, present because of the lack of muscles below the mucous membrane of the soft palate as well as aberrant muscle insertions. The levator muscles may not connect with the levator sling, their insertion being into the hard palate; this leads to a foreshortening of the soft palate.
3. A bifid-uvula is present in almost all cases. This symptom is easily recognisable and should alert the clinician to examine carefully for other features.

Clefts in the bony hard palate only will not be functionally significant; however, muscle defects may be of considerable significance giving rise to velopharyngeal incompetence and subsequent speech problems.

Early surgery offers the best outcome for muscle defects. However, some authorities are opposed to this approach because cases may develop to be symptom-free (Weatherley-White et al 1972). Some surgeons recommend surgery to safeguard middle ear function. Speech problems found in sub-mucous clefting may be as severe as those found in overt clefts. The prevalence of asymptomatic cases is hard to establish because they are less likely to be identified. Stewart et al (1971) found an incidence of 1:1200 births. These authors report that around 38% of cases have speech problems. Hearing problems often occur and may be another obstacle to the development of normal communication. Excellent and extended accounts of sub-mucous cleft can be found in Bzoch (1979), Edwards & Watson (1980) and McWilliams et al (1984). The most frequently used classification of cleft lip and palate is that by Kernahan and Stark (1958) (see Table 1.1).

**Table 1.1** *Classification of clefts of lip and palate* (Kernahan & Stark 1958)

| Clefts of primary palate | II Clefts of secondary palate | III Clefts of primary and secondary palate |
|---|---|---|
| Lies anterior to the incisive foramen. May involve both lip and alveolus | Cleft of palate only. Lies posterior to the incisive foramen. Ranges from bifid uvula to complete hard and soft palate | Affects both primary and secondary palate. Wide range of manifestations and degrees of severity. |
| 1. Unilateral (Rt or Lt)<br>2. Median<br>3. Bilateral | 1. Total<br>2. Sub-total<br>3. Sub-mucous | 1. Unilateral (Rt or Lt)<br>2. Median<br>3. Bilateral |

## OTHER CONGENITAL PROBLEMS AFFECTING VELOPHARYNGEAL FUNCTIONS

Speech problems related to inadequate velopharyngeal function can be found in cases which do not have either an overt or a submucous cleft. These conditions, when of a congenital nature, are termed congenital palatopharyngeal incompetence (CPI), and have been described by different medical specialisms. Of note is the work by Worster-Drought (1974), a neurologist, and Calnan (1956 & 1971), a plastic surgeon. Knowledge of such conditions is of particular importance to the speech clinician as in the absence of this knowledge the clinican may be confused by the speech symptomatology and so fail to consult appropriate team members to aid differential diagnosis and plan appropriate management. The author has received a number of referrals from general practitioners in speech therapy where there has been uncertainty about the nature of the presenting speech problems. This is understandable as few cases will be encountered in general speech therapy practice.

The speech clinician has a particular interest in CPI or indeed any condition, congenital or acquired, that leads to velopharyngeal incompetence. Efficient functioning of the velopharynx is central in normal speech production. Malfunction may create major disturbance in speech especially at the articulatory, phonatory and resonatory levels. Speech therefore shows many of the features found in cleft palate cases. Knowledge of the whole range of causes of velopharyngeal problems, developmental and acquired, is essential for the speech clinician because symptomatology such as hypernasality in speech may be a first presenting symptom in some acquired disorders, while some congenital problems may not be apparent until speech develops. The speech clinician possesses high level skills in the description of speech and through these may identify problems where the velopharyngeal mechanism is implicated. Investigations undertaken by speech therapists have often accelerated the diagnosis of an acquired neurological disorder. It is important that speech clinicians are aware of the unique skills and knowledge they contribute to the diagnostic process. Minami et al (1975) provide a useful classification of velopharyngeal incompetence. Bradley (1979) reviews the reports of CPI cases, claiming that many 'find their way to cleft palate teams for treatment of palatopharyngeal insufficiency, even though they do not have associated cleft palate'. This is the situation in the States and is also true in the UK. It is not known what happens to the other cases who are presumably unrecognised; some may be having speech intervention or may be seen by medical specialists who are not equipped to recognise the precise nature of the problem. Management by the cleft palate team is in fact entirely appropriate as this team provides the appropriate specialists for evaluation and remediation.

McWilliams et al (1984) treat the congenital anatomical and neurological problems leading to velopharyngeal incompetence separately; this may be confusing as anatomical and neurological features may both occur in the same individual. The groupings are most simply described by Kaplan (1975); he classifies the causes of congenital velopharyngeal incompetence under four different aetiologies:

1. Anatomical disproportion with normal palate function.
2. Muscle dysfunction with normal proportions.
3. A combination of both muscle dysfunction and anatomic disproportions.
4. Another group which does not fit clearly into the above three categories.

Group four indicates how difficult it may be for even the specialist team to reach a conclusion regarding the exact nature of the problem and therefore in deciding appropriate management.

Worster-Drought (1974) provides an in-depth description of the nature and causes of these problems with illustrative case studies.

He describes two main groups: those with the condition termed *congenital supra-bulbar paresis* and those with *palato-pharyngeal disproportion*, one group with neurological causes and one with anatomical causes.

### Congenital supra-bulbar paresis

Supra-bulbar paresis is characterised by paralysis or muscle weakness in those muscles supplied by the vagus (tenth) and hypoglossal (twelfth) cranial nerves. The function of the face, tongue and palate may therefore be impaired in varying degrees. The soft palate and tongue are most frequently affected but all organs in the vocal tract, including the pharynx, may be involved. The lesion is upper motor neurone and is located above the pons or medulla. Worster-Drought (1974) describes a developmental defect of the motor tract, which runs from the cerebral cortex to the cranial nerves. Spontaneous improvement is sometimes reported in less severe cases indicating a delay in neurological maturation. There is frequently a history of sucking, swallowing and drooling problems. The drooling problem may be the primary reason for referral. Speech development may be late and exhibit hypernasality and a range of phonetic problems resulting from velopharyngeal insufficiency and poor tongue, lip and palate movement. Although the condition is usually congenital, it may be acquired prior to speech development such as through head injury or virus infections, for example, measles encephalitis.

### Palatopharyngeal disproportion

In some children problems of velopharyngeal closure relate to the size and shape of structures involved in the velopharyngeal mechanism, rather than to their innervation. These are Kaplan's group one, having anatomical disproportion with normal palate function. The mechanism is not competent either because the soft palate is too short or the pharynx capacious; in both instances the soft palate is unable to reach the posterior pharyngeal wall. Some investigators include reduced palatal bulk as a cause of incompetence as well as aberrant insertion of the levator muscles. Many cases of velopharyngeal incompetence remain undiagnosed until well on into speech development. The author has seen cases at referral from 3 years to 42 years; the appropriate differential diagnosis had not been reached in the adults although several medical specialists had already been consulted. In the 42-year-old, a diagnosis of 'psychogenic voice disorder' had been made and had led to inappropriate management. The speech problem which included articulatory, phonatory and resonatory problems was so severe that the woman was frequently unintelligible. The phonatory aspect had been perceived as the centre of the problem, because the medical specialists describing the disorder were not equipped to recognise or describe all the speech parameters and were therefore unable to hypothesise on the relationship between these disordered parameters and their cause. In some instances children are given lengthy periods of unsuccessful speech therapy, whereas more appropriate first stage management would be surgery to provide a competent velopharyngeal mechanism.

Shprintzen (1979) challenges the diagnostic categories of CPI as discussed above. This claim is on the basis of his study of 116 patients with 'hypernasal speech of previously undescribed origin'. 21 of these cases had normal appearing palates on oral examination. However, objective measurements revealed anatomical defects, 20 involving the musculus uvuli. He found that the majority of the subjects (71) revealed anatomical problems on full investigation. These findings stress the importance of carrying out full investigative procedures, now available, when the speech symptomatology indicates that the velopharyngeal mechanism is implicated. These investigations will be described in Chapter 3 of this volume.

### Velopharyngeal problems after adenoidectomy

Adenoids are most commonly located in the

concavity of the nasopharynx. When adenoids become hypertrophied, during development, the child adjusts gradually to the change in nasopharyngeal dimensions, with auditory feedback providing the regulator to maintain the already established speech patterns. Adenoidectomy requires sudden adjustment of the velopharyngeal mechanism.

In some children speech may develop normally until adenoidectomy is performed. Here the adenoidal pad had helped to occlude the nasopharynx and the potentially incompetent velopharyngeal mechanism remained undisclosed. This situation can occur in children both with apparently normal velopharyngeal sphincters and those with repaired congenital cleft palate. ENT surgeons will be well aware that in cases of repaired cleft palate complete adenoidectomy and tonsillectomy needs extreme caution (Lawson et al 1972).

The reported incidence of VPI diagnosed following adenoidectomy or tonsillectomy is very low, an incidence of one in 3000 in tonsil and adenoidectomy, and 1 in 10 000 in adenoidectomy only has been reported by Van Gelder (1964). The ENT specialist and the speech clinician need to be aware of the possibility of this condition. Although temporary increased nasality frequently occurs following adenoidectomy, children usually quickly adjust to the change in structure, through auditory feedback monitoring. Hypernasality occasionally persists up to a few weeks. If a return to the pre-operative speech pattern does not occur there may be cause for concern. If at follow-up the parents still report poor speech, further investigations should be implemented. If too much time elapses the child may make inappropriate adjustments to try to compensate for the increased nasality and may, through maladaptive use of the vocal tract, cause greater malfunction. For example, increased effort to speak clearly may lead to tension, vocal abuse and dysphonia. Facial tension may be used to stop the nasal airflow. A nasal grimace may restrict the airflow and thus increase turbulence. Furthermore, adverse reaction by the child to the acquired speech difficulties may lead to personal interactional problems.

Children with congenital velopharyngeal incompetence are as much at risk in relation to their speech and language development as the cleft palate cases. Indeed they may be more at risk because of the delays in the identification of the true nature of the problem.

The speech clinician requires a knowledge of the whole range of congenital and acquired conditions which affect the velopharyngeal mechanism.

For further accounts the reader is directed to Aronson (1985), Bzoch (1979), Darley et al (1975), Edwards and Watson (1980). Trost (1981) in *Communication Disorders, The Audio Journal of Continuing Education* provides a tape-recorded lecture which includes examples of the effects of velopharyngeal insufficiency on speech. The reader new to this field may find the audio examples particularly helpful. Hirschberg (1986) provides a review of the nature, assessment and treatment of velopharyngeal insufficiency in both adults and children.

## THE POTENTIAL FOR A COMMUNICATION DISORDER

The first part of the chapter outlined those congenital conditions of the vocal tract which put the infant at risk in relation to the development of adequate and acceptable communication. It is now necessary to consider these risk factors in more detail, as well as to explore the concept that the original medical condition of cleft lip and palate or velopharyngeal malfunction is not self-contained, but may be causative for other potentially disabling conditions. Sociological and psychological factors may also contribute to or maintain communication problems, both at interpersonal and linguistic levels.

As indicated earlier, the speech clinician should not anticipate that all children with cleft of lip and palate will develop with a communication problem. In Western society post-primary surgery, the majority of children will develop acceptable speech and language without requiring the specialist intervention of the speech therapist. In some countries children may not be fortunate enough to receive early surgery. The best time for palate surgery appears to be around 12 months. Ideally the speech therapist should be a member of the team in all cases, providing support and assurance to parents regarding the development of their child's communication.

The speech therapist's role in the context of the infant and toddler is fully explored in Chapter 2.

## Speech as an adaptive behaviour

The respiratory and digestive tracts are basically designed to carry out the life-supporting activities of breathing, chewing and swallowing, together with the protection of the airway. Although these tracts can naturally produce sounds, in man they have become highly adapted in their functions to produce sounds to subserve man's communicative needs, speech being used as the most rapid and efficient means of communication. The acquisition and development of speech involves advanced development of physiological, neurological, psychological neurolinguistic and neurophysiological processes. These processes enable man to adapt structures designed for life-support processes to produce intelligible sustained speech activities.

## Producing speech sounds

The glottis (vocal folds), designed to protect the lungs, has been adapted in its function to modify the air flow generated by the lungs. Air flow may be completely closed off, allowed to flow freely (vocal cords abducted) as in voiceless phones, or vocal folds may be brought together (adducted) to produce vibrations, as in vowels and voiced consonants. The organs above the glottis modify the air flow further by constricting or completely closing the vocal tract to produce different phonetic realisations, such as stops and fricatives. The air stream is directed into the mouth through the

function of the velopharyngeal mechanism. The function of the velopharynx is the main factor determining whether or not a sound is perceived as oral or nasal. Phonetically the velum fulfils a number of different functions and is central to the production of normal speech. *The functions of the velum in speech may be summarised as follows:*

### 1. Manner of articulation

Sounds produced with velic closure are oral. When air flows freely through the velopharyngeal port, by lowering the velum a nasal phone is produced. Oral closure accompanied by a lowered velum produces a nasal consonant. For each voiced or voiceless plosive there can therefore be a voiced or voiceless nasal made at the same place of articulation (homorganic) as in:

|  | Voiceless plosive | Voiced | Voiceless nasal | Voiced nasal |
|---|---|---|---|---|
| Bi-labial | [p] | [b] | [m̥] | [m] |
| Alveolar | [t] | [d] | [n̥] | [n] |
| Velar | [k] | [g] | [ŋ̊] | [ŋ] |

Voiceless nasals do not usually occur in English.

### 2. Place of articulation

Sounds are produced by raising the back of the tongue close to or to contact the velum, producing velar sounds. As in:

|  | Voiceless | Voiced |
|---|---|---|
| Plosives | [k] | [g] |
| Fricatives | [x] | [ɣ] |
| Nasals | [ŋ̊] | [ŋ] |
| Affricates | [kx] | [gɣ] |

### 3. Secondary articulations

The articulations described in (1) and (2) above are primary articulations. Secondary articulations involve a lesser degree of closure and may be added to the primary articulation. When secondary articulation involves raising the velum, velarisation results. An example in English is the 'dark ł' as in [mitk]. When the velum is lowered nasalisation occurs. It is likely to occur, even in normal speakers, in vowels between nasal consonants, e.g. [mãn].

The above descriptions are occurrences in normal speakers. However, some of these features, not usually occurring in a given language, may appear in a speaker with disordered speech. For example, poor function of the velum may lead to the nasalisation of vowels as a persistent feature, while oral sounds may be accompanied by nasal emission resulting from the secondary feature of a lowered velum, e.g.

$$[f] \rightarrow [\tilde{f}^F]$$
$$[s] \rightarrow [\tilde{s}^F]$$

In English for all consonants, except [m], [n] and [ŋ], sufficient closure of the velopharyngeal isthmus must prevent air passing into the nose to achieve air pressure within the mouth. Vowels require varying degrees of closure, from open in nasalised vowels when occurring next to nasals, to complete velic closure such as in the high vowel [i:]. In English the nasalisation of vowels is not phonemic, that is it does not affect meaning contrasts. In connected speech the movement of the velum is extremely rapid. In addition to velopharyngeal function, perceived nasality in speech is also influenced by tongue height, degree of mouth opening and the position of the mandible (Fletcher 1978).

When air passes into the mouth it is further adapted by the shape, movement and contacts made by the articulators. The tongue tip is capable of and is required to make extremely rapid and precise movements. Lips and tongue are very mobile structures and must achieve a wide range of rapid and highly co-ordinated movements. Normally, the intrinsic constraints of any organ play an important role in determining how that organ is used in speech sound production. Furthermore, the vocal tract is a dynamic mechanism, each part inter-relating with another. For example, tongue movement will alter the height of the larynx and width of pharynx, and movement of the velum may alter the shape and position of the back of the tongue. It is essential that speech clinicians and others in the team have full awareness of the adaptive functions and dynamic features of the vocal tract. Readers are referred to texts in articulatory and physiological phonetics which deal with the functions of the vocal tract for speech sound production in greater detail (Catford 1977, Hardcastle 1976, Ladefoged 1985).

In spite of the recent advances in knowledge in articulatory and physiological phonetics it is still extremely difficult to establish the exact relationship between the structure of any individual's vocal tract and the speech produced. It is therefore essential to take into consideration all those factors which may lead an individual with an anomaly of the vocal tract to being able to adapt a poor structure to an adequate level of speech function. It is valuable for the clinician to have an opportunity to meet an adult with an unrepaired cleft. A number of individuals in this group achieve a remarkable standard of speech.

## FACTORS AFFECTING THE DEVELOPMENT OF COMMUNICATION IN THE CLEFT PALATE INDIVIDUAL

The child with a congenital cleft of lip and palate is subject, like all children, to the possibility of having a problem in the development of communication. The major causes of developmental speech and language problems can be summarised as follows:

1. Sensory impairment, in particular hearing impairment and/or auditory perceptual problems
2. Anatomical/physiological problems in the peripheral speech mechanism
3. Neurological factors
4. Cognitive factors
5. Environmental factors
6. Emotional (psychogenic disorders).

The child with a cleft palate may be at risk in relation to a number of these factors. Those areas where they are particularly at risk will now be discussed.

### The timing of the surgery

The majority of infants with cleft lip and palate have their surgery in infancy. In some centres lips are repaired at a few hours, although it is more usual for this to be undertaken between 3 and 6 months. Some surgeons carry out the lip and palate repair concurrently at around 6 months. The repair of the palate will more usually be undertaken between 6 and 18 months. A range of procedures are used in the initial repairs of lip and palate; an introductory account of these can be found in Albery et al (1986) while specialist texts deal with the subject in greater detail (Edwards & Watson 1980, McWilliams et al 1984). Debate continues regarding the ideal timing of surgery as it relates to speech results and the potential hazard to growth centres. Palate repair carried out at around 12 months of age is generally preferred.

In some cases further surgery, referred to as secondary surgery, may be required. This need arises where the cosmetic outcome of lip and nose repairs is not satisfactory, the function of the velopharyngeal mechanism is not adequate for speech or there is blockage of the nasal airway. As surgery is usually undertaken in infancy it is very difficult for the team to predict the long-term growth outcomes. These will not be evident until the late teens, when growth is almost complete. At this age problems with the nose and dental arches may be particularly evident and may require management through surgery or orthodontics. Orthodontic management will be of major importance throughout the entire growth period of the individual from infancy to the final outcomes in adulthood. From the point of view of speech outcomes it is now generally agreed that early surgery is desirable. Unfortunately for some children early surgery may not be possible because of the presence of other handicapping conditions, or

the extensiveness of the cleft of palate. It is beyond the scope of this volume to describe the many operative procedures undertaken. Some are outlined in case studies later in the volume.

### Hearing

Speech is an aural/oral activity and for its normal development is dependent on a high level of auditory processing. The high incidence of middle ear disease and consequent hearing loss in individuals who have a cleft palate is now well documented. Masters et al (1960) proposed three possible explanations for hearing loss:

*1. Mechanical.* The abnormal reflux of food into the nasal cavity can set up chronic inflammatory changes around the Eustachian orifices—with oedema, hypertrophy of adenoids, low grade infection and secondary middle ear disease. Cases with unrepaired clefts or velopharyngeal incompetence, for any cause, are subject to nasal reflux.

*2. Infection.* If the break in the mechanical barrier between the mouth and the nasopharynx with its chronic inflammatory change alters the bacterial flora in the region to permit overgrowth of predominantly pathogenic bacteria, invasion of the middle ear and otitis media could result.

*3. Dynamic.* The dynamic factor in Eustachian tube and middle ear physiology depends upon the intact anatomy of the Eustachian apparatus and its associated musculature. In the cleft case there is frequent malfunction of the tensor palati muscle which governs the opening and closing of the Eustachian tube.

There is also some evidence of a synergistic action between the tensor tympani and tensor palati in swallowing. Research shows that changes in the middle ear are apparent in cleft palate infants. A world-wide study by Paradise (1975) found otitis media in virtually all unrepaired cleft cases under 2 years. There is some evidence that hearing becomes progressively impaired if palate repair is delayed (Masters et al 1960). Hearing loss is usually of a conductive type and is therefore subject to fluctuation. Conductive loss arises because of the poor conduction of the sound pressure across the middle ear space, in which there is a collection of infected material and fluid. The variation in conductive loss means that children's level of hearing will vary from month to month (Harrison & Philips 1971). Sensori-neural losses are occasionally present where there is an anatomical abnormality such as is found in some syndromes, e.g. Treacher-Collins. Table 1.2 provides a summary of information on syndromes in which cleft palate may occur.

Team members need to be alert to the potential for hearing loss. Although the palate repair is likely to improve hearing, it should be routinely checked and re-checked because of the possibility of intermittent loss. The presence of any loss will be a handicap in the development of language and speech and may be detrimental to academic progress.

In addition to an ENT examination and pure tone audiometric assessment, impedance audiometry, which may be used with small children, will reveal abnormal negative pressures in the middle ear space. Hearing loss tends to improve with age as the pathologies of childhood diminish. Cranio-facial growth may also contribute to improved hearing. A study by Heinemann-de Boer (1985) showed that in a group of 5-year-old cleft palate children, 38.7% had hearing impairment, while only 25.2% of the 7-year-olds had hearing loss. Lower incidence is reported in adults (Maue-Dickson 1977).

Hypertrophied adenoids are frequently implicated in relation to hearing impairment. However, as there is some evidence of incompetent velopharyngeal closure following adenoidectomy, adenoidectomy needs careful consideration. Removal of the lateral elements nearest to the Eustachian tube orifice is sometimes recommended. The surgical decision should be reached by the team and based on careful assessment of speech and the status of the velopharyngeal mechanism. Where the child is old enough a range of diagnostic procedures such as described in Chapter 3

may be undertaken. The insertion of drainage tubes (grommets) into the ear drum is frequently used; this allows air into the middle ear so that drainage takes place through the Eustachian tubes.

Hearing impairment is significant, not only for speech and language acquisition but in relation to intervention procedures undertaken in speech therapy. Auditory discrimination may be particularly affected (Finnegan 1974) and may be helped by the use of amplification in therapy, even if a hearing aid is not worn.

A review of the nature and causes of otological and audiological disorders in cleft palate is given in McWilliams et al (1984); this review indicates that the mechanisms by which middle ear disease occurs in cleft palate is the subject of continued research. Like the congenital cleft cases, other children, such as those with sub-mucous cleft or velopharyngeal incompetence, are also at risk in relation to ear disease. The presence of hearing loss may be a major handicap to the development of communication.

### The status of the vocal tract

The congenital anatomical defects associated with cleft lip and palate have been outlined earlier in the chapter. It is important to note, however, that the surgical repairs of lip and palate do not necessarily achieve a perfect result in terms of appearance, anatomy and speech function. Furthermore in some instances, for example where there is a wide cleft or other handicapping conditions are present, surgery may have to be delayed until speech development is well underway (see Table 1.2). Once deviant speech patterns are established they may be difficult to modify. The pattern established will already be acceptable to the speaker and will be maintained through auditory and kinaesthetic feedback. In cases where the repair has been carried out in infancy, the surgical result will not necessarily produce a mechanism which is able to achieve a degree of velopharyngeal closure sufficient for normal speech. This may not be

**Table 1.2** *Summary of syndromes in which cleft palate commonly occurs*

| Name and nature | Features | Factors which may put the development of communication at risk |
|---|---|---|
| *APERT'S* Premature fusion of the sutures of the skull affects both brain and facial growth | *Main features* Craniosynostosis. Syndactyly of hands and feet | Facial and hand disfigurements may lead to psychosocial, including poor interaction and communication problems. |
| | | Conductive hearing loss—speech and language problems. Mental retardation may lead to speech and language delay. |
| Incidence: 160 000 live births | *Other features* Forehead is high, steep and broad, occiput flattened. Nasal deformities, underdevelopment of mid-face. Fixation of stapes. Mental retardation may be present. *Palate high arched and narrow clefts of soft palate reported in 30% of cases* | Palatal clefts will need to be repaired. |
| | | The Class III malocclusion and high arched narrow maxilla will cause reduction in space for tongue movement in speech. |
| | | Deformities of nose such as saddle nose, sometimes reported, may lead to hyponasality and forward tongue carriage to protect the airway. Adenoids should be removed with caution as post-operatively hypernasality may be revealed. |
| NB. *CROUZON'S DISEASE*—similar to Apert's but less severe. No hand and feet involvement. The hazards to communication development relate to the presenting features. | | |
| *KLIPPEL-FEIL* | *Main features* Fusion of cervical vertebrae therefore shortness of neck and limited head movement | Degree of hearing loss may severely affect the development of speech and language. |
| | Hairline extends to shoulders Trapezius muscle flares from mastoid to shoulders Bi-manual synkinesis | Palatal cleft may cause long term problems because of difficulty of repair related to lack of neck extension and limited mouth opening. |
| | *Other features* Hearing loss Palatal cleft Facial asymmetry | Psychosocial factors may lead to interactional and communication problems. |
| *VAN DER WOUDE* | *Main features* Lower lip pits Cleft lip may be bilateral *Other features* 80% cleft palate may be bilateral. Syndactyly | Appearance, especially if there is cleft of upper lip as well as lip pits, may cause communicative problems. Speech problems will be similar to those generally associated with palatal clefting. |
| *PIERRE ROBIN* Caused by arrested embryonic development Incidence: 1 in 30 000 births. May be part of a more complex sydrome such as *Trisomy 18* in which there is antero-posterior skull elongation, micrognathia and microstomia). Glossoptosis — | *Main features* Mandibular hypoplasia (small lower jaw—micrognathia & microstomia). Glossoptosis— low tongue attachment, which tends to be drawn back, and block the pharyngeal airway. Midline cleft of palate | The palatal cleft tends to be 'U'-shaped and extensive, may be difficult to repair effectively. Small mouth opening may mean palate repair is delayed. Limited degree of mouth opening may exacerbate hypernasality. Congenital heart defect may be a further reason to delay palate repair. |
| | *Other features* Abnormally small tongue, tongue tie (the author has observed this in sisters both with syndrome), ear defects, heart defect, occasional mental retardation | If respiratory obstruction has been severe cerebral anoxia may have caused brain damage. There may consequently be learning, including language learning, difficulties. |
| | | Natural growth of the lower jaw leads to a balanced maxilla-mandible relationship and normal occlusion. |
| | | Ear defects may be associated with hearing impairment. |

**Table 1.2** (contd)

| Name and nature | Features | Factors which may put the development of communication at risk |
|---|---|---|
| | | Tongue tie and associated poor tongue development may limit tongue tip use for articulation, surgery may be indicated for tongue tie. Prolonged hospitalisation for respiratory problems may adversely affect mother-child bonding and have consequences for communication development. All children with repeated periods of hospitalisation will be at risk for language development. |
| *TREACHER COLLINS* or *MANDIBULO-FACIAL DYSOSTOSIS* Condition affects the structures derived from 1st and 2nd branchial arches. Strong hereditary factor in aetiology | *Main features* Antimongoloid slant to eyes. Notching of eyelids—usually lower lids. Deficient or absent eye lashes Underdevelopment of facial (malar) bones Deformities of external and middle ear Large mouth with malocclusion and dental irregularities Low hairline extending to cheeks. *Other features* 30–40% with cleft palate reported. Risk of mental retardation | Appearance may cause psychosocial problems including communicative difficulties Hearing loss may be a considerable handicap, amplification needs to be provided early. Cleft of palate needs surgery. Speech difficulties may be hampered further by malocclusion. Language development will be affected by mental retardation. |

Further accounts of syndromes may be found in Gorlin et al 1976, McWilliams et al 1984, Travis 1971.

obvious during early speech development but will be a central factor needing further investigation and appropriate management if speech does not progress towards a normal pattern. The speech therapist should not continue to work on speech if knowledge of the potential for velopharyngeal closure is uncertain. Although the velopharyngeal mechanism is central in speech production there are other features in the vocal tract which, if present, will place the child at considerable disadvantage in relation to speech development; these include oro-nasal fistulae, dental and occlusal problems, and changes in sensation and perception. These will now be discussed.

### Oro-nasal fistulae

In some cases a small breakdown in the primary palate repair results in incomplete separation of the nose and mouth; an oro-nasal fistula is present, most commonly in the area of the incisive foramen. Fistulae may vary from pin-hole size to the size of a thumb nail. Figure 1.6 shows fistulae in different locations and sizes. There is some evidence that fistulae occur more frequently following certain forms of surgery (McWilliams et al 1984). Every effort is made by surgeons to adopt procedures which will not lead to fistulae. The relationship between oro-nasal fistulae and speech is not yet clearly established. Stengelhofen & Foster (1979) studied the speech and dental factors in a group of 23 children with oro-nasal fistulae. Of the 23 children, 16 had audible nasal emission while the remaining 7 did not. However, all 23 children had speech problems mainly at the phonetic level. The fistulae were closed with an acrylic plate (obturator) and the spontaneous changes in speech studied over time. The findings showed that there was no

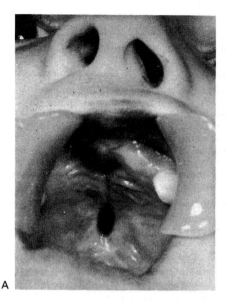

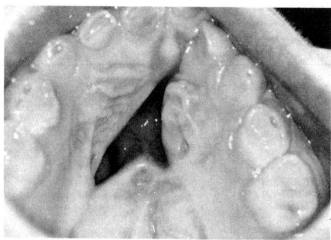

**Fig 1.6** (A) Oro-nasal fistula at junction of hard and soft palate. (B) Large oro-nasal fistula in anterior part of hard palate

A

B

significant correlation between the size of the fistula, the relative widths of the upper and lower dental arches and the depth of the palate on the one hand, and the original speech condition and changes in speech with obturation on the other. The position of the fistula in the palate did not vary sufficiently for correlations to be tested. The study provided some evidence that 'the more the lower jaw is positioned forward in relation to the upper jaw, the more the nasal escape occurs'. The findings of some aspects of this research have been confirmed by the study by Shelton & Blank (1984) who found that only the largest fistulae allowed loss of intra-oral air pressure to a degree to weaken obstruents. Although many smaller fistulae revealed nasal airflow during the production of syllable strings, Shelton and Blank considered that good speech was maintained through increased respiratory efforts and varied according to fistula size.

Clinicians and researchers are gradually paying greater attention to the presence of fistulae as they affect tongue function, rather than purely as a source of nasal airflow. If tongue function is adapted in an attempt to stop air passing through the fistula into the nose, it will be impaired in its function for speech sound production. This view was supported by the study of Stengelhofen & Foster (1979) and more recently by Cosman & Falk (1980). Their study showed that the subjects used the correct manner in consonant production but tended to shift placement further back in the vocal tract. The subjects in Cosman and Falk's study did not have oro-nasal fistulae following complete palate repair but were subjects with delayed hard palate repair. These authors recommend that caution is taken regarding the approach of delayed hard palate repair. Although this procedure is of value in not affecting maxillary growth, the study showed that the majority of children failed to achieve acceptable speech by five years. The findings regarding tongue function are further supported by the palatographic studies in Chapter 6 of this volume. Figure 1.7 shows a palate where the repair of the hard palate has been delayed. The plate to obturate the hard palate is also shown.

The most frequently reported speech problem in cases with oro-nasal fistulae is audible nasal emission. This may be severe enough to mask friction produced in the oral cavity. In the study of Stengelhofen & Foster (1979) of the 23 children evaluated, 14 showed a significant reduction in nasal emission with

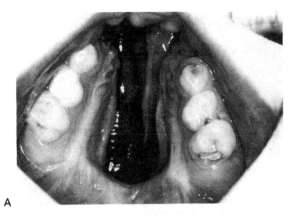

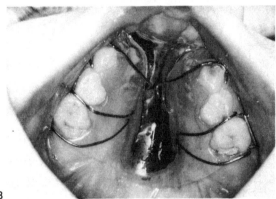

**Fig 1.7** (A) Delayed hard palate repair. (B) Hard palate defect closed by obturator

a fistula may be closed for a short period with dental wax (Albery et al 1986, Shelton & Blank 1984). It can also be closed temporarily, or for indefinite periods with an acrylic plate; this may be a preferred approach in subjects who may become long-term dental plate wearers. Alternatively, various surgical procedures may be undertaken (Jackson 1972, Jackson et al 1976).

Naso-labial fistulae are also found in some cases, but are not likely to give rise to speech problems.

## Dental and occlusal problems

The child with a cleft palate is at risk both in relation to dental problems and malocclusion between the upper and lower jaws. As Foster (1980) says: 'in cleft lip and palate there is usually a potential for gross deformity of the dento-alveolar structures as well as the basal elements of the upper jaw and palate'. If the cleft involves the alveolar ridge there may be disturbance of the structures in the region of the cleft. Lateral incisors may be malformed, malpositioned or absent, both at the deciduous and permanent stages of development. A missing lateral incisor may have only a minimal effect on speech, sometimes causing the tongue to protrude through the space, resulting in a fronted realisation of fricative and plosive sounds normally articulated against the alveolar ridge.

In clefts involving the alveolus, especially bilateral, the pre-maxilla may become severely misplaced in a forward position (Fig. 1.8). The normal forward growth of the pre-maxilla results in gross protrusion in bilateral clefts. This may be checked through pre-surgical orthodontics (Foster 1980). Nevertheless in severe cases, even after surgery, there may still be some distortion, making precise articulatory placement at the alveolar ridge difficult to achieve (Fig. 1.9). This may be in part due to scarring, but may also be related to poor sensory awareness in the alveolar ridge. Where tongue tip to alveolar ridge contacts are imprecise, the articulation of a number of fricatives and plosives may be affected.

obturation. Speech help was not provided. Furthermore, 15 subjects showed spontaneous phonetic improvement with obturation, while 3 remained unchanged and 6 regressed in their phonetic realisations. The tongue function appears to be inevitably implicated. This view on tongue function is supported by Warren (1986) who claims that individuals 'manipulate their tongues and maintain aerodynamic equilibrium' because only in this way is it possible for the system to maintain the required pressures for speech.

The speech clinician should try to establish whether or not the presence of an oro-nasal fistula is significant for an individual's speech or feeding. Diagnostic investigations should be undertaken with other appropriate team members. Where the fistula is considered detrimental, management to close the fistula should be carried out. For diagnostic purposes

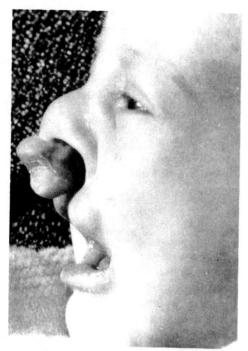

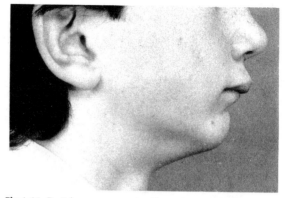

Fig 1.10 Facial appearance in Class II malocclusion

**Fig 1.8** Protruded pre-maxilla in infant with unrepaired bilateral cleft of lip and alveolus. (From Edwards and Watson 1980 *Advances in Cleft Palate Management.*)

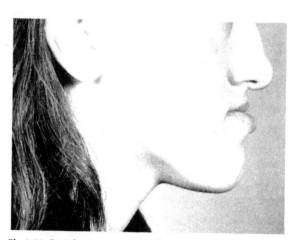

Fig 1.11 Facial appearance in Class III malocclusion

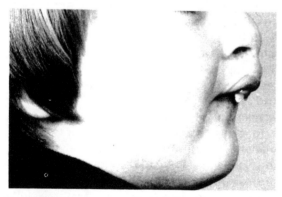

**Fig 1.9** Protruded pre-maxilla in child with repaired lip and alveolus

The tongue, although related to the size of the mandible (lower jaw), functions within the maxilla (upper jaw) in speech. This fact leads us to an awareness of the importance of the relationship between maxilla and mandible. When teeth erupt they are strongly influenced by the forces of the soft tissues—lips, tongue and cheeks—as well as by the bony base from which they erupt. Texts on cleft palate and orthodontics deal in detail with normal occlusion and occlusal variations (Albery et al 1986, Edwards & Watson 1980, McWilliams et al 1980, Foster 1975). The alveolar processes on which the teeth are based, are inherited features. The skeletal base is usually classified as follows:

Class I   The maxilla lies slightly forward of the mandible and is considered normal, the maxillary arch is slightly larger than the mandibular arch.

Class II  The mandibular base is set back in comparison to the maxilla (Fig. 1.10).

Class III The mandibular base is set too far forwards or the maxillary base is set too far back (Fig. 1.11).

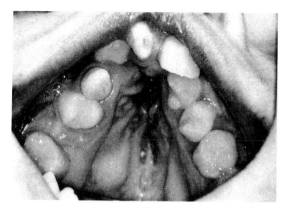

**Fig 1.12** Narrow maxillary arch with oro-nasal fistula

In post-operative repaired cleft cases the maxilla is frequently lacking in width or is underdeveloped and a Class III malocclusion results. There is therefore a lack of maxillary space in which the tongue has sufficient space to function for speech activities (Fig. 1.12). Fronting and lateralisation of a number of consonants may result. As the tongue is developed from and related to mandibular size, in a Class III malocclusion, the tongue tip tends to remain behind the lower incisors in a passive posture, the blade of the tongue taking over the articulatory functions normally undertaken by the tongue tip. The tongue blade is comparatively insensitive and inflexible, and imprecise articulations inevitably result. In severe Class III malocclusions, because the maxillary teeth rest inside the mandible, it may be difficult for the individual to achieve a labio-dental articulatory placement for /f/ and /v/ and bilabial fricatives [Φ] and [β] may be substituted. A Class II malocclusion may occasionally be found, but is not so likely to have a marked effect on speech; alveolar contacts may become fronted or dentalised. A detailed description of speech is essential in trying to establish the exact relationship between speech patterns and any anatomical features which may be observed.

Malocclusions are present in a number of syndromes and the presence of malocclusion in addition to any cleft condition will place the child at greater risk in the development of speech.

*Oral sensation and perception*

In the developing infant, the sensations passing between the tongue and the rest of the oral cavity, and the oral cavity and the rest of the environment are highly sensitive and important. Bosma (1970) describes the mouth of the infant as 'an organ for laying hold of the environment'. Therefore any malfunction of the mouth may have severe consequences. The tongue in particular is of central importance in speech and is supplied with a highly sensitive exteroceptor system. The touch endings provide information to the CNS on the location and pressure of contacts, the direction of movement and onset time of contact (Hardcastle 1976). The tongue tip, which is the most highly sensitive and mobile part of the whole oral cavity, plays a key role in speech sound production. Although there are fewer receptors in the palate, the alveolar ridge has a high level of sensitivity. Oral sensation and perception is involved in the speech servo-system and is therefore intimately involved in both its development and maintenance. During the development of a speech sound system, the central nervous system is informed of the auditory and visual characteristics of a target sound. Motor adjustments are gradually made through proprioception and tactile senses, and auditory feedback guides further adjustment during production. Gradually sounds produced are matched with the target sounds of the environment and to previous productions by the individual until a schema is eventually established. The schema involves auditory, visual and proprioceptive information. If sensory awareness in the mouth is impaired it is likely to make the precise and rapid movements required in speech more difficult to achieve. Andrews (1970), Edwards (1974), and Hochberg & Kabcenall (1967) in testing oral form discrimination all found significantly poorer ability in cleft palate subjects than in the normals. However the relationship between oral form discrimination (oral stereognosis) and the ability to perform complex articulatory movements is not well established and is an area of continuing research. Nevertheless as a high level of oro-sensory awareness is the norm, especially in the tongue and alveolar ridge, individuals with lowered awareness may be disadvantaged. Those with repairs involving the hard palate may have particular problems in this respect. The role of oral sensory function in speech production and its possible role in remediation is fully explored by Shelton (1979).

## Social factors and the communication context

Research evidence does not indicate a high degree of social maladjustment in the cleft lip and palate population, especially by the time individuals reach adulthood. It is not difficult, however, to understand that infants with clefts, especially those involving a facial defect, may be at risk in relation to the development of communication, especially initially with their care-givers. The feelings of parents towards their infants with clefts of lip are reported later in this volume. If there are feeding difficulties the usually satisfying time of feeding may be disrupted. Although some cleft babies manage to breast-feed, this is unusual. Some babies may not even be able to bottle-feed. The difficulties and the length of time needed for feeding may give rise to tension in mother and baby. Reports of feeding difficulties are as high as 73% (Slutsky 1969) and 85% (Spriestersbach 1973). Feeding which is usually constructive in establishing bonding and early interaction, becomes an anxiety provoking experience where early communication interactions are unlikely to be fostered. Sometimes extended time in hospital is necessary and mother and baby may be deprived of essential opportunities for communicating and bonding may be endangered.

The appearance of a cleft lip and palate, before repair (Fig. 1.13), can be very distressful to both parents, who themselves are under pressure in a society where high value is placed on physical attractiveness, and stigma is attached to physical anomalies. Clifford (1969) found that cleft palate adolescents had a lower perception of parental acceptance than some other groups with potentially

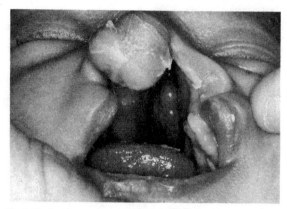

**Fig 1.13** Severe unrepaired bilateral cleft of lip and palate in infant

disabling conditions. Acceptance by parents is established very early in a child's development. The time of waiting for surgery, either for lip or palate, will be very stressful for the family.

As well as the problems of appearance, if poor speech becomes evident, parents may be discouraged from providing the usual reinforcements given to infants in their attempts to communicate. At 4 to 5 years of age children become aware of their physical differences. This is at the same time as they become exposed to a wider social context and the need to communicate effectively becomes extremely important. Poor speakers may become self-conscious and therefore less willing to communicate. Although the research evidence is that cleft palate individuals are, on the whole, quite well adjusted (Spriestersbach & Sherman 1968, Spriestersbach 1973), clinicians from all fields will be aware that in dealing with those cases where speech and language is not developing well, consideration must be given to all the factors which may put the development of effective communication at risk.

The following list provides pointers to factors needing careful monitoring by the team:

1. Feeding problems: difficulties parents will have in showing new baby to family, friends, neighbours, etc.

2. Family reactions to the problem, especially to appearance.

3. Parental encouragement to the child to talk. Research evidence is that cleft children are given less opportunity to talk at home and school (Spriestersbach 1973).

4. How do the parents cope with poor speech? Do they discourage, over-correct, or by-pass their child as a communicator?

5. Is the parents' view realistic about the long-term outcomes for their child? Both over-optimistic and pessimistic attitudes can be harmful.

6. What is the reaction of playgroup leaders and teachers to the child? Cleft palate children are sometimes viewed as more inhibited in class by teachers than parents view them. Although parents may view their children as behaviourally normal, children may react differently in certain contexts. It is therefore important for the team to be aware of the effect the clinical context may have on a child.

7. Does the child avoid any situations? Is this because such situations involve negative reactions from others?

8. How do peers respond to the child's speech difficulties? There is some research evidence that negative responses may increase nasal resonance (Blood & Hyman 1977) while nasal resonance elicits a negative peer response.

9. Do teachers give the child opportunities to participate in communicative activities to the same extent as peers? Spriestersbach's (1973) research showed that compared with their peers, fewer cleft children liked school or volunteered to recite in school.

There is some evidence that cleft palate individuals' personality characteristics tend to be compliant, passive and self-effacing. Characteristics of low gregariousness, shyness, quietness and being ill at ease with strangers have been described. All these characteristics may either be the result of poor communication skills or could exacerbate communication inadequacies already present. The team, especially the speech therapist, needs to identify problems which occur in individual cases and attend to those characteristics which may be detrimental to the development of effective communication. The cleft palate population is not a homogeneous group; it is therefore essential that each child and family is approached individually with regard to the appraisal and the provision of management directed to physical, psychological and social aspects of the problem.

Where communication problems occur in addition to any physical anomalies, either related to the cleft or other conditions, the individual may be gravely disadvantaged in a social context. If psychological and social maladaptions do develop they may be more handicapping than the original condition (Lencione 1980). Children with other abnormalities of the cranio-facial complex may be particularly at risk.

Individuals who have severe difficulties in the development of acceptable speech may be involved with the team into early adulthood. They may require surgery to the lip and nose into adolescence and young adulthood. Others may still need secondary operative procedures to improve the velopharyngeal mechanism. Orthodontic treatment may not be completed until school leaving or later. The persistence of speech problems may require continued intervention. Differences in appearance and communicative skills mark out these individuals from their peer group, while frequent attendance at clinic appointments disrupts progress at school or work and further identifies their differences. The psychosocial problems are fully discussed in a number of texts, especially Bzoch 1971, Edwards & Watson 1980, McWilliams et al 1984, and Spriestersbach 1973.

### Intellectual factors

Intellectual handicap is one of the major causes of developmental speech and language problems in the population as a whole. In the past there was a tendency to attribute intellectual impairment to cleft palate individuals; such a view, if unfounded, is detrimental to the child and his family. Heineman-de Boer (1985) pleads that 'The old judgement that cleft palate persons are intellectually impaired must either be confirmed with statistical facts or dismantled as prejudice'. Intellectual ability in cleft palate cases has a long history of controversial and inconclusive research findings. An excellent review is given by Heineman-de Boer (1985). Her study draws the conclusion that as a group cleft palate persons have an average to high average intellectual potential. She did, however, find evidence to support some earlier findings that there is some depression of verbal ability compared to performance ability (Lamb et al 1972). The lower verbal ability was not supported by a study by McWilliams & Matthews (1979) and is therefore still a controversial area.

The findings of Heineman-de Boer that slightly lower IQ levels were found in the group with cleft of palate only, supports the earlier study by Goodstein (1961). This finding may relate to the fact that children with clefts of palate only, are more likely to suffer from other congenital abnormalities. However, the mean IQs of these children still fell within the average range.

There is a good deal of evidence that the abilities of cleft palate children improve over time. This should encourage the team not to come to premature conclusions about any individual's intellectual potential. Cleft palate children are not a homogeneous group and therefore need to be thoroughly observed as individuals. Formal intellectual testing of young children, fortunately currently unfashionable, should not be sought in young cleft palate children whose development may lag initially because of the interruptions in their early development (Starr et al 1977). Nonetheless cleft palate individuals with low intelligence will be further handicapped in relation to speech and language development. Every support should be given so that handicapping conditions are reduced as far as possible. The occasionally encountered suggestion that surgery may not be worthwhile in children with severe intellectual handicap, cannot be supported. Unfortunately it is easy to presume

that the poor communicator is intellectually retarded, a view that is often held by the general public, but may also be a trap that professionals may be drawn into.

Earlier studies reporting low IQ scores in cleft palate cases may not have accounted for variables such as socio-economic status and parental intellectual levels, or may have been influenced by sampling problems and the use of verbal tests.

The range of speech and language problems which may be met in the cleft palate individual is outlined in the next section.

## PROBLEMS IN ORAL COMMUNICATION

In an interactive situation the first factor which will be evident to the listener is whether or not the speaker can be understood. The listener in the communicative context is put to great disadvantage if the speaker is unintelligible. This may be one of the reasons why there is a tendency to attribute low intelligence to poor speakers, thus placing the appearance of stupidity onto the speaker, rather than the listener. The new clinician needs to be aware of this problem and should endeavour to develop strategies to deal sensitively with the difficulties in understanding clients.

### Intelligibility

Intelligibility is a variable measure, greatly influenced by social context. It may vary from one speech sample to another. For example, connected speech may be intelligible in general, but specific vocabulary items may present problems, such as a surname, an address or an item requested in a shop. Intelligibility should therefore be evaluated from a range of samples and in different contexts. It is influenced by a number of variables, including phonetic, phonological, phonatory and resonatory factors, together with rate, volume, accent and prosodic features. Listener variables are also significant.

Although phonetic and resonatory problems may have the greatest influence on intelligibility (Moore & Somers 1975), all the variables should be considered as these may require attention in intervention. Improvement in areas such as rate and volume may be of primary importance in enabling an individual to become a more effective communicator. This is extremely important in the context of Fletcher's finding (1978) that intelligibility is likely to plateau at seven years of age. The concurrent disturbance of several speech parameters, found in many cleft palate individuals, is likely to have severe consequences. Problems of intelligibility may arise in other cases with velopharyngeal problems from different aetiologies.

A full analysis of all the variables affecting intelligibility will prevent the speech clinician from focussing only on the phonetic and resonatory aspects of speech, which may be grossly deviant but not of greatest consequence in relation to intelligibility (Subtelny et al 1972). Some speech features may be severely distorted but intelligibility may be preserved.

## Phonatory and resonatory problems

When listening to any speaker it is difficult to distinguish between the phonatory and resonatory aspects of voice. This may be a particular problem for the new clinician, although there is evidence that the subjective judgement of voicing is not easy, even for the experienced assessor. Where the speaker exhibits problems in a number of speech parameters, the task becomes extremely difficult. Nevertheless it is necessary to try to differentiate the phonatory and resonatory aspects, because this differentiation will lead to a greater understanding of the nature of the presenting problems. A consideration of the dynamic interplay between the larynx and vocal tract may lead to alternatives in management. The exact relationship between the functions of various areas of the vocal tract is complex and still not fully understood (Laver 1980).

*Phonatory disorders*

The reported incidence of voice disorders in children, generally described as 'hoarseness' ranges from 6% (Wilson 1979) to 23% (Silverman & Zimmer 1975). Clinically, dysphonia (voice disorder) has been reported in a number of cleft palate individuals. Breathiness, hoarseness, weakness and pitch changes have all been reported. Although there is little evidence that the incidence of dysphonia in cleft palate children is any higher than in the population as a whole, it is nevertheless important to note its occurrence. It is generally found in those children facing considerable difficulties in achieving acceptable speech, and where, therefore, the adequacy of the velopharyngeal mechanism is in question. These cases will also exhibit hypernasality (too much nasal resonance) and probably articulation problems. The suggested explanation for dysphonia is that speakers with velopharyngeal incompetence have to expend excessive effort to achieve a given intensity; this extra effort leads to vocal misuse (Bzoch 1964). Furthermore, children with poor speech may automatically try to speak louder in an attempt to make themselves understood, thus causing further misuse and increased phonatory disorder. This view is supported by the observation that some cleft palate speakers present with an extremely quiet voice; this is either a strategy to compensate for loss of air through the velopharyngeal isthmus or it may be that they do indeed have difficulty in achieving an adequate degree of intensity (Bzoch 1979, McWilliams et al 1984). Furthermore the glottis may be used as an articulator, inappropriate glottal sounds occurring in the speech pattern, adding to the vocally abusive behaviour.

Hoarseness and associated laryngeal pathology in cleft palate children was reported in a study by McWilliams et al (1969). 84% of the children with hoarseness had laryngeal pathology, most frequently bilateral vocal fold nodules. These problems were already present in 4 year old children. Hoarseness should be seen as a danger signal by the clinician requiring further investigations, both of the state of the larynx and the velopharyngeal mechanism. If velopharyngeal problems are leading to misuse of the vocal tract and larynx, initial management should be directed to improving the velopharyngeal mechanism; surgery may well be required.

There is inconclusive evidence regarding the effects of velopharyngeal incompetence on the fundamental frequency of voice (pitch). It is nevertheless important to describe this parameter in each case. The author recently observed an adult with an unrepaired cleft. When the obturator, normally worn, was removed there was a marked drop in pitch as well as in volume. This example illustrates further the importance of the dynamic relationship between the laryngeal structures and the supra-laryngeal tract.

Many types of voice disorders have been described in the cleft palate population; some of the parameters are supported by research, others noted in clinical examples. The speech clinician, ENT specialist and plastic surgeon need to be aware of the possible occurrence of dysphonias and how these may relate to inadequacy of the velopharyngeal mechanism.

### Resonatory disorders

If speech clinicians are not always in agreement in making subjective judgements about phonation, they are probably even less reliable in judging resonance. This may be some comfort to the new clinician who is likely to find these aspects difficult to recognise and evaluate. The area of resonance is also surrounded by terminological problems. In this discussion the following terms are adopted:

*1. Hypernasality.* This is the quality perceived auditorily which results from the inappropriate coupling of oral and nasal cavities. In normal speech the velopharyngeal valve controls the amount of air passing into the nose. Varying degrees of closure have been noted, from full opening in nasal sounds [m, n, ŋ] to complete closure in stops and fricatives. Resonance will be most easily perceived

in vowel sounds; if too much air is deflected into the nasal passages, hypernasality results. This is a common problem in individuals with velopharyngeal problems from various causes.

*2. Hyponasality.* This is the quality perceived auditorily which results from insufficient coupling of oral and nasal cavities so that insufficient air passes into the nasal cavities. It results from blockage either at the entrance to or in the nasal cavities, and reduces nasal airflow in [m, n] and [ŋ] and the surrounding vowels.

*3. Cul-de-sac resonance* is perceived auditorily when air passes into the nasal passages but cannot continue to pass out of the nose because of some obstruction. It is the sound produced when the nose is pinched to occlude the passages; the nose, which should be an open tube, becomes closed anteriorly.

The term rhinolalia, used in the description of resonatory conditions is not generally in current usage.

From the preceding sections it can now be understood that in cleft palate individuals the function of the velopharyngeal valve is at risk, and conditions where the velopharyngeal mechanism is implicated may present with *hypernasality.* Hypernasality is influenced by factors other than velopharyngeal function. These include auditory perception, degree of tension in all structures involved in speech, tongue position, relationship of maxilla and mandible, the degree of mouth opening, phonetic context and intensity.

Fletcher's extensive research (1978) found evidence that the degree of speech impairment tends to parallel the extent of the original cleft. Although Fletcher found 'Males higher in nasalance' he indicated that data for isolated clefts of secondary palate only, most common in females, suggest a totally different distribution between sexes. The rates of co-ordination implicated in the study are of particular note. Fletcher suggests that there may be a generalised motor impairment of the pharyngeal and oral structures in cleft palate subjects.

The above findings should help the clinician to guard against focussing on the velopharyngeal sphincter as the only contributor to hypernasality. Hypernasality is not a constant feature but may be present in varying degrees. Many speakers with repaired clefts will have normal balanced resonance. Others may exhibit a range from mild to severe hypernasality.

Examination of the velopharynx by endoscopy has shown that vowels require varying degrees of closure of the velopharynx and are therefore differentially influenced by the inadequacies of the mechanism, with low vowels such as [a:] being hardly affected but the high front vowel [i:] being seriously impaired. Differences in vowel sounds alone do not generally lead to marked intelligibility problems. However, it will be realised that speakers exhibiting hypernasality will usually have speech problems at the phonetic level resulting from a decrease in intra-oral air pressure, as well as resulting from any of the contributory factors discussed earlier.

The speech clinician should guard against an expectation of hypernasality in the cleft palate speaker, as this expectation may predispose perception of hypernasality whenever the resonatory quality deviates from the norm. In some cases *hyponasality* may be present. This may result from some degree of occlusion of the nasal passage, perhaps adenoidal growth, a deflected nasal septum or a collapsed nostril. Even in instances of hyponasality the efficient functioning of the velopharynx cannot be presumed, as blockage of the airway at some point may reduce the effects of air flow into the nasal passages. Hyponasality is not an isolated phenomenon, but will be associated with mouth breathing and if persisting over time may lead to: (1) lax oro-facial musculature; (2) permanent open mouth posture with mandible hinged down; (3) forward tongue position; (4) imprecise articulation.

Although the perception of resonatory factors is psychologically real to the listener, it is a difficult area to evaluate objectively. The clinician may be helped by a deeper understanding of the physiological and acoustic correlates. Further discussion can be found in

Bzoch (1979), Fletcher (1978) and McWilliams et al (1984), as well as in texts on acoustic and physiological phonetics.

### Nasal emission

Nasal emission is dealt with in this section because the term is frequently used synonymously with hypernasality. This is a misleading and incorrect concept. The likening of the speech mechanism to a wind instrument (Anthony 1980) is helpful in considering problems resulting from anatomical and physiological differences in the supra-glottic structures. The velum has the special function of enabling or preventing the use of the nose as an additional air cavity. In normal speech the flow of air through the nose is much less than that through the mouth, from being small in amount in vowels, to virtually no air flow in consonants, especially fricatives and plosives. Small amounts of nasal air flow are therefore evident in normal speakers. Inability to prevent the air stream passing into the nose, because of palatal deficiency or oronasal fistula causes extreme difficulty in building up sufficient intra-oral air pressure in the oral cavity for the production of fricatives, plosives and affricates.

Nasal air flow occurs appropriately in the nasal phones [m] [n] and [ŋ]. It can be demonstrated by the clouding of a mirror held under the nose. In some speakers exhibiting speech problems, clouding may be visible in the production of some other phones. The context should be noted. Nasal emission may be associated with weakened production of fricatives and plosives.

In some instances the nasal emission of air becomes audible. This arises because turbulence is set up and generates noise in the nose. The *audible nasal emission* resulting may mask a sound otherwise articulated in the correct manner and place. A number of cleft palate subjects may spontaneously try to inhibit the air flow through the nose. They attempt this through increased tension in the oro-facial region especially around the nares. The increased tension, by restricting the nasal air flow, actually increases the nasal turbulence and exacerbates the audible nasal emission. The clinician should not only listen carefully but also watch for evidence of *nasal or facial grimace*. Clinical observation suggests that the presence of nasal grimace is an indicator that the individual may have anatomical and physiological limitations, such as a poor velopharyngeal closure or an oro-nasal fistula. Audible nasal turbulence may also be exaggerated by blockage of the nasal airway, either temporarily with mucus or permanently by a deflected septum.

The phenomenon of audible nasal emission is probably most easily identified as part of the articulatory pattern. In some cases the degree of turbulence in the nose may set up such a disturbance as to result in what may be termed a *nasal snort*, which may be evident in both vowel and consonant production and tends to become very intrusive in the speech pattern. It is indicative of poor velopharyngeal function. Friction of the velum against the pharyngeal wall is also found in some cases. Even after appropriate surgical management features such as nasal emission and nasal snort may persist as habits within the speech pattern.

There is a close relationship between resonance and phonetic problems. These features will often co-occur. Resonatory problems alone may not require further surgery, but persisting phonetic problems may be caused by velopharyngeal incompetence and will require surgical intervention. Karnell & Van Demark (1986) considered that articulation is the most important factor in deciding whether or not individuals have velopharyngeal competence. The nature of the phonetic/articulation problems will now be outlined.

## Phonetic problems

The study of phonetic problems in cleft palate cases is a complex area because the ability to articulate 'normally' is influenced by a large number of variables. Those factors which affect the anatomical structures of the vocal tract or produce limitations in function may be especially significant, while the presence of conditions such as hearing impairment will compound the problems. Additionally other factors such as phonetic context, syllable structure, rate and length and complexity of utterance may all be influential. McWilliams et al (1984) provide a thorough review of the literature in this area.

In this section of the chapter, the term phonetic has been chosen to identify the speech parameter under discussion. Some writers use the general term phonology to subsume both the phonetic and phonological aspects. However, if the phonetic level is viewed as the basic foundation, as it were the building block for signalling meaning through phonological contrasts, it is essential that it is examined separately. This is an important distinction because problems at the phonetic level may require different procedures to the remediation of phonological problems. With individual cases it will be necessary to evaluate both the phonetic and phonological levels. In children, evaluation in the context of the normal developmental processes should be undertaken.

In some cases articulatory difficulties may persist and be resistant to remediation. Although normal children have mature articulatory patterns by 8 years of age, Van Demark et al (1979) in a longitudinal study of cleft palate cases found articulatory problems persisting up to 18 years. It is helpful for the inexperienced clinician to understand this, so that management can be approached with a view of possible long-term involvement. The possibility of a long-term need for provision applies not only to the speech clinician but to others in the team, especially the ENT specialist, plastic surgeon, orthodontist and oral surgeon. Intervention for speech may need to be provided at different points of time and will need to be co-ordinated with management provided by other team members.

### Change in manner

Using a phonetic description, consideration of changes in both manner and place is important. There is a good deal of research evidence regarding problems of manner in the cleft palate population. The overall findings can be summarised as follows:

1. It is rare to find any problems with the production of *nasals*.
2. Problems with *liquids* [l, r] have occasionally been reported; however, because of their infrequent occurrence in connected speech in English, they may not cause a great problem in communication if they are the only consonants presenting problems. [r] is a consonant subject to considerable variation in individuals classified as normal speakers. It is subject to variation in regional accents and is late to mature.
3. *Fricatives* and *affricates* then *plosives* present the greatest difficulty. Fletcher (1978) analysed manner of articulation in cleft palate speakers using three categories:
   a. Sibilants [s, z, ʃ, ʒ, tʃ, dʒ]
   b. Non-sibilant fricative [f, v, θ, ð]
   c. Plosives [p, b, t, d, k, g].

The sibilants showed the highest mean error percentages (47.4), non-sibilant fricatives next (24.0) and the least errors in plosives (17.3).

*Change in place*

The maintenance of manner but a shift of place is frequently observed; this results from the individual's natural attempt to achieve what is most like the target sound. For example, oral plosives may be substituted by glottal stops. This may occur because the glottis may be the only place in the vocal tract where plosion can be achieved. Stopping attempted higher up the vocal tract may result in air escape into the nose. The production of glottal stops may be accompanied by correct placement elsewhere in the vocal tract but with the audible articulation at the glottis. In some instances glottal stops may be introduced liberally and intrusively into the speech pattern. Here the manner is contravened in all instances except the plosives. Because greater air force is required for the fortis (voiceless) plosives, these are generally found to be more difficult than their lenis counterparts (voiced plosives) in individuals where the velopharyngeal sphincter is inadequate. The use of glottal stops for both voiced and voiceless plosives is sometimes very resistant to change.

The interplay between manner and place of articulation is complex, the ability to achieve correct place being influenced by a large number of factors. The backward shift of place, to the glottis, to achieve plosion is already noted. Tongue tip and blade to alveolar and post-alveolar positions include many plosives, fricatives and affricates [t, d, s, z, ʃ, ʒ, tʃ, dʒ] and are frequently disordered on the basis of manner of articulation because weak intra-oral pressure makes them difficult to produce. These sounds may be disordered further in cases of clefts of the pre-palate in which there is poor alignment of the alveolar ridge and possibly a lowered level of sensory awareness. Lawrence & Phillips (1975) found deviant contacts to be in a posterior direction, thus palato-alveolar consonants [ʃ ʒ] may be produced palatally to become [ç ʝ] or even velar [x or ɣ] or pharyngeal [ħ ʕ].

Where malocclusions are present other deviant articulatory patterns may result. Class III malocclusion, with consequent forward tongue position, makes it difficult to achieve precise tongue tip placements within the maxilla. The maxilla may in itself be small, due to maxillary collapse (see Fig. 1.11). When it is difficult to achieve tongue tip to alveolar ridge placement, the blade of the tongue may be used as the main articulator, therefore imprecise contacts and lateralisation may result (Foster & Greene 1960). Furthermore a forward position of the mandible may make the labio-dental position difficult to achieve, and a reverse position of lower incisors to upper lip may be used, resulting in [p̪, b̪, m̪, f̪, v̪]. In a Class II malocclusion, apart from a tendency to fronting, severe effects on speech are not usually found. Trapping of the lower lip under the upper incisors may lead to a labio-dental placement for bi-labials. Fletcher (1978) suggests that precise articulatory placement may be handicapped further by deviant tongue positions during vowel sounds. There is some evidence that tongue position may also be influenced by the presence of a fistula, the altered tongue position leading to articulatory changes. The tongue may undertake manoeuvres in an attempt to prevent air escape through the fistula.

The potential range of problems in cleft of lip and palate may be summarised as follows:

1. Changes in breath direction
2. Inadequacy of breath support because of air waste
3. Weakened fricatives, plosives and affricates
4. Audible nasal emission
5. Tendency for contacts to be to the back of the oral cavity
6. Preponderance of lamino contacts and imprecise tongue tip movements.
7. Use of double articulation, e.g. alveolar and glottal
8. Secondary articulations such as pharyngealisation and velarisation.
9. Frequent use of glottal stop.
10. Fricatives may be retracted in place to become velar, pharyngeal or glottal.

**Phonological problems**

The phonological processes as well as the phonetic patterns need to be considered in cleft palate individuals. In children developmentally immature, phonological processes will be found according to the child's age as well as in relation to a number of factors affecting phonological development. In some children, difficulties at both the phonetic and phonological levels may be found. From the above discussion on phonetic problems it can be understood that the maturation of phonology will in some cases be handicapped by a child's inability to produce the target adult phone.

Crystal (1980) describes phonology as a bridge level between the phonetic and other levels of language. It is an essential level of development for the child in being able to signal differences in meaning. Inability to signal distinctive features leads to reduced phonological contrasts and may be a factor strongly influencing intelligibility. Work by Singh et al (1981), which studied distinctive features in the analysis of articulation problems in a range of cases, found the cleft palate group showed different patterns in their use of distinctive features to other groups. Of note was the poorness of front-back distinction. Other researchers suggest that articulatory patterns used lead to poor differentiation of the voiced and voiceless pairs. In such instances phonemic distinction becomes dependent on contextual cues. Some young children who are having severe difficulties in achieving velopharyngeal closure may have a system consisting purely of nasalised vowels, nasals and glottals. Consequently it will be impossible for them to signal phonological contrasts, even when it can be shown that perceptually they understand these contrasts. The presence of perceptual awareness may be a good prognostic indicator for the child to mature into adult phonology, providing the anatomical structures make this possible.

Identification of the stage of phonological development is particularly relevant to the management of the young child. Phonetic and phonological development in infants will be discussed further in Chapter 2.

**Language problems**

The child with a cleft palate does not belong to a homogeneous group, and is not exempt from other communication problems. Like all children he may be subject to language delay from a range of possible causes. There are, however, a number of reasons why these children may be especially prone to language deficit. The early mother–baby bonding in which early interaction takes place, is under stress and may therefore provide a poor start. A number of other factors could be detrimental to language development. For example hearing loss, if present, will slow the development of language comprehension and in consequence expressive language will also be delayed. Periods of hospitalisation may interrupt periods of normal experience, so vital for language learning. Furthermore if a child's speech efforts are not easily understood it will be difficult for parents to reinforce communication efforts. Parents may be prevented from expanding utterances because they cannot understand the child's intended meaning, consequently usual language-stimulating opportunities may be curtailed. The child who is lacking in confidence may not be willing to use language interactively. The natural protectiveness of parents may discourage children from expressing themselves.

Although the actual incidence and nature of language delay in the cleft palate child is a matter of continuing controversy, it has been reported as a finding in a number of studies over a considerable period. Phillips and Harrison (1969) in assessing pre-school children found that the cleft palate group functioned below their normal peers in both receptive and expressive language skills.

Faircloth & Faircloth (1971) examined the natural language of cleft palate children between 6 and 11 years. They found that children with articulation problems also showed reductions in word and sentence length and reduced sentence complexity. The authors hypothesised that children confine themselves to simple utterances to maintain intelligibility. However some other studies have not necessarily found reduced length and complexity in cleft palate speakers.

In general there seems to be support for the incidence of a mild language delay in many but not all cleft palate children. The relationship between hearing loss and language deficit is the variable most clearly established. Intelligence is another variable which is highly relevant to linguistic development and has been discussed earlier.

The involvement of the speech clinician in the early management of the cleft palate infant so that appropriate help can be provided regarding language, as well as speech develop-ment, should help to promote good language skills in such children. These ideas are discussed more fully in the following chapters.

There is some evidence that restricted language skills are also evident in the adult cleft palate speaker. Pannbacker (1975) compared adults with repaired clefts to normals. She found significant correlations between intelligibility and mean length of utterance, the adults with cleft palate tending to use shorter and more consistent responses. Syntactic and vocabulary differences were not found. More recent studies do not give such clear evidence of language delay; this could relate to changes in research methods, but could also be a valid finding related to the provision of early advisory management on language stimulus for these children, as well as the earlier identification and treatment of language handicapping factors such as hearing impairment.

## GENERAL COMMUNICATION AND INTERACTION

Linguistic abilities will be seen within the child's general abilities to interact and communicate. Some will appear language deficient because they are just unwilling to talk, either because they know they have poor speech or their appearance is poor, or both. Spriestersbach's (1973) findings show that cleft palate children tend not to be treated in the same way as their potentially normal communicating peers. For example, they are given less encouragement to babble; given less chances to talk as much as they want; take less part in family conversations; talk less frequently than their peers; are less willing to talk to strangers and have less speaking parts in school. This list of factors gives clear indication that they may become poor communicators, less because of their specific speech problems, but more because they are given a role as a poor communicator and deprived of usual encouragement and opportunities.

The author has frequently met adolescent cleft cases who are extremely reluctant to communicate in most situations. They exhibit such behaviour as unwillingness to talk, situation avoidance, hiding behind their hair, head lowering and lack of use of eye contact. In their speech they may use low intensity and talk very quickly, hoping that if they do this they will not be noticed; in fact their whole demeanour and unintelligible speech draws attention to themselves. In normal communication the listener's attention is largely focussed on the speaker's face. Where the speaker is concerned about his facial appearance communication may be disturbed. The problem will be exacerbated by the presence of speech difficulties, especially if they lead to lack of intelligibility. Features such as nasal grimace will also be distracting for the listener.

A study by McWilliams & Paradise (1973) showed that cleft palate adolescents are less willing than their peers to communicate outside their homes. At a time when all adolescents are very aware of all aspects of the physical self, there will be increased awareness of facial disfigurement. Concern over this may take precedence over concerns about other problems, including speech (Richman 1983).

It is evident that there is close interaction between speech and communication in general. Any intervention to improve speech and thus enhance the individual's self-image should lead to better communication, while management to improve self-image and the development of communication skills may in fact lead to an improvement of functional speech. The interactions between these areas therefore need to be carefully evaluated, especially by the speech clinician. Team management can then be targeted on those aspects which are considered to be central in causing or maintaining the communication problems at all levels.

## REFERENCES

Albery E H, Hathorn I S, Pigott R W (eds) 1986 Cleft lip and palate: a team approach. Wright, Bristol

Andrews J R 1970 Oral form discrimination in individuals with normal and cleft palates. Cleft Palate Journal 10: 92

Anthony J F K 1980 Aerodynamic and phonetic analysis. In: Edwards M, Watson A C H (eds) Advances in the management of cleft palate. Churchill Livingstone, Edinburgh

Aronson A E 1985 Clinical voice disorders, 2nd edn Thieme, New York

Blood G W, Hyman M 1977 Children's perception of nasal resonance. Journal of Speech and Hearing Disorders 42: 446

Bosma J F (ed) 1970 Second symposium on Oral sensation and perception. Charles C Thomas, Springfield, Illinois

Bradley P 1979 Congenital and acquired velopharyngeal insufficiency. In: Bzoch K R (ed) Communication disorders related to cleft lip and palate. Little Brown and Company, Boston

Bzoch K R 1979 Communication disorders related to cleft lip and palate. Little Brown and Company, Boston

Bzoch K R 1964 The effects of a specific pharyngeal flap operation upon the speech of 40 cleft-palate persons. Journal of Speech and Hearing Disorders. 29 (No 2): 111

Calnan J S 1956 Diagnosis, prognosis and treatment of palato-pharyngeal incompetence with reference to radiographic investigation. British Journal of Plastic Surgery 8.4: 265

Calnan J S 1971 Congenitally large pharynx. British Journal of Plastic Surgery 24: 263

Catford J C 1977 Fundamental problems in phonetics. Edinburgh University Press, Edinburgh

Clifford E 1969 The impact of a symptom: a preliminary comparison of cleft lip palate and asthmatic children. Cleft Palate Journal 6: 221

Cosman B, Falk A S 1980 Delayed hard palate repair and speech deficiencies: a cautionary report. Cleft Palate Journal 17: 27

Crystal D 1980 An introduction to language pathology. Edward Arnold, London

Darley F L, Aronson A E, Brown J R 1975 Motor speech disorders. W B Saunders Co, Philadelphia

Edwards M 1974 Perceptual processes underlying speech. Unpublished MPhil Thesis, University of Aston in Birmingham

Edwards M, Watson A C H (eds) 1980 Advances in the management of cleft palate. Churchill Livingstone, Edinburgh

Enderby P, Philipp R 1986 Speech and language handicap: towards knowing the size of the problem. British Journal of Disorders of Communication 21: 151

Faircloth S R, Faircloth M A 1971 Delayed language and linguistic variations. In: Grabb W, Rosenstein S, Bzoch K (eds) Communication disorders related to cleft lip and palate. Little Brown and Co, Boston

Finnegan D 1974 Speech sound discrimination skills of

seven and eight year old cleft palate males. Cleft Palate Journal 11: 111

Fletcher S G 1978 Diagnosing speech disorders from cleft palate. Grune and Stratton, New York

Foster T D, Greene M C L 1960 Lateral speech defects and dental irregularities in cleft palate. British Journal of Plastic Surgery X11 4: 367

Foster T D 1975 A textbook of orthodontics. Blackwell Scientific Publications, Oxford

Foster T D 1980 The role of orthodontic treatment. In: Edwards M, Watson A C H (eds) Advances in the management of cleft palate. Churchill Livingstone, Edinburgh

Goodstein L D 1961 Intellectual impairment in children with cleft palates. Journal of Speech and Hearing Research 4: 287

Gorlin R J, Pindborg J J, Cohen M M 1976 Syndromes of the head and neck. McGraw Hill, New York

Hardcastle W 1976 Physiology of speech production Academic Press, London

Harrison R J, Philips B J 1971 Observations on hearing levels of pre-school cleft-palate children. Journal of Speech and Hearing Disorders 36, 2: 252

Heineman-de Boer J A 1985 Cleft palate children and intelligence. Swets and Zeitlinger, Lisse

Hirschberg J 1986 Velopharyngeal insufficiency. Folia Phoniatrica 38: 22

Hochberg I, Kabcenall J 1967 Oral stereognosis in normal and cleft palate individuals. Cleft Palate Journal 4: 47

Jackson M S, Jackson I T, Christie F B 1976 Improvement in speech following closure of anterior palatal fistula with bone grafts. British Journal of Plastic Surgery 29: 295

Jackson I T 1972 Closure of secondary palatal fistulae with intra-oral tissue and bone grafting. British Journal of Plastic Surgery 25: 93

Kaplan E N 1975 The occult sub-mucous cleft. Cleft Palate Journal 12: 356

Karnell M P, Van Demark R D 1986 Longitudinal speech performance in patients with cleft palate; comparisons based on secondary management. Cleft Palate Journal 23: 278

Kernahan D A, Stark R B 1958 A new classification for cleft lip and palate. Plastic and Reconstruction Surgery 22: 435

Ladefoged P 1985 A course in phonetics, 2nd edn. Harcourt Brace Jovanovich, San Diego

Lamb M M, Wilson F B, Leeper H A 1972 A comparison of selected cleft palate children and their siblings on the variables of intelligence, hearing loss and visual perceptual-motor abilities. Cleft Palate Journal 9: 218

Laver J 1980 The phonetic description of voice quality. Cambridge University Press, Cambridge

Lawrence C A, Phillips B J 1975 A telefluoroscopic study of lingual contacts made by persons with palatal defects. Cleft Palate Journal 12: 85

Lawson L I, Chierci G, Castro A, Harvold E P, Miller E R, Owsley J Q 1972 Effects of adenoidectomy on the speech of children with potential velopharyngeal dysfunction. Journal of Speech and Hearing Disorders 37: 390

Lencione R M 1980 Psychosocial aspects of cleft lip and palate. In: Edwards M, Watson A C H (eds) Advances in the management of cleft palate. Churchill Livingstone, Edinburgh

McWilliams B J, Bluestone C D, Musgrave R H 1969 Diagnostic implications of vocal cord nodules in children with cleft palate. Laryngoscope 79: 2072

McWilliams B J, Paradise L P 1973 Education, occupational and marital status of cleft palate adults. Cleft Palate Journal 10: 223

McWilliams B J, Matthews H P 1979 A comparison of intelligence and social maturity in children with unilateral complete clefts and those with isolated cleft palates. Cleft Palate Journal 16: 363

McWilliams B J, Morris H L, Shelton R L 1984 Cleft palate speech. B C Decker Inc, The C V Mosby Company, Saint Louis

Masters F W, Bingham H G, Robinson D W 1960 The prevention and treatment of hearing loss in the cleft palate child. Cleft Palate Journal 5: 44

Maue-Dickson W 1977 Cleft lip and palate research: an updated state of the art. Section II. Anatomy and physiology. Cleft Palate Journal 14: 270

Minami R T, Kaplan E N, Wu G, Jobe R P 1975 Velopharyngeal incompetence without overt cleft palate. Plastic and Reconstructive Surgery 55.5: 573

Moore W H, Somers R K 1975 Phonetic contexts: their effects on perceived intelligibility in cleft palate speakers. Folia Phoniatrica 27: 410

Pannbacker M 1975 Oral language skills of adult cleft palate speakers. Cleft Palate Journal 12: 95

Paradise J L 1975 Middle ear problems associated with cleft palate. Cleft Palate Journal 12: 17

Phillips B J, Harrison R J 1969 Language skills of pre-school cleft palate children. Cleft Palate Journal 6: 108

Pigott R W 1969 The nasendoscopic appearance of the normal palatopharyngeal valve. Plastic and Reconstructive Surgery 43,1: 19

Richman L 1983 Self-reported social, speech and facial concerns of adolescents with cleft palate. Cleft Palate Journal 20: 41

Shelton R L 1979 Oral sensory function in speech production and remediation. In: Bzoch K R (ed) 1979 Communicative disorders related to cleft lip and palate. Little Brown & Co, Boston

Shelton R L, Blank J L 1984 Oronasal fistulas, intraoral air pressure and nasal air flow during speech. Cleft Palate Journal 21: 91

Shprintzen R J 1979 Velopharyngeal insufficiency in the absence of overt or submucous cleft palate: the mystery solved. In Ellis R L, Flack F C (eds) Diagnosis and treatment of palatoglossal malfunction. The College of Speech Therapists, London

Silverman E M, Zimmer C H 1975 Incidence of chronic hoarseness among school-age children. Journal of Speech and Hearing Disorders 40: 211

Singh S, Hayden M E, Toombs M S 1981 The role of distinctive features in articulation errors. Journal of Speech and Hearing Disorders 46: 174

Slutsky H 1969 Maternal reaction and adjustment to birth and care of cleft palate child. Cleft Palate Journal 6: 425

Spriestersbach D C, Sherman D 1968 Cleft palate and communication. Academic Press, New York

Spriestersbach D C 1973 Psychological aspects of the 'cleft palate problem', vol I. University of Iowa Press, Iowa

Starr P, Chinsky R, Canter H, Meier J 1977 Mental, motor and social behaviour of infants with cleft lip and/or cleft palate. Cleft Palate Journal 14: 140

Stengelhofen J, Foster T D 1979 An investigation into the effects of residual oro-nasal fistula in repaired cleft palate. Proceedings of the 8th National Conference of The College of Speech Therapists, London

Stewart J, Ott J, Lagace R 1971 Sub-mucous cleft palate. Birth defects VIII, 7: 64

Subtelny J D, Van Hattum R J, Myers B A 1972 Ratings and measures of cleft palate speech. Cleft Palate Journal 9: 18

Travis E L (ed) 1971 Handbook of audiology and speech pathology. Appleton Century Crofts, New York

Trost J E 1981 Differential diagnosis of velopharyngeal disorders. In: Bradford L J, Wettz R T (eds) Communication Disorders, An Audio Journal of Continuing Education. Grune and Stratton, New York

Van Demark D R, Morris H L, Van de Haar C 1979 Patterns of articulation in speakers with cleft palate. Cleft Palate Journal 16: 23

Van Gelder L 1964 Open nasal speech following adenoidectomy and tonsillectomy. Journal of Communication Disorders 7 (3): 263

Warren D W 1986 Compensatory speech behaviours in individuals with cleft palate: a regulation/control phenomena? Cleft Palate Journal 23: 251

Weatherley-White R C A, Sakura C Y, Brenner L D, Stewart J M, Ott J E 1972 Sub-mucous cleft palate: its incidence, natural history and indications for treatment. Plastic and Reconstructive Surgery 49,3: 297

Wilson K D 1979 Voice problems in children. The Williams and Wilkins Co, Baltimore

Worster-Drought 1974 Supra bulbar paresis and its differential diagnosis. Supplement to Developmental Medicine and Child Neurology. No 30 Vol 16 No 1

*Influences on the beginnings of communication*
*Early vocalisation*
*Early communication development*
*Aims of early management*
  *Parent support through counselling*
  *Feeding*
  *Problem recognition and prevention*

*Assessment of communication development*
  *The case history*
  *Language development*
    *The checklist of communicative competence*
    *Receptive expressive emergent language scale*
  *Speech assessment*
    *Articulation*
    *Phonetic and phonological analysis*
    *Resonance and phonation*
  *Assessment of velopharyngeal function*

*Intervention*
  *Intervention strategies*

*Case studies*
  *Peter: complete unilateral cleft of primary and secondary palate*
  *Philip: bilateral cleft of primary palate and complete cleft of secondary palate*
  *Susan: unilateral cleft of primary and secondary palate*

# 2

# Early intervention

*J. Russell*

This chapter describes the role of the speech therapist in the management of children with cleft lip and palate from birth and during the first 3 years of life. Methods of assessment and suggestions for intervention are discussed as well as the theory behind early intervention. The discussion focusses on the speech therapist's counselling activities and on treatment strategies which can be adopted to facilitate the acquisition of age-appropriate communication skills.

The cleft condition which is known to have consequences for normal speech and language development is usually diagnosed at or soon after birth. The nature of the condition and possible communication difficulties have been outlined in the first chapter. From birth, therefore, children with cleft lip and palate can be identified as an 'at risk' population vulnerable to factors known to be detrimental to the acquisition of communication skills. Once the parents have an awareness of the condition and have coped with initial problems such as feeding and plans for surgery, their next major concern is often associated with speech. Sometimes they are worried that the child will not talk at all, let alone normally.

INFLUENCES ON THE BEGINNINGS OF COMMUNICATION

In addition to the parental concern and the implications of the cleft itself, it is also

31

necessary to consider the importance of the first year of life in the establishment of the prerequisites for normal communication development. Recent research into child language has indicated that the communication process commences from birth and that during the first year of life significant events are occurring which are of vital importance to future language development (Anisfeld 1984, Bower 1977, Bates 1979, Bullowa 1979, Fletcher & Garman 1979, 1986, McCormick & Schiefelsbusch 1984). The presence of a cleft palate may influence these events, thus affecting the development of communication at a very early stage.

The initial, most obvious effect of a cleft, except when the physical defect is of a very minor nature, is related to feeding (Campbell & Watson 1980). In severe cases, such as the Pierre Robin syndrome, there may also be respiratory difficulties (Campbell & Watson op cit). Feeding problems are caused by the abnormal physical structures which prevent the infant from being able to suck in the normal manner. This in turn also affects oral motor and oro-sensory development. Edwards (1980) comments that 'however successful the surgical intervention, early oral sensation derived from feeding and sucking will be different' as of course will be the method of feeding. Bzoch (1979) suggests that abnormal neuromotor patterns will also develop because 'auditory decoding and neuromotor encoding skills are learned when the vast majority of infants with a palate defect have an abnormal mechanism'. Both the abnormal physical structures and neuromotor patterns have the potential to cause delayed or deviant phonetic development.

Another important aspect of the regular and frequent feeding episodes in infancy is the opportunity for mother–child interaction which is vitally important for pragmatic development (Carpenter et al 1983). The infant's sucking behaviour follows a regular temporal pattern. Sequences of sucks described as a 'burst' are followed by pauses with 'the number of sucks per burst ranging from about 5 to 20 and the pauses lasting between 4 and 5 seconds' (Shaffer 1985). Kaye (1982) studied the 'burst-pause' patterns of infant feeding. One of his conclusions is that 'this phenomenon is the earliest example of infants and mothers learning to give and take turns'. This is an important part of early social development. It arguably leads to the later establishment of interactive play (Bruner 1975) which directs the child's attention to turn-taking and communicative exchange, thus establishing the pattern of conversational interaction. If feeding the cleft palate baby is a slow and arduous process and causes anxiety, a pattern of negative interaction may develop. Because of having to deal with orthopaedic appliances and strapping (Foster 1980), and having to cope with the frustrations of the feeding situation, the parent and child may both become exhausted and have neither the time nor the inclination to indulge in pleasurable communicative interaction. Thus the natural opportunities for the initiation of and response to communication may not occur. As McWilliams et al (1984) comment, 'it is difficult for the mother to look at her baby and talk gently during feeding if the baby is experiencing difficulties that are frightening to the mother'. The parents may also be under pressure because no one else is willing or able to feed the child for them. These ideas are explored further in Chapter 7 of this volume.

A further physical effect of the cleft palate is related to hearing problems, as already outlined in the previous chapter. Otitis media is frequently present from birth in children with cleft palate and is thought to be due to Eustachian tube malfunction (Heller 1979, Lencione 1980, McWilliams et al 1984, Maw 1986). The resulting conductive hearing loss may fluctuate and be intermittent in nature, thus having the potential seriously to interfere with the development of auditory skills and later language development (Bamford & Saunders 1985). Kent (1981) pointed out that 'it is clear that the neonate has considerable capacity to make discriminations of speech or speech-like sounds'. In an infant with a cleft palate and associated otitis media it is possible that this ability is diminished. Unfortunately studies investigating the incidence of otitis media in children with clefts have not addressed this particular issue.

Less tangible than the physical effects of the cleft palate is the possible influence of parental reactions on subsequent speech and language development. The existence of a cleft may affect the parents' attitude to the child and thus their response to, and initiation of communication. Parental reaction has been shown to be related to some extent to the severity of the deformity, but as McWilliams et al (1984) discuss there are a number of other influencing factors, many of which are difficult to evaluate objectively. Therefore the clinician needs to be alert to the possibility of individual differences and needs.

Tobiasen & Hiebert (1984) investigated parents' tolerance for misbehaviour in their cleft lip and palate children. They used a standardised questionnaire to record the parents' ratings of the occurrence of behaviour problems and their perception of the severity of the problems. The ratings of a group of parents of 41 cleft lip and palate boys were compared with those from a group of 512 non-cleft children (also boys). Unfortunately these were not matched controls and the data were based solely on parental report. Tobiasen & Hiebert were therefore appropriately cautious in the interpretation of their results because of weaknesses in the research design. The results do suggest that parents of cleft palate children may be more tolerant of misbehaviour than parents of children who do not have facial clefts, but further research is required to substantiate this conclusion.

Hospitalisation at the time of palatal surgery may be a traumatic time for both parents and children. The parents' chapter in this volume supports this view. Such trauma has the potential to affect parent–child relationships, interaction and subsequent pragmatic development. The palate repair itself has been shown to have an effect on the amount and range of vocalisations used by the child (Grunwell & Russell 1987a). It is possible that the experience of hospitalisation may also temporarily affect communication development.

Much will depend on the age of the child and on the attitude of the parents. The latter is partly determined by the relationship between the parents and the hospital staff and on the accuracy and amount of information the parents have been given (MacDonald 1979, Smith 1986).

Edwards (1980) points out that 'it has been shown that parents of children with congenital handicap tend to regard them as being different long after they have in fact moved towards normality'. In the early stages this may mean that parental expectations of the child's potential are an underestimate. Attempts by the child to communicate may pass unnoticed, particularly because the effects of the cleft on articulatory development can cause different vocal output from that which might be expected from the normal child.

## EARLY VOCALISATION

Until recently there were few studies of the pre-speech vocalisations of cleft palate children. Westlake & Rutherford (1966) and Ross & Johnston (1978) both cite Olsen's 1965 study of the vocalisations of unoperated cleft palate babies between the 5th and 30th month. This study indicated a delay in the onset of babbling and a tendency to articulate sounds using the 'posterior part of the vocal tract' rather than the lips and front of the tongue.

More recent studies of the babbling patterns of cleft palate children have also indicated delay and differences from the normal pattern of development (Grunwell & Russell 1987a, O'Gara & Logemann 1985). Henningsson (personal communication) described the pre-speech vocalisations of cleft palate children as being characterised by 'glottal babble'. Grunwell & Russell (1987a) and O'Gara & Logemann (1985) also report a predominance of glottal articulations as well as the frequent occurrence of glides.

The use of glottal substitutions and backing, i.e the production of consonants further back in the mouth than normal, is reported in the speech patterns of older cleft palate children

(Edwards 1980, McWilliams et al 1984, Morris 1979) and is described in the previous chapter. Although this has often been associated with velopharyngeal insufficiency, it is possible as Edwards (1980) discusses, that it could also be related to the effects of the abnormal learning patterns associated with feeding, as outlined above. Because of the physical defect and modified methods of feeding, the cleft palate infant is unable or does not need to create a reduced intra-oral pressure in order to suck milk from a teat. Gornall et al (1983) describe one type of feeding method in which a long teat with a larger than normal hole is used. This allows a free flow of milk to be delivered to the posterior part of the mouth without requiring the infant to create a reduced intra-oral pressure. There is, therefore, little use of the tip and front of the tongue during feeding; this may subsequently influence phonetic development.

With regard to normal speech development there is an established link between the phonetic repertoire of babbling and the basic sound system of a child's language, whatever that language may be (Locke 1983, Oller 1980). The detection of abnormal patterns in the pre-speech vocalisations of cleft palate children is a further indication of the need for early intervention. Ways can then be suggested whereby mothers can provide auditory and oro-sensory stimulation in order to encourage the infant to make the appropriate tongue and lip movements for the development of more normal articulatory patterns.

## EARLY COMMUNICATION DEVELOPMENT

It has been recently observed that dialogue between mothers and their older language-impaired children is different from that between mothers and children with normal language development (Conti-Ramsden & Friel-Patti 1984). It is also possible that impairment to this interaction is present in the cleft palate population. This could be prevented if early differences in mother–child interaction are detected. The importance of mother–child interaction for pragmatic development has been outlined above in relation to feeding. A delay in the expressive language skills of cleft palate children is well documented in the literature (see McWilliams et al 1984 for a comprehensive survey). This has already been referred to in Chapter 1 and will be further discussed later in this chapter. It is perhaps speech therapists' failure in the past to pay sufficient attention to early pragmatic development in the cleft palate population that is at least partly responsible for this delay. In monitoring early pragmatic development particular attention also needs to be paid to how the child learns to convey meaning, or communicative intention (Carpenter et al 1983). One particularly important facet in the pre-speech stage is the way in which the child learns to use gesture with vocalisation in order to convey a particular message.

The combination of gestural and vocal development is not only prerequisite for early pragmatic development, but is also linked to the origins of grammar. Griffiths (1979) describes how single word utterances are combined with intonation patterns and with gestures in order to convey different meanings. This combination provides the foundation for the emergence of two-word utterances which mark the beginnings of grammar. Long & Dalston (1982) specifically addressed this issue of 'paired gestural and vocal behaviour' in cleft palate children. Their findings from comparing groups of 10 normal and 10 cleft palate children at 12 months of age indicated significant differences between the two groups, and suggested that the children with cleft lip and palate were already showing deficits at this stage of development. This study thus provides direct evidence of the need for early intervention by the speech therapist.

From the preceding discussion, it can be appreciated that the physical effects of a cleft palate, combined with its functional influence on developments occurring during the first year of life, can have a significant impact on communication skills at an early stage. The speech therapist who has a detailed knowledge of normal development is able to observe and monitor the child's development in order to detect potential problems as they arise. In maintaining regular contact with the cleft palate child and his family, the speech therapist is also in an ideal position to detect other problems connected with the child's general development, for example, signs of developmental delay, auditory impairment and family social difficulties. Early appropriate action can therefore be initiated with reference to other members of the cleft palate team. This responsibility for identifying factors detrimental to the child's personal and social development is part of the speech therapist's traditional role with older cleft palate children, and indeed with all children who present with communication problems. Involvement with the much younger child means that the cleft palate team is now able to operate a policy of total care which is designed to give the cleft palate child the best possible opportunity for achieving overall normal development from birth.

In some centres this early intervention role is undertaken by a therapist who is an integral member of the cleft palate team. However, in addition to this, and in places where such a service is not available, early intervention can be provided by the therapist in the child's home locality. All speech therapists are equipped with the necessary expertise to carry out this role. A specialist knowledge is not required and it is usually possible to consult more experienced colleagues who work routinely in the field of cleft palate, except perhaps in developing countries. In the author's experience, an ideal situation is when both the therapist from the cleft palate team and the child's local therapist liaise together about management of the child's communication development.

## AIMS OF EARLY MANAGEMENT

There are three main aims of early management which are:

1. Parent support

2. The identification and prevention of problems
3. The facilitation of normal communication development.

These are achieved through counselling the parents, monitoring the child's development and arranging early appropriate intervention, should this prove necessary.

The parents will, of course, have individual needs depending on personal resources, their circumstances and environment (MacDonald 1979), but there are broad areas of counselling which are applicable in every situation. Initial counselling is vitally important as it helps to initiate the long-term relationship between the parents and the professional team and lays the foundations for future intervention (Gornall et al 1983). Ongoing counselling is required to develop and maintain the relationship and to respond to parents' individual needs. There are also times when specific advice is required, for example with regard to feeding. The speech therapist's counselling role will be discussed in detail below.

The monitoring of development generally and communication development in particular, is an integral part of early intervention. In cleft palate individuals, as in any at risk population, it is important to identify potential problems as soon as possible so that early appropriate management can be implemented. Fox et al (1978) measured the development of cleft palate children and concluded that 'these children appear to be at increased developmental risk and deserve to be carefully and routinely evaluated'. They provide evidence to show that even below the age of three years cleft palate children are performing less well than their peers on both linguistic and non-linguistic tasks. The most significant areas of difference were found to be receptive and expressive language and some motor subtests. It proved possible to classify the children into cleft and non-cleft groups on the basis of the results of the developmental tests. Influencing factors such as hearing problems and the severity of the cleft were also correlated with the test results and a significant correlation was found with the extent of the cleft. Fox et al (op cit) suggest that early intervention is required in order to identify potential areas of concern and to prevent secondary social and educational problems.

In some cases, for example when children are referred from outlying geographical areas, initial contact with members of the cleft palate team will not take place until the first out-patient clinic appointment. However, in most instances the parents' first contact with the 'professional' team will be with the surgeon and/or orthodontist who will visit the maternity unit within 24 hours of the child's birth. The parents can then be given appropriate practical advice about feeding and general management, and treatment can be initiated if pre-surgical orthopaedics is required. There will also be discussion of future surgery and the long-term implications of the cleft.

Pre-surgical orthopaedics, which is undertaken by the orthodontist, involves the use of an intra-oral appliance and external strapping (Foster 1980, Gornall et al 1983). Its primary purpose is to protect exposed nasal mucosa during feeding and to influence the alignment of the cleft segments of the lip and alveolus. It helps to reduce the alveolar gap and is also thought to be important socially in that it involves the parents actively in their child's treatment (Gornall et al, op cit).

As a supplement to this initial visit, many centres will also provide written information for the parents. Such material, however, can only convey a limited amount of information, and although every effort is made to ensure accuracy, it is subject to individual interpretation. Written information should, therefore, be used cautiously (Gornall et al 1983, MacDonald 1979, Pannabacker 1976, Wylie & McWilliams 1965) and should not be considered a substitute for the initial interview or any subsequent counselling. A simple leaflet which describes the personnel and procedures of the cleft palate clinic which the child will be attending, is not only helpful to the parents but also to the staff of maternity units who may lack experience of the cleft palate child. Names and telephone numbers of people who

can be contacted for advice should be included. Some parents, such as those of Peter (see case study later in this chapter), will actively seek out further written information. In such instances the cleft palate team can use this material as a basis for discussion.

In the U.K., local branches of the Cleft Lip and Palate Parents' Association (CLAPA) maintain a register of parents who are willing to contact and/or visit new parents in order to offer support, and where possible, practical advice. CLAPA makes every effort to liaise closely with the professionals who are treating their children. They offer invaluable feedback about parents' views, make constructive suggestions and support centres through fund raising activities, in addition to fulfilling their primary aim of supporting each other. This will be taken up in Chapter 7 of this volume.

Following the visit to see the parents and newborn child by members of the professional team, an initial appointment at the cleft palate clinic is arranged to take place within the following few weeks. This early clinic appointment is particularly important for parents who are meeting the team for the first time. At this appointment much of the ground covered at the first meeting may need to be reviewed, as the parents have had time to begin to adjust to their reactions to the birth of their child. They will be learning to cope with any feeding difficulties and will have experienced the reactions of friends and family. While appreciating the reassurance provided by that early visit, they may now have more specific questions about surgical management and the consequences of the cleft for the child's future development. The emphasis should always be on helping the parents to realise that they are vital members of the team caring for their child (Gornall et al 1983).

An ideal time for the speech therapist to be introduced as a member of the cleft palate team is at this initial clinic visit. The feasibility of this will depend on circumstances. If a child is not being closely monitored by a cleft palate team from birth, then a speech therapist may need to be involved earlier in order to help with feeding problems in liaison with the midwife or health visitor, and to provide accurate information and support to the parents. In some localities, it may be possible to establish a system whereby the speech therapy service is advised of all children born with a cleft lip and/or palate, so that early contact can be made with the child's family.

**Parent support through counselling**

Whenever and wherever the speech therapist carries out early counselling of parents the underlying philosophy is the same. There is the need to establish the foundations of a long-term relationship with the parents and to provide them with accurate and comprehensible information. As Gornall et al (1983) comment 'early inaccurate information is very often difficult to overcome with later counselling'. MacDonald (1979) provides insight into the parents' needs and suggests some excellent guidelines for those undertaking counselling. She emphasises that professionals should make 'positive comments about the *total* baby' and listen carefully so that they can be guided by the parents themselves. This helps to prevent the situation in which professionals 'seem to be suggesting to parents what they should be experiencing' because they are telling them what not to do, for example 'not to feel guilty . . .' (MacDonald 1979).

At the initial meeting with the parents, after personal introductions, a brief explanation is given of the speech therapist's involvement with cleft palate children, namely, that there is a possibility that any physical defect affecting the mouth may have implications for speech and language development, that many children will develop normal communication skills with little or no help, but others may need greater involvement from the speech therapist. The therapist is therefore going to adopt an observation and monitoring role in order to help the parents and to ensure that the child receives any help required at the appropriate time.

Then, following MacDonald's suggestions, the speech therapist can ascertain what the

parents knew about cleft palate before their child was born and what they have learnt since. This provides the opportunity to find out if they have been given accurate information and to get some idea of their attitudes and the reactions of family and friends. Because the speech therapist has been present in the clinic when the child was seen by other team members, there is an excellent opportunity to check that the parents have fully understood the information they have been given and that their questions have been satisfactorily answered. When the parents' first language is not English and problems of interpretation may arise, it is doubly important to check that the parents understand the extent and nature of the problem and the treatment plan. In the author's experience, it has often been particularly helpful to bring in experienced interpreters who have some understanding of the situation to assist in the counselling process, especially with mothers.

Once the parents' level of knowledge has been established the speech therapist will begin to have some idea of the accuracy of their information. As the interview progresses counselling can then be based on their individual needs. Accurate, honest answers should be given in response to the parents' questions. If the speech therapist is unable to answer any particular point other team members will be consulted or advice sought from more experienced colleagues and reported back to the parents.

Hahn (1979) gives a detailed description of a first meeting between the 'speech specialist' and the family of a child with a cleft. She emphasises the importance of treating the child as a child and not as a child with a defect, which supports the paediatric approach of Gornall et al (1983).

Ongoing counselling should continue at subsequent joint clinic visits or speech therapy appointments. The parents' need for support will change over time and they may require more help at times of stress, such as when children go into hospital for lip and palate operations (MacDonald 1979). This is illustrated in the case study of Susan at the end of this chapter. The speech therapist should continue to be guided in counselling activities by listening to the parents. For the therapist working in a hospital setting, it is often helpful to see the parents when the child is an in-patient. There is often more time available for discussion than during busy out-patient visits and parents seem to appreciate the contact with a non-surgical member of the cleft palate team. On some occasions it may be desirable and possible to make appointments for parents on their own.

## Feeding

Despite the increasing amount of information available concerning feeding methods and different teats etc. (for example the CLAPA leaflet 1987), it is unfortunate that this is often still not readily available to those who need it most, i.e. the parents of a newborn child with a cleft lip and/or palate. Most specialist centres have a team member, often a paediatric nurse, who offers specific advice on feeding, but many parents struggle alone before they meet this person and others never encounter her. Phillips comments, later in this volume, that most of the initial approaches made to CLAPA are associated with feeding.

The level of involvement with feeding varies according to the situation, but because of the possible link with later speech development, the speech therapist may be approached for help. If the situation is beyond an individual therapist's expertise or experience then advice can be sought from appropriate sources, for example, from specialist centres. In the U.K. the College of Speech Therapists holds a list of specialist advisers on cleft palate who may be approached. The primary aim is to support the parents and help them to establish a feeding routine suitable for them and their baby. At the same time, emphasis can be placed upon using feeding time to provide, as far as is possible, a pleasant experience where patterns of interaction are laid down.

## Problem recognition and prevention

In the team situation, the child's general development is monitored through regular clinic visits. These will tend to be more frequent initially, especially if pre-surgical orthodontic treatment is provided (Foster 1980). Longer intervals between visits occur once a feeding pattern has been established and the baby is gaining weight and growing satisfactorily.

At these clinic visits, the speech therapist is also involved with regard to feeding and can use these opportunities for monitoring communication development in particular. The overall aim is to detect any signs of delay or deviance so that appropriate action can be taken as soon as possible. Once again, if the speech therapist is not involved in the cleft palate clinic this role can be undertaken at a local level. In either case there should be an established procedure for referral to other medical and social agencies as appropriate.

Ideally an otolaryngologist will be either an integral member or closely associated with the cleft palate team. It is then possible for the children to have routine and regular hearing tests and otological examinations. In circumstances where this is not the case, the speech therapist should ensure that regular hearing checks are carried out and appropriate referrals made if problems are suspected.

Most monitoring of early development is carried out through observation and discussion with the parents. Any cause for concern should then be investigated in greater detail. A knowledge of normal development is obviously essential. In this regard it can be useful to refer to development checklists which will be discussed further below. In a cleft palate or screening clinic, constraints of time and adequate facilities make it difficult to carry out anything more than a brief assessment. However, this is usually sufficient to identify children who need further investigation and parents who require more specific counselling. When this occurs, the speech therapist in the specialist clinic can either make a specific appointment to see the parents and child (as in the case study of Peter), or liaise with the child's local therapist who will be carrying out any treatment needed.

A continuing part of the observation and

monitoring role of the speech therapist is to provide the parents with information about normal communication development. At the same time the parents are shown how to observe their child and how to help him progress on to the next stage of communication development. Parents can be helped to recognise their child's attempts at communication and shown how to encourage these attempts. The importance of maintaining interaction and giving the child positive feedback even when the child's vocalisations may not sound speech-like can be demonstrated. The speech therapist can also help the parents to have realistic ideas about what their child can achieve. Attention should also be focussed on how the parent responds to the child and provides a model for communicative interaction and vocalisation.

## ASSESSMENT OF COMMUNICATION DEVELOPMENT

While recognising that post-surgery some cleft palate children will achieve normal speech and language skills with little or no active speech therapy intervention, it is important to identify as soon as possible those who will require specific help and/or further surgery. In some cases direct intervention may not prove to be necessary because of the ongoing advice and help the speech therapist has given the parents while monitoring the child's progress.

It should be remembered that, as well as being vulnerable to speech and language problems because of the cleft condition itself, cleft palate children are also subject to influences which affect the development of communication in the normal population. For example, a child with a cleft lip only may have a language disorder or delay which is unrelated to the physical abnormality. In other words the speech therapist must consider all areas of communication development and not focus solely on the physical defect. Factors relating to the cleft itself which may be relevant should be taken into account, but

these must not prevent the speech therapist from being open-minded until a differential diagnosis is reached. It should be stressed that a specialist knowledge of cleft palate is not required. All speech therapists are equipped by their training to assess and manage children of all ages and in the first instance that is what is required here.

If there has been no previous concern about the communication development of a cleft palate child, a routine assessment should be carried out at about the age of 18 months to 2 years. The aim of this assessment is to make sure that the child is making satisfactory progress along normal lines. All areas of communication development should be screened and those which give cause for concern should then be investigated in greater detail. The speech therapist needs to consider the whole child in relation to his environment.

As with all speech therapy assessments of young children, the results are compared to the normal model of development and considered in the light of any influencing factors, for example, hearing loss, physical effects of the cleft and family social problems. The child's speech and language skills are compared to his abilities in other areas of development. If there is any evidence of general delay, referral should be made to an appropriate source such as a paediatrician.

### The case history

Taking a case history is always a good starting point, even though there may already be information about the child available from the medical notes and previous speech therapy contact. It helps to review that information with the parents, and by discussing it with them, the speech therapist is able to reach a greater understanding of their concerns and attitudes towards their cleft palate child. It should be explained to the parents why this information is needed by the speech therapist and how it helps to build up a complete picture of the child.

In addition to the information which the speech therapist usually requires when dealing with a young child (Warner 1984a), there will be some which relates specifically to the child with a cleft. It is important to know the size and extent of the cleft and whether the child had pre-surgical orthodontic treatment. Details of early feeding, including feeding methods, the type of bottles and teats used and the success of these are required. The medical history should include information about operations to repair the cleft lip and/or palate and the child's age at the time of operation. Parents usually know if there are any palatal fistulae and the speech therapist will need to observe the site and size of these later when carrying out an oral examination. The child may also have had other operative procedures such as grommet insertion to alleviate otitis media and conductive hearing problems.

## Language development

In the many studies of the language development of cleft palate children, there is considerable variation in the aspects of language investigated and in the variables taken into account. There is, however, general agreement that the language abilities of cleft palate children are delayed, particularly the development of expressive language (Bzoch 1979, Fox et al 1978, McWilliams et al 1984, Nation 1970, Pannbacker 1971, Philips & Harrison 1969). McWilliams et al (1984) comment that 'because of the increased risk of language impairment which children with clefts have in their pre-school years, their early linguistic development should be carefully monitored'. Studies which involved younger children have shown that it is possible to detect delay in the pre-linguistic period of development (Bzoch 1979, Fox et al 1978, Long & Dalston 1982).

The speech therapist, therefore, needs to consider all areas of communication development. This includes non-verbal, pragmatic and comprehension development as well as expressive abilities. The procedure followed by the speech therapist will depend on the age of the child but a variety of informal and formal assessments are available. Initially the speech therapist may carry out an informal play session with the child and parent. Using observation and discussion, the aim is to 'build up a descriptive profile of the child's abilities and to estimate the developmental level in areas associated with language acquisition' (Warner 1984b). From this session the therapist is able to identify areas which need further investigation.

Checklists or developmental scales are particularly appropriate for assessing children under 2 years old as they rely on observation and parental interviews rather than requiring the direct co-operation of the child. 'They provide the clinician with insights from the parents' perspective and help to provide guidance for further observation and testing of the child,' (McWilliams et al 1984). In addition they help to identify children who are delayed in all areas, as well as those who are experiencing difficulty in one particular area, for example, expressive language.

### The checklist of communicative competence (0–2 years)

This checklist devised by Gérard (1986) includes all areas of communication development and is a very useful tool for the speech therapist when in-depth assessment is required. It is divided into four main sections—social, cognitive, comprehension and communication—all of which are sub-divided into further categories. For example, social development includes sections on attachment, turn-taking, and interactions with adults and other children. Thus pragmatic development is investigated in some depth. The age at which each behaviour usually appears is indicated and the checklist provides a profile of the child's development rather than specific age levels or scores.

### The receptive expressive emergent language scale (REEL)

The REEL scale (Bzoch & League 1971) 'was developed and has been used for the specific purpose of providing a quick and valid receptive and expressive language measure in children up to 3 years of age' (Bzoch 1979). It consists of detailed receptive and expressive language scales presented in tandem in developmental sequence. Scoring gives a receptive language age and an expressive language age, as well as other measures of the child's abilities in each area. The REEL has been used extensively with cleft palate children (Bzoch 1979). It can be used to measure changes in language skills over time and and helps the speech therapist to identify those areas which need particular attention.

The REEL and the Checklist of Communicative Competence both focus primarily on the child's behaviour. The speech therapist should also pay attention to how the parent responds to the child. It is important to observe whether the parent recognises the child's verbal and non-verbal attempts to communicate and the type of parental response to these attempts. Philips (1979) comments on this aspect of communication and describes how the child's attempts should be reinforced and rewarded by the adult.

With the 2-year-old or more co-operative child, the speech therapist can use formal assessment procedures in order to ascertain receptive and expressive language abilities. Examples are the Derbyshire Language Scheme (Knowles & Masidlover 1982) and the Reynell Developmental Language Scales (1985). Some linguistic profiles such as LARSP (Language Assessment, Remediation and Screening Procedure, Crystal et al 1976) which are constructed from a sample of spontaneous language can also be used with children who are under 3 years of age.

When any of the above measures indicate delay or deviant development the speech therapist will need to investigate areas of deficit in greater detail, advise parents and implement intervention as appropriate.

## Speech assessment

Earlier studies of the speech of cleft palate children focussed primarily on articulatory and phonetic ability (Bzoch 1979, Edwards 1980 McWilliams et al 1984). They tend to be lacking in specificity because they pre-date modern methods of phonetic and phonological analysis and because the descriptive terms used are ambiguous. Ingram (1970), however, commented that even these early analyses of cleft palate speech revealed systematic processes.

More recently, phonological analysis of cleft palate speech has begun to be reported (Lynch et al 1983, Hodson et al 1983, Grunwell & Russell 1987b). The importance of using phonological as well as phonetic analyses to study the speech of cleft palate children is succinctly indicated by Crystal (1981). He states that it is required in order to 'determine the extent to which an adequate phonological system is being obscured by purely phonetic deviance, or whether there is in addition an underlying disturbance of a phonological type; if the latter, whether it is something unique to the cleft palate condition, or a manifestation of some general pattern of delay'.

When the child is unable to or does not articulate specific speech sounds, this is described as phonetic deviance or delay. This may be due to abnormal articulatory structures, hearing impairment or abnormal learned neuromotor patterns (Bzoch 1979) as a result of the cleft, or may be developmental in origin (Grunwell 1982). When this phonetic deviance affects the child's ability to signal meaning differences and thus to communicate effectively there is also a resultant 'phonological deficit' (Grunwell, op cit).

Phonetic deviance may occur without a phonological consequence which means that the child is able to signal meaning differences even though phonetic realisation is abnormal. An example is when the alveolar fricatives /s/ and /z/ are produced as palatal fricatives [ç] and [ʝ], which means that the child is able to communicate effectively and intelligibly, although he is not using the adult pronunciation of the intended target phoneme, for example, sea [çi] zoo [ʝu] bus [buç].

When there is a phonological deficit, in addition to or as a result of phonetic deviance, communicative adequacy is diminished and it may be very difficult to understand what the child is saying. An example is when a child produces both the alveolar fricative /s/ and the post-alveolar fricative /ʃ/ as the palatal fricative [ç] with resulting confusion in meaning.

| sea | | sue | | sew | |
|-----|------|------|------|------|-------|
| | [çi] | | [çu] | | [çəʊ] |
| she | | shoe | | show | |

In this example the phonetic deviance is causing a phonological deficit as the child's ability to signal meaning differences is reduced.

A delay in phonetic development will cause a corresponding delay in phonological development. Distinction must be made between delay as a result of phonetic deviance and normal though delayed development. A child who is using velar but not alveolar or bilabial plosives will exhibit Backing which is an unusual process in normal development and can be attributed to the physical defect, for example, daddy [gægi] sue [ku]. If a child uses Stopping of fricatives and Cluster reduction, however, for example, sue [tu] spoon [pun] scar [ka], these are processes which occur in normal development (Grunwell 1985).

It should be stressed that a child with a cleft lip and/or palate may also present with a phonological delay or disorder in the absence of, or in addition to, any phonetic deviance. It is, therefore, important for the speech therapist to investigate the child's articulatory ability and also the phonetic and phonological aspects of speech. Firstly, the therapist needs to determine how the child uses the articulators in imitation and in non-speech as well as speech tasks, as described below. Secondly, a phonetic inventory of the sounds which the child uses in his speech is constructed. Thirdly, the therapist needs to establish how the child uses the sounds in his phonetic inventory to signal meaning. The results of these procedures are then evaluated with regard to any influencing factors, such as abnormal intra-oral structures and conductive hearing loss, in order to determine the extent and nature of any deviance or delay.

## Articulation

The principles and procedures of oro-facial examination are described in Chapter 3. While this is usually a straightforward procedure with the very young infant who is unable to resist (though he may protest!) and the older co-operative child, toddlers often require a less direct approach. Some cleft palate children are very accustomed and willing to allow intra-oral examination, but others may be less forthcoming.

The speech therapist can use observational skills to note obvious facts such as lip scars or nasal grimace, and can take advantage of the opportunity to obtain an intra-oral view when the child is yawning or laughing (Warner 1984b, or being examined by the surgeon or orthodontist in the cleft palate clinic. Randall (1980) describes such an examination. In other situations when information from an intra-oral examination is needed, the procedure must be approached as a game. Speech therapists will be very familiar with the appropriate games of pretence and imitation, for which time and patience are prerequisite.

Information about the child's articulatory ability for verbal and non-verbal imitation tasks also contributes to the overall assessment of articulation. This can also be obtained from an appropriate imitation game in which the child gets some reward, for example a shape to put in the posting box. The therapist will encourage the child to attempt to imitate consonant and vowel sounds in isolation, consonant-vowel and vowel-consonant combinations as well as lip and tongue movements. Knowledge of the child's ability for imitation tasks helps in treatment planning. It may be necessary, for example, to encourage use of the lips and front of the tongue.

## Phonetic and phonological analysis

At any age, the speech therapist needs to evaluate the type and range of sounds used by the child both in pre-speech vocalisations and speech. With children who are not yet using recognisable words the speech therapist will listen to their vocal output and discuss their babbling patterns with their parents. From this an inventory of the consonant-like sounds used can be established and compared with normal development (Stark 1979). In particular the speech therapist should ascertain whether the child is using plosives other than the glottal plosive. Mousset & Trichet (1985) recommend intervention for those children who are not producing any of the voiceless plosives [p] [t] and [k] at 15 months of age. (Appropriate procedures are outlined in Chapter 4). Although this advice is based on a French population it is also applicable to English speakers.

When children are using recognisable speech, the therapist can carry out a phonological, as well as a phonetic analysis, in order to determine which consonants are being used contrastively in the child's speech. In addition to constructing a phonetic inventory the speech therapist assesses 'the child's use of his phonetic inventory in order to establish which sound differences function contrastively' (Grunwell 1985). The child's contrastive system can then be compared with the adult target system and also with characteristics of normal developmental patterns. This includes an assessment of the organisational structure of the child's phonological system, in other words the child's use of different phone combinations in syllables and words, in order to detect whether there are any simplification processes operating in the child's speech indicating delay, deviance or normal development. The principles and procedures for carrying out phonetic and phonological analysis are explicitly described by Grunwell (1985) and will be illustrated in the case studies later in this chapter.

## Resonance and phonation

In addition to articulatory, phonetic and phonological factors the speech therapist also needs to consider the resonatory and phonatory aspects of speech. Inappropriate nasal escape and hypernasal resonance during speech may indicate velopharyngeal insufficiency (VPI). This has been described in the previous chapter.

Albery (1986) comments that 'the significance of the identification of velopharyngeal insufficiency between 2 and 3 years of age is variable' and describes four different types of problem. Two of these are likely to require surgery and two therapy. Albery (op cit) also stresses that the speech therapist 'should always be aware of the possibility of potential competence' of the velopharyngeal sphincter and recommends a period of diagnostic therapy for children with 'a total glottal stop pattern'. The child therefore learns to produce some consonants, such as bilabial plosives, with the correct articulatory placement. In the author's experience, this approach is particularly applicable to young children.

Even in cases where children have gross nasal escape indicating VPI which will require surgery, the speech therapist can usually continue to work on other aspects of speech and language development while waiting for investigations of velopharyngeal function to be implemented, or for the child to have secondary surgery. Work on delayed language and deviant articulatory placement, for example, should continue.

## Assessment of velopharyngeal function

All speech parameters including the phonetic and phonological analysis are important in the diagnosis of VPI. The speech therapist needs to determine whether inappropriate nasal escape occurs consistently in the child's speech, on certain consonants only, or because the child is only using nasal consonants. (See, for example, the case study of Philip at 18 months.) Nasal escape on all consonants and nasalised vowels probably indicates VPI and requires further investigation. If nasal escape occurs on certain consonants only, for example fricative consonants, it can be indicative of deviant sound production due to abnormal learned neuromotor patterns such as those described earlier in this chapter. If the child is using predominantly nasal consonants, the speech therapist will need to establish whether there is any evidence of oral/nasal contrast in the child's speech or whether it can be introduced through therapy. Context should also be considered, as discussed by Crystal (1981) who comments on the 'interference of nasal consonants, and the differing degrees of nasal perceptibility on the range of vowel qualities'.

A battery of procedures is required in order to evaluate VPI (Van Demark et al 1985) and is outlined in Chapter 3. Only some of the procedures may be used with pre-school children. It is possible to persuade children under 3 years old to co-operate for nasal anemometry (Ellis 1979) which helps the therapist to confirm the initial auditory evaluation. Confident children may also be willing to take part in radiography investigations.

## INTERVENTION

The speech therapist's intervention role with the young cleft palate child is very closely linked with the monitoring and advisory role described above. With younger children, in particular, intervention is usually implemented through the parents. The speech therapist may demonstrate how an activity should be carried out with the child and will then advise the parents about how to continue this at home. This approach has two main advantages. Firstly, there is benefit to the parents who are the child's 'natural teachers' and who thus become actively involved in their child's therapy. Secondly, it means that help can be provided on a consistent basis as part of the child's daily routine. Even when therapy is carried out by the therapist working with the child on a one-to-one basis, the parent should continue to be involved in the intervention process and encouraged to work with the child at home.

In the author's experience, most intervention with young cleft palate children is carried out on an individual basis with the child and his parents. It may, however, be appropriate to include some slightly older children, from the age of about 2 and a half to 3 years, in groups. The feasibility of this will depend on whether the needs of the children are similar and if there are sufficient children to consti-

tute a group. Cleft palate children can be included in groups of non-cleft palate children if their needs match those of the other children. This may occur, for example, when they present with delayed language development.

Intervention is geared to the needs of the individual child and his parents. The speech therapist will identify specific aims for each child based on the results of the assessment. Procedures appropriate to that child's developmental level and to his environment will then be selected. As McWilliams et al (1984) point out 'the parents should be directed to encourage activities that are appropriate to the child's developmental level' and they will need to be guided in this by the speech therapist.

When working with parents, all suggested activities should be introduced with demonstration and explanation. The speech therapist needs to be clear about the aims and objectives required and should discuss these with the parents. The parents themselves may provide suggestions about how particular aims can be achieved during the child's daily routine. Bathtime, for example, may be a good time to encourage and participate in 'vocal play' (Hahn 1979).

### Intervention strategies

In the literature a number of strategies for intervention with the cleft palate infant and young child are described (Brookshire et al 1980, Hahn 1979, McWilliams et al 1984, Philips 1979). It may help the speech therapist to consult some of these references and to use some of the strategies described while tailoring them to the needs of the individual child.

Brookshire et al (1980) provide detailed objectives and activities for facilitating speech and language development from birth up to three years of age. These are presented in six-monthly stages. This programme is a valuable resource for therapists who lack experience with younger children. It offers specific ideas rather than vague suggestions, but attention should still be paid to the suitability of any activity for the individual child and his parents.

Philips (1979) describes a programme for 'stimulating syntactic and phonological development' which she recommends is initiated when the child is 18 months to 2 years old. The purposes of this programme are to:

1. Develop the child's confidence in his ability to achieve intelligible verbal communication
2. Allay parental anxiety concerning the child's development of verbal communication
3. Encourage development of communication skills to the maximum of the child's potential
4. Minimise or prevent the development of undesirable compensatory articulation and voice patterns when physical inadequacies interfere with the normal development of communication skills
5. Determine velopharyngeal competence for oral communication as early as possible.

In order to achieve these objectives, Philips suggests informal sessions in which advantage is taken of the child's spontaneous behaviour during play. Parent participation is also encouraged. The stimulation programme is illustrated with case studies in which play situations are used to demonstrate how the child is encouraged to use verbal language, to develop articulatory placement and to use the appropriate sounds in his speech.

In the author's experience some work on sound production can be carried out with children under 3 years old, provided that it is introduced as a game. It should be monitored closely by the speech therapist and should not cause parent or child any frustration if exact results are not achieved. Details of work on articulation are provided in Chapter 4.

Some intervention strategies which have been found to be useful in work with cleft palate children are described below. This is by no means a comprehensive list and is designed only to provide a few guidelines. The therapist must select those strategies which are applicable to the child's needs and developmental level. Here the main focus is on vocal output, but these activities should be integrated with any others which are required for different aspects of communication development, as described above.

The overall philosophy is based on taking advantage of what the child is doing naturally to reinforce and encourage appropriate development. In this way suitable activities become part of the daily routine. Appropriate methods of reinforcing the desired behaviour must be selected according to the individual child and his parents. Very young children, for example, will be rewarded by the pleasure of participating in vocal imitation with a parent, whereas those of 2 years and over may require a more specific reward, perhaps involving a simple activity. The child should be helped to realise when the required target has been achieved.

*1. To encourage a wider range of speech-like vocalisations and for the child to 'experiment' with his articulatory ability*

This may be required both at the pre-speech and speech stages of development. In the former, it is achieved by participation in the child's spontaneous babbling and encouraging imitation of different lip and tongue movements in order to produce 'new' consonant-like sounds. Visual stimulation is provided by parent and child looking at each other and may be supplemented by the use of a mirror. The adult may make exaggerated facial movements and use language-appropriate consonant and vowel combinations. In particular, the adult should use the speech-like sounds which the child is already producing in his babbled utterances. The speech therapist should teach the parent how to recognise non-speech sounds such as glottal plosives and not to reinforce them. Tactile stimulation is also helpful; the mother can, for example, put her hand or finger against the child's mouth while he is vocalising in order to produce different sounds. The child's hand can also be taken to the mother's mouth for the same purpose. Many parents naturally engage in such games with their children.

With toddlers who are using some speech, different strategies may be required. Imitation games involving making faces or particular 'noises' can be incorporated into pretend play. Materials such as face crayons supplement such games and may provide some tactile stimulation. In addition, tongue movements can be encouraged by using an appropriate food which the child has to lick from his top or bottom lip or from a spoon. The food should be of a suitable consistency and acceptable to the mother. It is often useful to use a mirror in some of these activities.

## 2. To encourage the development of auditory and discrimination skills

This is included here as it is considered to be a vital part of the preparation for the following objective of producing specific consonants. It is important for the child to be able to recognise different consonants in isolation and in different positions in words, particularly when phonological therapy is being undertaken. There are four main steps in this strategy, but it may not be necessary to go through all of them. The speech therapist will select those which are appropriate for the age and ability of the individual child.

(i) The child learns to recognise and associate everyday sounds with what they represent. The parent comments if the child is attracted by a noise and/or draws the child's attention to the noise, for example the sound of the telephone ringing.

(ii) Sounds are associated with symbolic representation. Animal noises, for example, are associated with toy animals and pictures of animals.

(iii) Consonants are associated with symbolic representation, for example, a snake represents an /s/ and a tap represents a /t/. Even 2-year-olds enjoy games in which they learn to select the appropriate object or picture, provided that the game itself is at their developmental level.

(iv) The child learns to identify consonants in different positions in words, having become familiar with them in stage (iii). It is possible to achieve success with this activity with some 3-year-olds.

## 3. To produce consonants with correct articulatory placement (and if possible the appropriate manner of articulation, that is plosive or fricative for example)

Many children when introduced to the discrimination games described above will attempt to imitate the consonants spontaneously. This can be encouraged further through imitation games in which the child is encouraged to produce different consonants for a reward. As Hahn (1979) comments 'visual and tactile stimulation are also helpful'. These have been described in (1) above.

It is advisable to concentrate on a range of different consonants including those the child does produce as well as those he does not. In this way some real success is built into the task which does not focus specifically on any particular consonant. When the game is introduced to parents it is important to stress that the child is not necessarily expected to succeed in imitating all the consonants. The aim is to encourage and reinforce his attempts at imitating the correct articulatory placement rather than the results per se, particularly when there may be velopharyngeal insufficiency.

## 4. To encourage the use of consonants which the child can produce correctly

This can be achieved by devising games and play situations in which, firstly, non-meaningful syllables are associated with particular objects, for example 'wobbly men' are named [ta] and [ti], and, secondly, words containing the appropriate consonant are used frequently. It is often helpful to contrast the words in minimal pairs starting from basic consonant vowel words and building up to longer words as the child progresses. This aspect of the therapy programme is based on the results of the phonetic and phonological assessment.

These strategies are only outlined in general terms in order to give the speech therapist some basic ideas on which to build individual therapy programmes. They and some of the other principles explored in this chapter are illustrated further in the following case studies.

## CASE STUDIES

### Peter (Table 2.1): Complete unilateral cleft of primary and secondary palate

Peter was born with a complete left-sided unilateral cleft of the primary and secondary palates which is illustrated in Figure 2.1A. There is no family history of clefting and the parents already had a 2-year-old boy with no problems who was developing normal speech and language skills. Feeding was difficult initially but improved in the first few weeks of life. Peter was bottle fed using a long 'anti-colic' teat which had a larger than normal hole in it. Pre-surgical orthopaedic treatment, as described above, was initiated soon after birth. Peter was fitted with an intra-oral plate and external strapping. The initial speech therapy counselling session followed the format outlined earlier in this chapter. Peter's parents asked appropriate questions about cleft palate and about future speech development. They were keen to have written information about cleft palate and subsequently purchased Albery et al (1986) which provided a focus for discussion in later counselling sessions.

When he was 6 weeks old, Peter's mother

**Table 2.1** Case summary: Peter complete unilateral cleft of lip and palate

| Age | Cleft clinic management | Speech status and management | Comment |
|---|---|---|---|
| 2 weeks | Complete unilateral cleft of lip and palate. Initial clinic appointment. Feeding—2 oz then 3 oz half hour later. Pre-surgical appliance and strapping | Counselled by speech therapist. Put in touch with local parent support group | |
| 6 weeks | Feeding going well, good weight gain | Mum reports good communication between Peter and herself | |
| 10 weeks | Pre-operative appointment. Nose and throat swabs taken. Recent antibiotics for ear infection | | Routine procedure re swabs. Otological exam normal: myringotomies not indicated |
| 3 months | Lip repair | Seen on ward by speech therapist | |
| 4 months | Post-operative check. Feeding well | Peter making lots of communicative noises | These checks are usually made at approx 6 weeks post-op |
| 7 months | Plans made for palatal surgery | | |
| 10 months | Palatal repair | Uses nasals and vowels and a range of mainly glottal 'growls' with varied intonation | Peter is trying hard to communicate despite the physical restrictions of the cleft |
| 11 months | Post-operative review making good progress | Lack of plosive and fricative articulations | |
| 1 year & 5 months | Routine review—satisfactory progress | Single words understood by Mum. Some new consonants | Mum concerned re speech development. Assessment appointment made |
| 1 year & 6 months | Speech therapy assessment | Comprehension and expressive language appropriate for age. Delay in phonetic development | Advice given to Mum. Continue to review regularly |

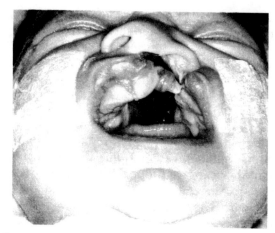

**Fig 2.1A** Peter at 2 weeks: complete unilateral cleft of primary and extensive cleft of secondary palate

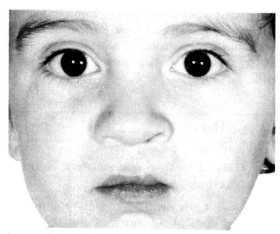

**Fig 2.1B** Peter at 1 year and 7 months

reported good communication between Peter and herself. She had observed good eye contact and smiling as well as vocalisation in response to her speech. At the post-operative review following lip repair, the speech therapist commented that Peter was 'making lots of communicative noises'. This was based on parental report and observation of Peter in the clinic. He had obviously learnt that vocalisation attracted adult attention and enjoyed responding vocally to his parents' verbal stimulation. By the age of 10 months this had developed into real attempts to communicate despite the physical restrictions imposed by the cleft. The latter meant that Peter did not produce the consonant-like sounds, for example, 'dada' and 'baba' which normally occur in the babbling patterns of non-cleft palate children at the same age. Peter compensated for this by using nasals, vowels and glottal 'growls' with a wide range of different intonation patterns.

At the age of 17 months, new consonant-like sounds such as the approximants /l/ and /j/ were routinely heard in Peter's vocalisations. In addition he was beginning to use a plosive /d/, articulated using the front of the tongue. This was a good sign as it indicated some potential for the production of pressure consonants. Peter's mother also reported a few identifiable single words. In the clinic she

mentioned that she was concerned about Peter's speech development but also commented that her elder son had been slow to develop speech. At the subsequent speech therapy assessment session, it emerged that Peter's mother had not been unduly concerned about his speech herself but had begun to wonder whether she should be as a result of the well-meaning comments of relatives and friends. There had been a tendency to interpret normal toddler behaviours, such as temper tantrums, as frustration because of an inability to communicate. In fact, Peter was communicating quite successfully with his family.

In this assessment which took place when Peter was 18 months old, the speech therapist carried out an informal play session. Using observation and information from Peter's mother, it was possible to ascertain that Peter responded appropriately to simple commands at an appropriate level for his age. Several single words were heard as well as jargon which Peter used in a conversational manner. The therapist concluded that Peter's language was developing satisfactorily along normal lines apart from a delay in phonetic development which could potentially affect subsequent phonological development, as outlined above. Peter's mother was advised about how to encourage further speech and language

**Table 2.2** Philip: Summary of management: Bilateral cleft of primary and secondary palate

| Age | Cleft clinic management | Speech therapy management | Comment |
|---|---|---|---|
| 4 months | Initial appointment. Receiving pre-surgical orthodontic treatment. Continued regular clinic visits with ongoing counselling and monitoring of development. Pre-surgical treatment continued | Initial counselling session | |
| 5 months | Lip repair. Millard type bilateral simultaneous closure | Making a variety of different sounds. Mainly vowels. Very 'chatty' | |
| 6 months | 6 weeks post-op review. Sleeping problems, constant dribbling. Not keen to take liquid from bottle or cup | Not putting objects to mouth any more. Advised about oral stimulation and how to encourage sound development. Telephone contact made 2 months later to ensure that feeding problem had resolved | |
| 10 months | Routine check—no problems. Date set for palate repair | Using nasals, [l] and a variety of vowels. Good intonation patterns | |
| 1 year & 2 months | Palate repair a difficult operation because of the extent of the cleft. Modified Langenbeck / Wardill procedure | | Still excessive dribbling. 14 months is quite late for palate repair but the surgeon was waiting for maximum growth of the palatal shelves |
| 1 year & 6 months | Surgeon pleased with results of operation | Trying to say many words. Advised re imitation, sound-making games | Mum worried that he sounds nasal |
| 2 years | Satisfactory progress | Using approx 50 words and some two-word phrases. Subjectively, resonance sounds normal | Mum considers that language development is delayed, but thinks this is not related solely to cleft |
| 2 years & 4 months | Speech therapist assessment | Comprehension and expressive language within normal limits. Phonology-backing of bilabials and alveolars | Advised Mum to encourage bilabial and tongue-tip sounds |
| 2 years & 6 months | Clinic review. Otitis media—to have bilateral grommets (at 2 years & 7 months) | Good progress in last two months. Now has alveolar and bilabial plosives—still some backing. Palatal fricatives occurring | In view of progress— decision to continue indirect versus direct intervention |
| 2 years & 9 months | Speech therapy review | Intelligible in context to those who know him. Further fricative development. Still some backing of bilabials | Further improvement in speech since grommet insertion |
| 3 years & 3 months | Speech therapy review | Bilabials have improved—now seem to be fully established. Excellent language. Slight tendency to palatal fricatives | Doing very well for a child who had bilateral cleft lip and palate, especially considering extent of original palatal cleft |
| 3 years & 6 months | Speech therapy review and cleft clinic review. Good occlusion. Some decay in upper dentition. Will probably require some cosmetic nose surgery in the future | Normal phonetic inventory but still a number of abnormal phonological mismatches with normal developmental patterns. Nasal anemometry: normal air flow during speech | Continuing advice to mother is sufficient to maintain progress |

development and the speech therapist decided to continue to monitor progress, particularly in phonetic and phonological development, at 2 to 3 monthly intervals.

### Philip (Table 2.2): Bilateral cleft of the primary palate and a complete cleft of the secondary palate

The lip repair was carried out when Philip was 5 months old. The palatal cleft was quite extensive as can be seen in the photograph which was taken when he was 5 months old (see Fig. 2.2A). This meant that the operation to repair the secondary palate was delayed until Philip was 14 months old. (In this centre palate repairs are routinely carried out between 9 and 12 months of age.) It was important to keep a particularly close eye on Philip's speech development because a more extensive initial defect can increase the potential for articulatory difficulties.

At 18 months Philip was reviewed in clinic following palate repair. The surgeon was pleased with the results of the operation. The palate had healed well and appeared to be of reasonable length. It should be noted, however, that a good intra-oral appearance does not imply adequate velopharyngeal closure. At this time, Philip's mother was concerned that he sounded 'nasal' but he was still using predominantly nasal consonants which could account for this. Indeed, as his sound system developed and he began to use

more plosive and fricative consonants, Philip's resonance began to sound more normal. Appropriate nasal airflow during speech was later confirmed by nasal anemometry when Philip was 3 and a half years old. At the 18 month review, Philip's mother was advised how to encourage imitation of speech-like consonants and 'vocal play' as described earlier in this chapter. Some games were suggested by the speech therapist and Philip's mother herself devised some more which suited their daily routine.

By the time he was 2 years old, Philip was using approximately 50 words which were understood by his mother. He was only just beginning to use two word phrases such as 'Daddy's car'. Philip's mother considered that his language development was not as good as that of other children at the same age, but she thought that this was not related to the cleft and would have followed this pattern in any case. Philip's understanding and use of language continued to develop to within normal limits with excellent stimulation from his mother.

With regard to phonetic development at 2 years 4 months, it can be seen from Figure 2.3 that Philip could produce a near normal range of consonants. However, when his phones are mapped onto the adult target phones (Fig. 2.4), it can be seen that there is some developmentally unusual variability and a Backing process operating on target bilabial and alveolar consonants. Philip's mother was

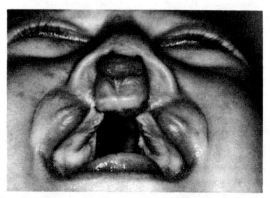

**Fig 2.2A** Philip at 5 months: bilateral cleft of primary and complete extensive cleft of secondary palate

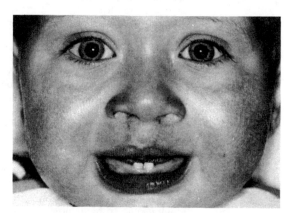

**Fig 2.2B** Philip at 15 months

# Phonetic Inventory

Name ....... PHILIP   2;4 ......................

| | Labial | Dental | Alveolar | Post-Alveolar | Palatal | Velar | Glottal | Other |
|---|---|---|---|---|---|---|---|---|
| **Nasal** | m | | n | | | ŋ | | |
| **Plosive** | p b | | t | | | k g | | |
| **Fricative** | | | s z | ʃ ʒ | ç | | h | |
| **Affricate** | | | | ʧ ʤ | | | | |
| **Approximant** | w | | l | | j | | | |
| **Other** | | | | | | | | |

Marginal Phones:  d̪  ~d   r̮

## Phonetic Distribution

| | Single Consonants | | | | | Consonant Clusters | | | |
|---|---|---|---|---|---|---|---|---|---|
| | **SIWI** | **SIWW** | **SFWW** | **SFWF** | | **SIWI** | **SIWW** | **SFWW** | **SFWF** |
| **Nasal** | m n | | n ŋ | m n ŋ | | | | | |
| **Plosive** | t b d k g | p t b k g | | p t d k g | | | | | ʔs ʔʃ bs |
| **Fricative** | s ʃ ç h | s ʃ | | s z ç ʒ ʃ | | | | | |
| **Affricate** | ʧ ʤ | ʤ | | | | | | | |
| **Approximant** | w l ʎ j | w l j | | | | | | | |
| **Other** | | | | | | | | | |

Fig 2.3

# Systems of Contrastive Phones and Contrastive Assessments

**PACS** © Pamela Grunwell, 1985.
Published by
The NFER-NELSON Publishing Company Ltd.,
Darville House, 2 Oxford Road East, Windsor,
Berkshire SL4 1DF.

Name ...... PHILIP  2;4 ......

**Syllable Initial Word Initial**

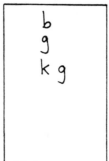
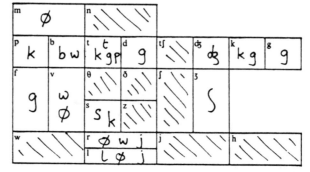

**Syllable Initial Within Word**

**Syllable Final Word Final**

Fig 2.4

advised how to encourage the use of bilabial and tongue tip articulations using consonants associated with symbolic representation as described in activity 2 (iii) above.

At Philip's next clinic check when he was 2 and a half years old, the otolaryngologist diagnosed bilateral secretory otitis media. Despite the presence of the associated conductive hearing loss Philip's speech had continued to develop. His vocabulary was increasing steadily and he was using more appropriate word-final and within-word plosive, fricative and affricate consonants. The Backing process operated on alveolar fricative targets which were produced as palatal fricatives. As Philip was continuing to evidence good progress, the speech therapist decided that direct intervention was not required. It was sufficient to continue indirect intervention, that is, seeing Philip at regular intervals and advising his mother.

The speech therapist monitored phonological development in particular. At 2 years 9 months Philip's mother reported that he was intelligible to those who knew him, but the Backing was still in evidence, particularly on word-initial bilabial plosives, for example, boy [gɔɪ] bath [gæx]. Six months later at 3 years 3 months bilabial phones matched the normal adult targets in all word positions but there was still some velar/alveolar confusion and continued use of palatal fricatives for some alveolar fricative targets, for example, ship [ʃɪp] sheep [ʃip] balloons [blunç] boat [bəʊt] daddy [gægi] dirty [dɜti] cup [tʌp] television [kelibɪʒn]. Further phonological assessment was carried out when Philip was 3 and a half years old. The phonetic inventory (Fig. 2.5) shows a normal pattern overall, but there are still a number of mismatches with the adult system. There is Backing of some alveolar targets and also Fronting of some velar targets. Backing still occurs on those words which Philip acquired early in his language development, for example, daddy [gægi]. Fronting is another systemic process which occurs in the developing phonological systems of normal children and which is 'usually suppressed by 2;6–3;6' (Grunwell

1987). Both these processes only occur on a few phones in Philip's 3 and a half year-old data, with all other targets of the same phones matching the normal adult targets (Fig. 2.6). In view of Philip's near normal phonological development it was concluded that continued advice to his mother would be sufficient to maintain progress. Future speech therapy review would be required in order to monitor the possible effect of changes in dentition on speech.

### Susan (Table 2.3): Unilateral cleft of primary and secondary palate

In Susan's family there is a history of clefts of the secondary palate, but Susan is unusual in that she also had a primary palate cleft as illustrated in the photographs (Fig. 2.7A). Consequently, Susan received pre-surgical orthopaedic treatment. Feeding was initially slow but improved when a larger hole was made in the teat. More extensive counselling was required at the time of lip repair when Susan's mother became very concerned about the operation itself, the effects of hospitalisation and how Susan would feed post-operatively. Parents are asked to accustom their children to taking some milk from a spoon, as this is how they will be fed immediately post-operatively, and Susan's mother had been finding this difficult. She was counselled by the surgeon, speech therapist and ward staff about the different aspects of Susan's care, and at the post-operative clinic appointment it emerged that she had coped well.

At the time of palate repair the speech therapist noted that Susan was only using the nasal bilabial [m] and a variety of glottal and pharyngeal sounds. She did, however, incorporate these with varied intonation patterns and appeared to be using them in a communicative manner. Unfortunately, Susan was sick in the immediate post-operative period because she developed gastroenteritis. This caused some dehiscence of the posterior palatal muscles. At the post-operative clinic review it appeared that the palatal muscles were well united anteriorly but the uvular part

# Phonetic Inventory

© Pamela Grunwell, 1985.
Published by
The NFER-NELSON Publishing Company Ltd.,
Darville House, 2 Oxford Road East, Windsor,
Berkshire SL4 1DF.

Name ...... PHILIP 3;6 ......................

| | Labial | Dental | Alveolar | Post-Alveolar | Palatal | Velar | Glottal | Other |
|---|---|---|---|---|---|---|---|---|
| **Nasal** | m | | n | | | ŋ | | |
| **Plosive** | p b | | t d | | | k g | ʔ | |
| **Fricative** | f v | ð | s z | ʃ | ç | | h | |
| **Affricate** | | | | tʃ dʒ | | | | |
| **Approximant** | w | | l | | j | | | |
| **Other** | | | | | | | | |

Marginal Phones:

# Phonetic Distribution

| | Single Consonants | | | | | Consonant Clusters | | | |
|---|---|---|---|---|---|---|---|---|---|
| | **SIWI** | **SIWW** | **SFWW** | **SFWF** | | **SIWI** | **SIWW** | **SFWW** | **SFWF** |
| **Nasal** | m n | m n | m n ŋ | m n ŋ | | pl (s)pw fw bw bl (s)tw | pl | | mp nt ŋd |
| **Plosive** | p b t d k g | p b t d k g | b | p b t d k ʔ g | | gw st sk | bw | nt ŋk nʔ | ŋk nʔ nz |
| **Fricative** | f v ð s z ʃ ç h | f v s z ʃ h | | f v s z ʃ ç | | nn̥ mm̥ sp sm | | ʔs | nʒ ns nz ps |
| **Affricate** | tʃ dʒ | tʃ dʒ | | dʒ | | sn sw sl | | | ʔs ds dz |
| **Approximant** | w l j | w l j | l | l | | | | | bz ʔps st |
| **Other** | | | | | | | | | |

Fig 2.5

# Systems of Contrastive Phones and Contrastive Assessments

**PACS**

© Pamela Grunwell, 1985.
Published by
The NFER-NELSON Publishing Company Ltd.,
Darville House, 2 Oxford Road East, Windsor,
Berkshire SL4 1DF.

Name ...... PHILIP 3;6 ......

**Syllable Initial Word Initial**

**Syllable Initial Within Word**

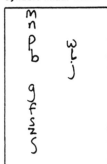

**Syllable Final Word Final**

Fig 2.6

**Table 2.3** Susan: Summary of management: Unilateral cleft of primary and secondary palates

| Age | Cleft clinic management | Speech therapy management | Comment |
|---|---|---|---|
| 1 month | Initial clinic appointment. Feeding slow about 1 hour. Larger hole in teat advised. Pre-surgical orthodontic treatment | Initial counselling | Family history of secondary palate clefts but Susan has cleft lip too. This is less common in females |
| up to 4 months | Continued regular clinic visits with ongoing counselling and monitoring of growth and development | | |
| 4 months | Lip repair. Millard type | 'Chatters' using vowels with varied intonation. Lots of smiles | Mother very concerned about the operation and hospitalisation |
| 6 months | Post-operative appointment. Good lip repair. Susan using muscles well | Monitoring of progress | |
| 10 months | Clinic review. Palate operation planned | Monitoring of progress | |
| 11 months | Palate repair: 4 flap closure | Only uses the nasal [m] and a variety of glottal and pharyngeal sounds | Susan had gastroenteritis and was very sick in the post-op period. This caused breakdown of the posterior part of the palate repair |
| 1 year | Post-operative review. Small residual fistula and bifid uvula which separates as palate lifts | Some lingual sounds now occurring but marked lack of anterior plosives | |
| 1 year & 10 months | Clinic review—some nasal regurgitation of liquids—from anterior fistula or velopharyngeal problem? | Using many single words and some phrases. Now has bilabial and alveolar voiced plosives. Development of range of abnormal back fricatives. Good comprehension | Surgeon decides on a 'wait and see' policy with regard to the posterior part of the palate |
| 2 years | Clinic review—satisfactory progress | | |
| | Speech therapy review Still some nasal regurgitation from fistula | Good language development. Speech intelligible to family Predominance of glottal and pharyngeal consonants. Overall nasal tone? | Normal development apart from speech. Mother advised how to encourage lip and tongue articulations |
| 2 years & 3 months | Clinic review. Surgeon decides to repair posterior part of palate | Speech sound development progressing-achieving plosives | |
| 2 years & 5 months | Re-repair of soft palate | Seen on ward | |
| 2 years & 7 months | Clinic review. Good operative result. Anterior fistula still present. | Parents think there is improvement in speech but despite more normal phonetic inventory there is a persistent backing process | Decision to implement direct intervention because of abnormal backing process |
| 2 years & 7 months to 3 years 3 months | | Direct speech therapy intervention | Therapy backed up very well by mother at home and good results obtained fairly quickly |
| 3 years & 6 months | Future plans: Surgeon plans to operate to close anterior fistula | Continued speech therapy review. Virtually within normal limits but still some difficulty with velar consonants | Susan is unlikely to need further direct speech therapy intervention. |

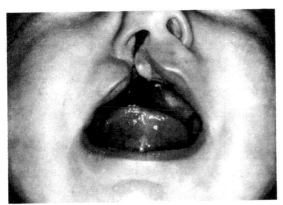

**Fig 2.7A** Susan at 3 months: cleft of primary and secondary palate

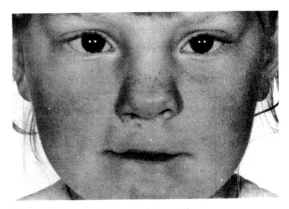

**Fig 2.7B** Susan at 4 years and 6 months

of the palate separated as the palate lifted. There was also a small anterior fistula just behind the alveolus. The surgeon decided on a wait-and-see policy initially, but later decided to re-repair the posterior part of the palate when Susan was 2 years 5 months. Despite the continued presence of the posterior defect, however, Susan's speech and language development had continued to progress. Her comprehension and use of language structures was within normal limits and her phonetic inventory was increasing. At the time of the second operation she was using plosive and fricative articulations, although the latter were an abnormal range of back fricatives. Phonological assessment also indicated that there was considerable variability and a Backing process operating on all target phonemes including velars. Subjectively, although an overall nasal tone had been queried at 1 year 10 months, this was not apparent to the speech therapist at Susan's 2 year 3 month review. It is possible, therefore, that adequate velopharyngeal closure was achieved despite the persisting posterior defect. The occasional regurgitation of liquids also continued to persist after the second palatal operation which indicated that, as had been suspected, this could be attributed to the anterior fistula.

At 2 years 7 months phonological assessment revealed that, despite a more normal phonetic inventory, there was still a persistent Backing process (Fig. 2.8 and 2.9). In view of this the speech therapist decided to imple-

ment a course of direct individual therapy. The aims of therapy were to encourage the use of anterior consonants which Susan could produce, to introduce new ones into her phonetic inventory and to eliminate the Backing process. These were achieved using imitation, auditory discrimination and production games as described above. Speech therapy sessions were at 2 to 3 weekly intervals and in the interim Susan's mother continued the games at home. Figures 2.10 and 2.11 show Susan's phonetic inventory and contrastive assessment at 3 and a half years. The phonetic inventory shows a much more normal pattern but there remains a phonological mismatch with the adult system. There has been a significant decrease in the use of velars for non-velar targets, but the Backing process for target velars is still evident. The speech therapist decided to discontinue direct intervention at this stage as there were signs that further spontaneous progress was being made. Susan is unlikely to need therapy in the future but the speech therapist will continue to review her speech at regular intervals until after her second dentition is established. When seen at 4 years and 6 months she was continuing to make good progress (Fig. 2.7B).

The case studies are provided to illustrate the effectiveness of the early involvement of the speech therapist with babies and toddlers with cleft palate. Counselling, monitoring and specific intervention early on helps to prevent the need for extensive speech therapy involvement later in the child's life.

## Phonetic Inventory

© Pamela Grunwell, 1985.
Published by
The NFER-NELSON Publishing Company Ltd.,
Darville House, 2 Oxford Road East, Windsor,
Berkshire SL4 1DF.

Name ...... SuSAN    2; 7 ......

| | Labial | Dental | Alveolar | Post-Alveolar | Palatal | Velar | Glottal | Other |
|---|---|---|---|---|---|---|---|---|
| **Nasal** | m | | n | | | ŋ | | |
| **Plosive** | | | | | | k g | ʔ | |
| **Fricative** | | | | | ç | x | h | ɦ x ʁ |
| **Affricate** | | | | | | | | |
| **Approximant** | w | | l | | j | | | |
| **Other** | | | | | | | | |

Marginal Phones: ⁻p

## Phonetic Distribution

| | Single Consonants | | | |
|---|---|---|---|---|
| | SIWI | SIWW | SFWW | SFWF |
| **Nasal** | m n | m | n | m n ŋ |
| **Plosive** | k g | k g | ʔ | k g ʔ |
| **Fricative** | ç x x | h | x | x ʁ ɦ |
| **Affricate** | | | | |
| **Approximant** | w l j | w j | | |
| **Other** | | | | |

| | Consonant Clusters | | | |
|---|---|---|---|---|
| | SIWI | SIWW | SFWW | SFWF |
| | gw kw n̥n nw | | | |

Fig 2.8

# Systems of Contrastive Phones and Contrastive Assessments

PACS © Pamela Grunwell, 1985.
Published by
The NFER-NELSON Publishing Company Ltd.,
Darville House, 2 Oxford Road East, Windsor,
Berkshire SL4 1DF.

Name ...... SuSAN  2;7 ......

### Syllable Initial Word Initial

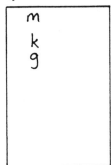

### Syllable Initial Within Word

### Syllable Final Word Final

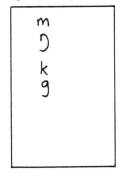

Fig 2.9

# Phonetic Inventory

© Pamela Grunwell, 1985.
Published by
The NFER-NELSON Publishing Company Ltd.,
Darville House, 2 Oxford Road East, Windsor,
Berkshire SL4 1DF.

Name ........ SuSAN 3;6 ........................

| | Labial | Dental | Alveolar | Post-Alveolar | Palatal | Velar | Glottal | Other |
|---|---|---|---|---|---|---|---|---|
| **Nasal** | m | | n | | | ŋ | | |
| **Plosive** | p b | | t d | | | (k)(g) | ʔ | |
| **Fricative** | f (v) | ð | s z | ʃ | | | h | |
| **Affricate** | | | | ʧ ʤ | | | | |
| **Approximant** | w | (r) | l | | j | | | |
| **Other** | | | | | | | | |

Marginal Phones: In parenthesis above

# Phonetic Distribution

| | Single Consonants | | | |
|---|---|---|---|---|
| | SIWI | SIWW | SFWW | SFWF |
| **Nasal** | m n | m n | m ŋ | m n ŋ |
| **Plosive** | p b t d (k) ʔ | p b t d (ʔ) | (b) (ʔ) | p b ʔt d g |
| **Fricative** | f ð v s ʃ h | s z ʃ | | s z |
| **Affricate** | ʧ ʤ | | | |
| **Approximant** | w l j r | w l | | l |
| **Other** | | | | |

| Consonant Clusters | | | |
|---|---|---|---|
| SIWI | SIWW | SFWW | SFWF |
| bl bw pw dw gw fw | | | nd nʒ nz ps ts ʔs st hl sl |

Fig 2.10

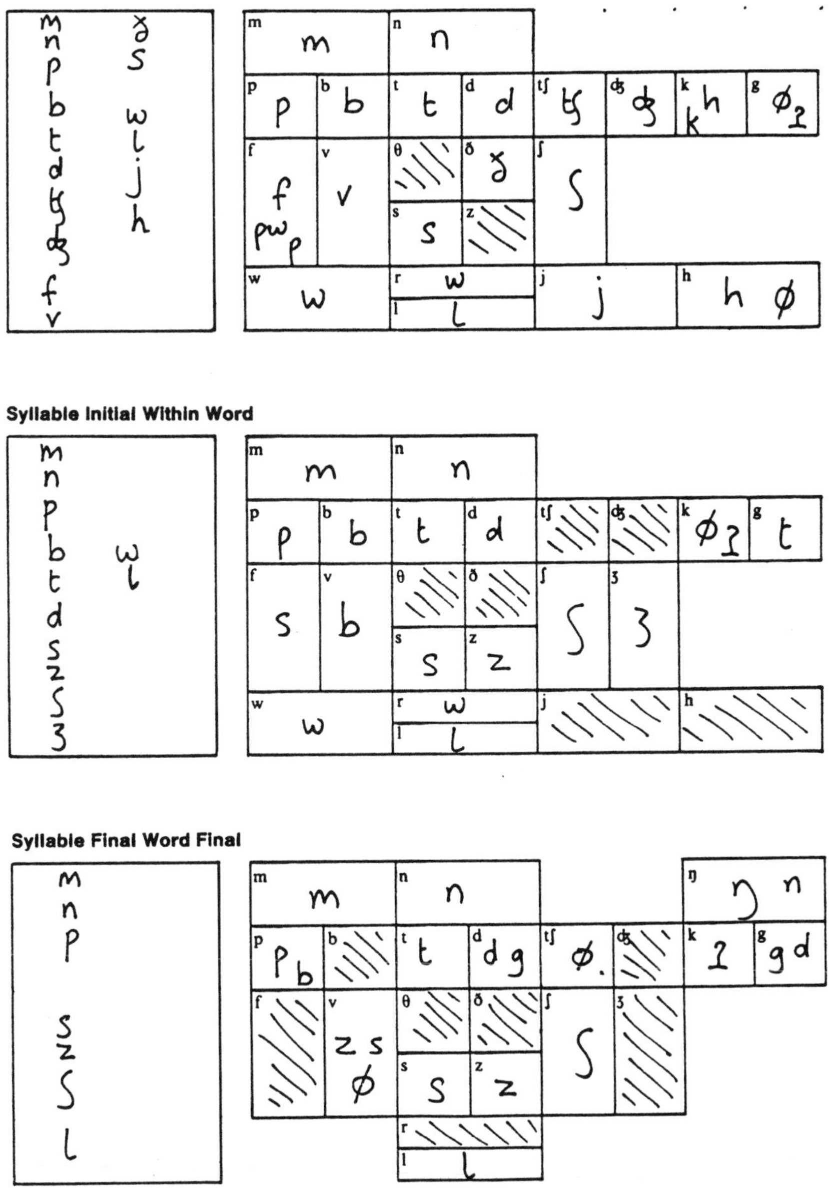

# Systems of Contrastive Phones and Contrastive Assessments

**PACS**

© Pamela Grunwell, 1985.
Published by
The NFER-NELSON Publishing Company Ltd.,
Darville House, 2 Oxford Road East, Windsor,
Berkshire SL4 1DF.

Name ......... SusAN  3;6 .............

**Syllable Initial Word Initial**

**Syllable Initial Within Word**

**Syllable Final Word Final**

Fig 2.11

ACKNOWLEDGEMENTS

I should like to thank Peter Gornall and the Cleft Palate Team at Birmingham Children's Hospital for their support; also the children and families whose co-operation enabled me to prepare the case studies. Thanks are also due to the Medical Illustration Department for the illustrations. I am especially grateful to Pam Grunwell for her support and valuable insights.

REFERENCES

Albery E H 1986 Type and assessment of speech problems. In: Albery E H, Hathorn I S, Pigott R W (eds) Cleft lip and palate: a team approach. Wright, Bristol

Anisfeld M 1966 Language development from birth to three. Lawrence Erlbaum, London

Bamford J, Saunders E 1985 Hearing impairment, auditory perception and language disability. Edward Arnold, London

Bates E 1979 The emergence of symbols: cognition and communication in infancy. Academic Press, New York

Bower T G R 1977 A primer of infant development. Freeman, Reading

Brookshire B L, Lynch J I, Fox D R 1980 A parent-child cleft palate curriculum: developing speech and language. C.C. Publications, Oregon

Bruner J S 1975 The ontogenesis of speech acts. Journal Child Language 2: 1

Bullowa M 1979 Before speech: the beginnings of interpersonal communication. University Press, Cambridge

Bzoch K R 1979 Etiological factors related to cleft palate speech. In: Bzoch K R (ed) Communicative disorders related to cleft lip and palate. Little Brown, Boston

Bzoch K R, League R 1971 Assessing language skills in infancy. University Park Press, Baltimore

Campbell M L, Watson A C H 1980 Management of the neonate. In: Edwards M, Watson A C H (eds) Advances in the management of cleft palate. Churchill Livingstone, Edinburgh

Carpenter R L, Mastergeorge A M, Coggins T E 1983 The acquisition of communicative intention in infants eight to fifteen months of age. Language and Speech 26: 101

Cleft Lip and Palate Association (CLAPA) Leaflet: Help with feeding. For details and support for parents contact The Dental Dept, The Hospital for Sick Children, Great Ormond Street, London WC1N 3JH

Crystal D, Fletcher P, Garman M 1976 The grammatical analysis of language disability. Edward Arnold, London

Crystal D 1981 Clinical linguistics. Springer Verlag, Wien

Conti-Ramsden G, Friel-Patti S 1984 Mother-child dialogues: a comparison of normal and language impaired children. Journal of Communication Disorders 17: 19

Edwards M 1980 Speech and language disability. In: Edwards M, Watson A C H (eds) Advances in the management of cleft palate. Churchill Livingstone, Edinburgh

Ellis R E 1979 The Exeter nasal anemometry system. In: Ellis R E, Flack F C (eds) Diagnosis and treatment of palato glossal malfunction. College of Speech Therapists, London

Fletcher P, Garman M (eds) 1979 Language acquisition. University Press, Cambridge

Foster T D 1980 The role of orthodontic treatment. In: Edwards M, Watson A C H (eds) Advances in the management of cleft palate. Churchill Livingstone, Edinburgh

Fox D, Lynch J, Brookshire B 1978 Selected developmental factors of cleft palate children between two and thirty-three months of age. Cleft Palate Journal 15: 239

Gérard K 1986 Checklist of communicative competence: 0–2 years (unpublished). Available from K Gérard, World's End Health Centre, 519 King's Road, London SW10 OUD

Gornall P, Bryan Jones W, Russell V J 1983 Paediatric aspects of pre-surgical care. Paper presented at 1st International Meeting, Craniofacial Society of Great Britain, Birmingham

Griffiths P 1979 Speech acts and early sentences. In: Fletcher P, Garman M (eds) Language acquisition. University Press, Cambridge

Grunwell P 1982 Clinical phonology. Croom Helm, London

Grunwell P 1985 Phonological assessment of child speech (PACS). NFER-Nelson, Windsor

Grunwell P, Russell J 1987a Vocalisations before and after cleft palate surgery: a pilot study. British Journal of Disorders of Communication 22: 1

Grunwell P, Russell J 1987b Phonological development in children with cleft lip and palate. Paper presented at Fourth International Congress for the Study of Child Language, Lund, Sweden

Hahn E 1979 Directed home training program for infants with cleft lip and palate. In: Bzoch K R (ed) Communicative disorders related to cleft lip and palate speech. Decker, Philadelphia

Heller J C 1979 Hearing loss in patients with cleft palate. In: Bzoch K R (ed) Communicative disorders related to cleft lip and palate. Little Brown, Boston

Henningsson G 1983 Personal communication

Hodson B W, Chin L, Redmond B, Simpson R 1983 Phonological evaluation of speech deviations of a child with a repaired cleft palate: a case study. Journal of Speech and Hearing Disorders 48: 93

Ingram D 1976 Phonological disability in children. Edward Arnold, London

Kaye K 1982 The mental and social life of babies. Methuen, London

Kent R D 1981 Sensorimotor aspects of speech development. In: Aslin R N, Roberts J R, Peterson M R (eds) Development of perception, Vol 1. Academic Press, New York

Knowles W, Masidlover M 1982 Derbyshire language

scale. Educational Psychology Service, Derby

Lencione R M 1980 Associated conditions. In: Edwards M, Watson A C H (ed) Advances in the management of cleft palate. Churchill Livingstone, Edinburgh

Locke J L 1983 Phonological acquisition and change. Academic Press, New York

Long N, Dalston R M 1982 Paired gestural and vocal behaviour in one-year-old cleft lip and palate children. Journal of Speech and Hearing Research 47: 403

Lynch J I, Fox D R, Brookshire B L 1983 Phonological proficiency of two cleft palate toddlers with school-age follow up. Journal of Speech and Hearing Disorders 48: 274

McCormick L, Schiefelbusch R L 1984 Early language intervention. Charles Merrill, London

MacDonald S K 1979 Parental needs and professional responses: a parental perspective. Cleft Palate Journal 16: 188

McWilliams B J, Morris H L, Shelton R L 1984 Cleft palate speech. Decker, Philadelphia

Maw A R 1986 Ear disease. In: Albery E H, Hathorn I S, Pigot R W (eds) Cleft lip and palate: a team approach. Wright, Bristol

Morris H L 1979 Evaluation of abnormal articulation patterns. In: Bzoch K R (ed) Communicative disorders related to cleft lip and palate. Little Brown, Boston

Mousset M R, Trichet C 1985 Babbling and phonetic acquisitions after early complete surgical repair of cleft lip and palate. Paper presented at the Fifth International Congress on Cleft Palate and Related Craniofacial Abnormalities, Monte Carlo

Nation J E 1970 Vocabulary comprehension and usage of preschool cleft palate and normal children. Cleft Palate Journal 7: 639

O'Gara M M, Logemann J A 1985 Phonetic analysis pre and post- palatoplasty. Paper presented at ASHA convention

Oller D K 1980 The emergence of the sounds of speech in infancy. In: Yeni-Komshian G, Kavanagh J, Ferguson C (eds) Child phonology, Vol 1. Academic Press, New York

Pannbacker M 1971 Language skills of cleft palate children: a review. British Journal of Disorders of Communication 6: 37

Philips B J W 1979 Stimulating syntactic and phonological development in infants with cleft palate. In: Bzoch K R (ed) Communicative disorders related to cleft lip and palate. Little Brown, Boston

Philips B J, Harrison R J 1969 Language skills of preschool cleft palate children. Cleft Palate Journal 6: 108

Randall P 1980 Secondary surgery. In: Edwards M, Watson A C H (eds) Advances in the management of cleft palate. Churchill Livingstone, Edinburgh

Reynell J 1985 The Reynell developmental language scales (revised). NFER-Nelson, Windsor

Ross R B, Johnston M C 1978 Cleft lip and palate. Krieger, New York

Schaffer R 1985 Mothering. Fontana Press, London

Smith J M 1986 Family support In: Albery E H, Hathorn I S, Pigot R W (eds) Cleft lip and palate: a team approach. Wright, Bristol

Stark R 1979 Prespeech segmental feature development. In: Fletcher P, Garman M (eds) Language acquisition. University Press, Cambridge

Tobiasen J M, Hiebert J M 1984 Parents' tolerance for the conduct problems of the child with cleft lip and palate. Cleft Palate Journal 21: 82

Van Demark D, Bzoch K, Daly D et al 1985 Methods of assessing speech in relation to velopharyngeal function. Cleft Palate Journal 22: 281

Warner J 1984a Assessment and evaluation: general information. In: Warner J, Byers Brown B, McCartney E (eds) Speech therapy: a clinical companion. University Press, Manchester

Warner J 1984b The developmentally young child: observational assessment procedures. In: Warner J, Byers Brown B, McCartney E (eds) Speech therapy: a clinical companion. University Press, Manchester

Westlake H, Rutherford D 1966 Cleft palate. Prentice Hall, Englewood Cliffs, NJ

Wylie H L, McWilliams B J 1965 Guidance material for parents of children with clefts. Cleft Palate Journal 2: 123

Subjective assessment
  Case history protocol
  Speech and language evaluation
  Examination of oral structure and function

Objective evaluation
  Nasal anemometry
  Speech radiography
  Nasendoscopy
  Summary of objective procedures

Case studies
  Elizabeth; cleft of secondary palate
  Lesley; cleft of soft palate with retrognathia
  Mary; acquired velopharyngeal palsy
  Angela; hypernasality: an early symptom of
  myasthenia gravis

Future developments
  Ultra-sound
  Computerised tomography
  Xeroradiography
  Nasopharyngoscopy: a therapeutic tool

# 3

# Assessment of speech and language status: subjective and objective approaches to appraisal of vocal tract structure and function

*C. F. Huskie*

It is generally accepted that one of the principal reasons to close a palatal cleft surgically or prosthetically is to facilitate normal speech. From the earliest days of medical interest in this condition, speech therapists have been closely involved in the management and treatment of individuals who present with cleft lips and/or palates. Borel-Maisonny worked closely with Veau, who described and compared anatomy of the normal and cleft palate in Division Palatine (1931). In her own right, Borel-Maisonny used a laryngopharyngoscope and then a nasopharyngoscope introduced over the tongue to examine the function of the velopharyngeal valve in the production of isolated sounds. Morley, an English speech therapist, is internationally recognised for her outstanding text, *Cleft Palate and Speech* (1958). It is a great privilege for the present generation of speech therapists who are interested in the cleft palate condition to continue the pioneering work of their distinguished predecessors.

This chapter aims to assist the speech clinician in accurate evaluation of the structure and function of the vocal tract and the resulting relationship to the speech and language status of the client. These related assessments which are undertaken by the speech therapist are essential if the need for further objective procedures is to be correctly identified. The resulting picture will decide the components of future management and remediation and the order in which treatment (surgical, orthodontic or speech therapy) should be undertaken.

## SUBJECTIVE ASSESSMENT

Ideally a speech therapist should have been involved with clients with congenital cleft lip and palate from the early stages: he will then be in an ideal position to monitor and influence speech and language development from its inception. There are many schools of thought as to the optimum age for palatal closure and the various stages in which this should be carried out, but it is reasonable to suggest that a child should be seen for a more formal speech and language assessment either at home or in clinic at any time between 18 months and 2 years of age. The age at which more formal assessment of speech and language is feasible will vary from child to child, but should be attempted before 2 years of age. In addition to assessing receptive and expressive language development with phonological and phonetic development, a subjective impression of hypernasality and nasal escape can be realised.

The majority of clients seen for subjective and objective assessment will be congenital cleft palate patients, but other problems involving resonance features will be referred by speech therapy colleagues and also by general practitioners, otolaryngologists and paediatricians amongst others. Cases will, for example, include submucous cleft palate, velopharyngeal disproportion, neurologically-based speech symptoms and hypernasal dysphonias: all complex problems which may include nasal escape. As the values of specialised subjective and objective assessments become recognised, an increasing number of more subtle problems will be referred for assessment to a specialist unit. The help of such a unit is continually available in making a diagnosis, then in the planning of speech therapy, or in referral to a plastic surgeon or other medical speciality as appropriate.

## Case history protocol

A detailed speech therapy case history will have been compiled (before more formal assessment is undertaken), by the speech therapist associated with the cleft palate group, but as any client suffering from vocal tract dysfunction may present in a generic speech clinic, the relevant areas in history-taking are outlined. Information about pregnancy, labour and birth history is all valuable, as problems there may give clues as to the possible basis for later developmental delay. Details of early feeding (by spoon, breast or bottle), the length of time taken to feed, any nasal regurgitation and information about any pre-surgical orthodontics which may have been undertaken, should be obtained. Early feeding difficulties and pre-surgical orthodontic treatment will influence the intra-oral physiology which is the basis for later speech development (Stuffins 1984). In addition, a description of the child's present diet, chewing and eating habits are important in establishing the nature of speech problems. Furthermore, the therapist should note any drooling, swallowing problems or nasal regurgitation while the client eats and drinks in clinic. From the developmental viewpoint, the ages of sitting up, walking and toilet training should all be ascertained. It is essential to see any child (cleft or non-cleft) who has a speech and language problem within a developmental setting and to relate the timing of his motor milestones to his speech development. In the case of the cleft palate child, the dates and details of all past and planned surgical procedures should be noted, together with results of otolaryngological examinations and audiological testing. The child's present state of health, with details of any past or recurring illnesses should be noted, along with information about his siblings and any relevant familial medical or speech history. The parents should be asked if any other medical or educational specialists are involved with this child, as information of any other congenital defects, e.g. heart condition, may influence other aspects of his development and progress. If applicable, progress at nursery or school should be discussed, together with any educational or social problems which may arise in these areas.

Observations should be made of the child's general appearance and co-ordination, with special note taken of any clumsiness for gross/fine movements. In conjunction with these aspects, any comments about facial asymmetry and proportions can be made. These areas are significant, as there is always a possibility of neurological deficit which is co-existing with a structural abnormality, and the presence of neurological handicap may well have significant influence on the presenting speech and language problem.

The parents should be asked about the dates of the inception of speech and language, then about its subsequent development. Spontaneous speech should be elicited to assess intelligibility, resonance balance, nasal escape, voice quality and fluency.

## Speech and language evaluation

Standardised phonetic, phonological and language assessments should be completed as appropriate and the results recorded. The choice of tests administered will depend on the preference of the particular clinician and the age and needs of the client, but general use seems to suggest that the Edinburgh Articulation Test and the Goldman Fristoe Test of Articulation are consistently useful. The Reynell Developmental Language Scales are a valuable tool for initial evaluation of receptive

and expressive language development. Additional speech data should be collected for phonological analysis. Further procedures for young children have been discussed in the previous chapter.

Tape recordings of spontaneous speech (and reading, if possible) should be made on high quality equipment in sound-dampened conditions. These base-line recordings can be used for analysis and augmented at a later date. The analysis of these recordings is an essential part of the clinical evaluation of the patient, and can be useful for other members of the team to evaluate progress, and for children and parents to have concrete evidence of improvement.

It can be useful to judge resonance balance using standardised phonetically-balanced sentences or passages (Van Demark 1974). It is generally accepted that it is very difficult to standardise listener judgements of resonance balance, but nevertheless a speech therapist should be better qualified to assess resonance than other team members.

It should be recognised that individuals assessed are considered to have a speech and/or language handicap, which implies that all the features of speech must be assessed, rather than limiting clinical judgement to seeking the more obvious features that are usually associated with cleft palate speech. Language skills along with phonetic, phonological and resonatory features all contribute to a comprehensive accurate clinical picture, essential to appropriate management.

## Examination of oral structure and function

When any client presents with a phonetic and/or resonance problem, it is essential to carry out an examination of the peripheral speech mechanism in both form and function, and this should be undertaken as early as is appropriate in diagnostic investigations. With young or shy children it may take a little time to gain enough of the child's confidence to enable this examination to be completed. Such an examination will help to reveal whether or not there are any aberrant features in the form and function of the vocal tract. If the precise aetiology of a speech problem is uncertain, this evaluation will help to establish if the problem is of a phonetic or phonological nature.

Where differences in structure and/or function are found, the next step is to try to decide whether there is a relationship between these and the speech symptomatology. The co-existence of two factors does not always mean that such factors are in a causal relationship. This can be confirmed or refuted by detailed speech analysis, anemometry, speech radiography and nasendoscopy. Other specialists may be able to help the speech clinician to establish the exact nature of any aberrations found. For example, the orthodontist will be able to describe dentition and occlusal relationships, and to predict growth potential and the options in future management. Speech radiography gives more objective information about intra-oral structure and activity, while nasendoscopy gives specific information about velopharyngeal function.

The correspondence between structure and function is tenuous; there are four possible outcomes:

1. Normal structure and normal movement = normal speech
2. Abnormal structure and normal adaptive movement = normal speech
3. Abnormal structure and maladaptive movement = abnormal speech
4. Normal structure and maladaptive movement = abnormal speech.

Some speakers are capable of surmounting seemingly major anomalies of the vocal tract to produce acceptable speech, while other speakers, with minimal structural defects present with marked dysfunction and atypical speech which appears to be out of proportion to the structural problem observed. It is essential to bear in mind the large numbers of additional factors which will influence the eventual standard of perceived speech. These include intellectual, motivational, psychological and social factors. Hearing and auditory perception and skills of neuromuscular co-ordination are also relevant to the eventual standard of speech.

Table 3.1 provides an outline of the examination of oral structures and function which should be undertaken. Functions should be assessed in vegetative and speech activities. The following equipment will be needed.
— Flexible examination torch
— Dental reflector
— Glass of water
— Tissues
— Stop watch
— Surgical gloves.

OBJECTIVE EVALUATION

It should be realised that the vocal tract functions as a co-ordinated whole to produce intelligible speech, and there is a particular inter-relation between all parts of the vocal tract and the velopharyngeal valve. Objective assessments must therefore examine the anatomy and physiology of the complete tract, and not isolate the velopharyngeal valve as if it was self-sufficient. Endoscopic studies of normal speakers demonstrate that tight, consistent velopharyngeal closure is not always a prerequisite for intelligible speech, and many clinicians will have seen clients with previously undiagnosed sub-mucous clefts where speech is acoustically satisfactory. The objective assessments described here should be used to facilitate understanding of vocal tract function, enabling us to offer the most appropriate solutions to clients.

The need for objective assessment is governed by the results of speech evaluation and surface examination of the vocal tract and must be undertaken, particularly if a choice is to be made between surgery to improve intra-oral structure and function or more directed speech therapy. The presence of audible nasal escape of air, weak intra-oral air pressure with correct tongue placement, or compensatory

**Table 3.1** Examination of oral structures and function

| Feature | Structure | Function |
|---|---|---|
| *Lips*<br>Lip structure and function can be observed informally | Upper lip length<br>Lower lip fullness/misproportion between upper and lower lips | Competence (seal) at rest<br>Retraction<br>Affect positioning for bilabial plosives and labiodental fricatives |
| Diadochokinetic rate should be assessed by repetition of bilabial plosives | Scarring, tightness inadequate anatomical cleft lip repair. Note relationship of lips to dentition—size of mouth opening | Swallow pattern, feeding chewing.<br>Diadochokinetic rate.<br>3.0 secs above average<br>5.50 secs below average<br>Immobility of lips may be neurological |
| *Dentition*<br>Need to carry out intra-oral examination | Regular conservation caries rate/fluoride treatment | Poor general health chewing efficiency |
| | Overcrowding/super-numerary teeth | May interfere with tongue movement for speech |
| | Orthodontic appliances | May reduce palatal surface area-affecting movement for chewing and speech |
| *Tongue*<br>Full examination will depend on co-operation of individual | Size and shape in relation to dental arches. Note tongue position at rest: may be interdental | Elevation to alveolar ridge and upper lip |
| | Symmetry | Pointing<br>Speech and swallowing |
| | Crenation | May be indicative of large tongue<br>Diadochokinetic rate repeated /t, t, t/ |
| | Increased size | May be related to poor co-ordination |
| | Observe lingual fraenum | Assess lingual-dental consonants |
| *Occlusion* | Occlusal patterns I, II, III | In Class II lip may become trapped under the upper incisors and help to maintain their proclination. In Class III—palatal surface area may be considerably reduced, with resulting lack of space for tongue. This may affect the place of articulation for some sounds |
| *Maxillary arch* | Premaxilla: present/absent/tongue mobile | May affect lip structure and function<br>Mobile pre-maxilla may be maintained movement |
| | Collapsed maxillary arches.<br>Alveolar fistula | Reduced intra-oral tongue space.<br>Possibly a route for nasal escape |
| *Hard palate*<br>Maximum mouth opening should be gained. Good light and intra-oral mirror essential to view hard palate | Height and width<br>Scarring<br>Fistula left/midline/right<br>Palatal notch | Reduced dimensions will interfere with tongue movement for speech<br>Reduced sensitivity<br>Route for escaping food or nasal air flow<br>Sub-mucous cleft? |
| *Soft palate*<br>Good mouth opening and low tongue position essential for satisfactory view.<br>Tongue depressor used only if view impossible without its use. Ask patient to say 'ah' to assess palatal movement | Length and depth of oropharynx<br>V-deformity<br>Bifid uvula/absent/scarring | Shortness may affect velopharyngeal valve function<br>May indicate inadequate previous repair or sub-mucous cleft<br>Affect muscle activity |

**Table 3.1** (contd)

| Feature | Structure | Function |
| --- | --- | --- |
| *Pharynx*<br>Low tongue position is required to view beyond soft palate | Pharyngoplasty type/position | Contribution to velopharyngeal closure—if in doubt proceed to speech radiography and endoscopy<br>Infected tonsils may indicate health problems |
| | Lateral wall movement<br>Passavant's ridge | Contribution to velopharyngeal closure. |
| | Tonsils | If enlarged, may interfere with velo-pharyngeal closure and tongue movement—speech radiography needed |
| *Nose*<br>Make sure nose cleared before examination | Note size and shape of nose | Small saddle-shaped nose becomes easily blocked |
| Observe resonance in speech | Collapsed nostril frequently associated with cleft lip and palate | Assess ability to use nasal airway. Habitual open mouth posture and mouth breathing? |
| | Catarrhal | Snorts, wheezing, snoring when asleep? |
| | Deflected septum | Inadequate air way<br>Note resonatory quality of speech. Hyponasality may indicate adenoid hypertrophy or blocked nasal airway |

articulation patterns with associated hyper-nasality are examples of features requiring objective evaluation. The case studies to follow at the end of the chapter give examples of assessment leading to appropriate diagnosis before surgical and/or speech therapy intervention.

### Nasal anemometry

Considerable effort has been invested in a search for accurate ways of measuring nasal and oral air flows in speech as described by Antony (1980) and Warren (1967 & 1976). However, much of the instrumentation described is complex and results are not easily interpreted by an isolated speech clinician who does not have access to specialist help in that area.

The Exeter Nasal Anemometry equipment was first described by Ellis (1979). It provides compact, easily-used equipment which is appropriate to the needs of a speech therapist. It is recognised that more sophisticated equipment is more suited to a research

phonetician than a practising speech therapist. The sensing head consists of a bead thermistor mounted in a plastic flow tube. The latter fits into a rubber anaesthetist's mask, or into a small acrylic mask for use with younger patients. When placed over the nose, the mask forms a seal, but if positioned correctly, does not obstruct the nares (Fig. 3.1). An indication of flow is registered on a meter on the front panel of the anemometry control unit (Fig. 3.2) which also provides a coded air flow signal to one channel of a stereo tape recorder. The second channel of the recorder is connected to a microphone and carries the speech sounds with which the air flow is associated. A phonetically-balanced word sample of 10 words is routinely used allowing air flow during consonants in different positions to be recorded. Following recording, the tape cassette is mailed to a processing centre where a dual trace chart is produced, showing speech along the upper trace and associated air flow on the lower. This chart and the original tape recording are then returned to the speech therapist for analysis.

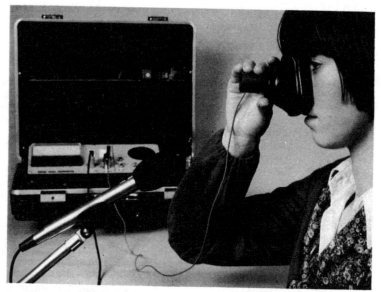

**Fig 3.1** Anemometry—mask positioning. Published by courtesy of College of Speech Therapists

**Fig 3.2** Anemometry control unit, tape recorder, mask and microphone. Published by courtesy of the College of Speech Therapists

## Clinical examples of anemometry

Figure 3.3 shows a chart obtained for a recording of a normal speaker, and this provides a useful comparison with the atypical examples which follow. Anemometry can show whether nasal air escape occurs consistently over non-nasal consonants or whether escape is inconsistent, perhaps revealing some timing and co-ordination problems in the velopharyngeal area. If a patient presents with audible nasal escape and has an anterior fistula, anemometry with the fistula open then

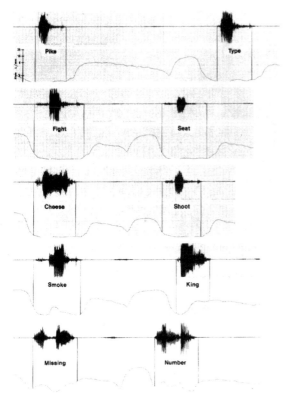

**Fig 3.3** Nasal air flow—anemometry trace of normal speaker

obturated can help to decide the route of the nasal air flow (Fig. 3.4). This simple, comparatively non-invasive assessment can help the surgeon and speech therapist to decide if the fistula should be closed or if the physiology of the velopharyngeal valve should be investigated.

Russell (1980) reported the management of a patient whose hypernasality was differently evaluated by two speech therapists using subjective criteria. This particular example highlights the unreliability of such subjective criteria and the need for more hard data in evaluating patients in a clinical setting.

In addition to its use for evaluation purposes, the visual display on the anemometer control unit can be a useful tool in therapy, giving the patient another biofeedback channel, and it may well be easier to 'see' than hear nasal escape, especially in the early stages of treatment.

### Speech radiography

This radiographic technique aids in the diagnosis and assessment of movements within

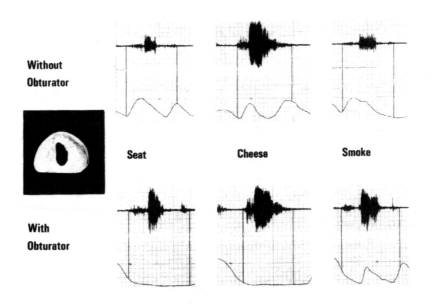

**Without Obturator**

**Seat**   **Cheese**   **Smoke**

**With Obturator**

**Fig 3.4** Comparative nasal air flows: Anemometry trace with and without obturation

the vocal tract during swallowing and speech. Current trends towards dynamic studies have superseded the static approach which can have an in-built degree of inaccuracy.

## Equipment for speech radiography

A unit suitable for head and neck work is based on a mobile X-ray machine, with an image intensifier and first television camera at one end of a c-arm and at the other an X-ray tube or source (Fig. 3.5). The c-arm can be positioned through any projection through the head and neck of the patient, but for speech assessment purposes lateral, basal and antero-posterior views are conveniently used. An aluminium filter placed in the beam allows soft tissue outline of the face and neck to be achieved. Barium coating can be applied nasally (Fig. 3.6) and to the tongue (Fig. 3.7). The second colour television camera provides the photographic image which is passed to a mixing unit where the radiographic and photographic views are shown in varying proportions. This is shown diagrammatically in

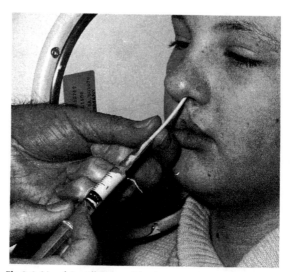

Fig 3.6 Nasal instillation of barium contrast

Figure 3.8. Sequences give radiation doses of 5–15 millirads per second to the skin surface nearer the X-ray tube. Twenty seconds exposure gives the same dose as an intra-oral periapical film. Simultaneous use of a video tape recorder (Fig. 3.9) allows repeated viewing and instant replay with no loss of

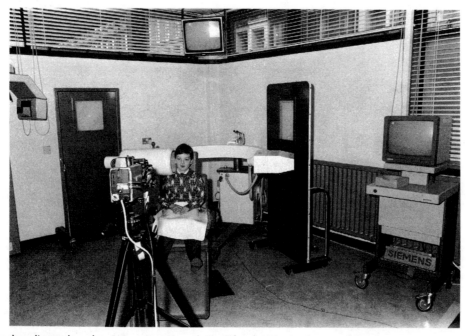

Fig 3.5 Speech radiography: showing patient X-ray unit with television camera and monitors

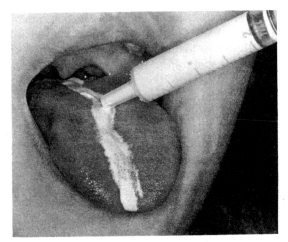

**Fig 3.7** Intra-oral application of barium to tongue

intensifier are positive, unlike a radiograph where they are negative: whites or radio-opacities on a still radiograph become black or radiolucent on movement studies.

*Technique*

Close co-operation between radiologist, radiographer and speech therapist is essential if these studies are to be carried out smoothly. The speech therapist should be able to decide from the speech evaluation if speech radiography is indicated, and will also be able to decide if the child's co-operation is likely to be forthcoming, i.e. a constant head position (head movement reduces the information obtained) and ability to speak on demand while the studies are being taken. It is important that the child is 'rehearsed' in this unfamiliar situation and that the required speech sample can be recorded quickly, so reducing the radiation dose. If a child is reluc-

quality. The moving picture can be stopped and held at any part of the sequence. There are two sound tracks—one for recording the patient's speech at the time and another for a commentary at a later date. Images from the

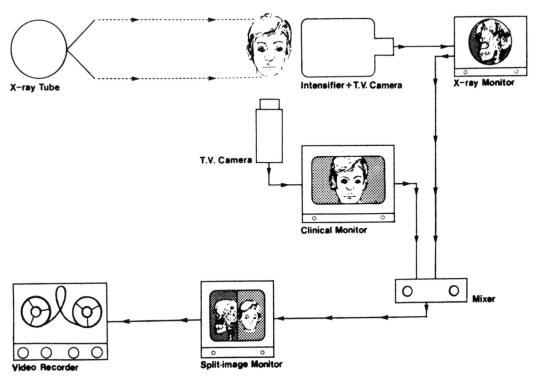

**Fig 3.8** Diagrammatic representation of radiographic equipment. Published courtesy of College of Speech Therapists

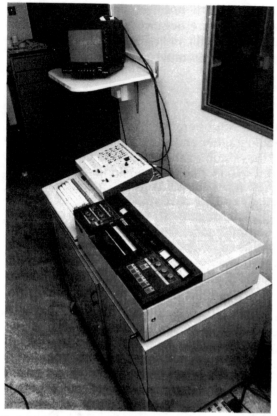

**Fig 3.9** Video recording and mixing units

tant to co-operate, it is possible for him to observe another child being radiographed and this often gives some confidence to proceed.

*Lateral radiographs* using a standard lateral cephalogram view (Fig. 3.10A) rather than a limited velopharyngeal view (Fig. 3.10B) give invaluable information about intra-oral dimensions and movement, especially of the tongue. In addition, lip movement, occlusion, palate length and movement of the posterior pharyngeal wall function can be seen, especially if barium coating is applied to tongue and nasopharynx.

*Image intensifiers* now have a magnification facility which is especially useful when examining palate and posterior wall laterally (Fig. 3.11) and view of the velopharyngeal valve basally. Use of a second colour television camera provides a *facial view* of the patient which is then combined with the lateral radiograph in variable proportions. This image is extremely useful as it records facial appearance at rest and behaviour during speech which can give some clues as to the effort invested in speech. In addition, full face and lip movement can be seen and compared to the radiographic profile of lip and tongue

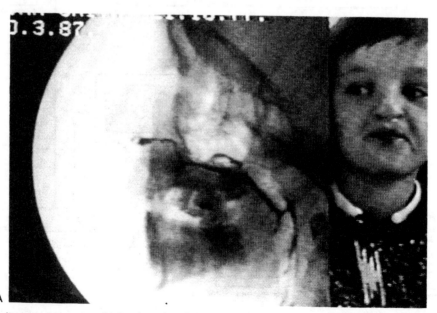

A

**Fig 3.10** (A) Split screen image combining lateral cephalogram view and facial image of patient. (B) Coned down view of velopharynx

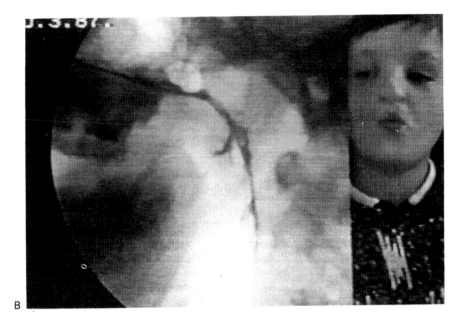

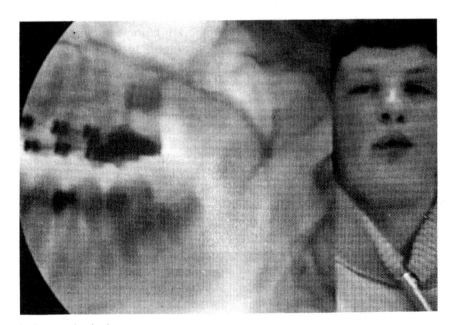

**Fig 3.11** Magnified view of velopharynx

movement together with occlusion.

In addition to information about intra-oral movements for swallowing and speech, clinicians are also interested in the *function of the velopharyngeal valve from below* (Figs. 3.12a & 3.12b). These views are useful, especially as lateral views show only palatal and posterior pharyngeal wall movements, and a basal view is essential if lateral pharyngeal wall movement is to be demonstrated. The patient is asked to hyperextend the neck and then the X-ray beam is directed up the pharynx from below. A small number of patients have significant deformities of the cervical spine which may preclude these studies, in which case endoscopy must be attempted. Movement of the velopharyngeal valve should be clearly seen, providing the patient is correctly positioned. If a pharyngeal flap procedure has been carried out, the competence of the lateral wall movements around the flap can be seen, and any remaining areas of incompetence noted.

*Antero-posterior views* (Fig. 3.13) can be useful to show movement of the lateral pharyngeal walls, especially if basal radiographs and endoscopy are impossible for any of the reasons suggested. Up to six patients can be screened in a half day session, and any other speech therapists who may have referred or are already involved with the clients can be invited to participate and discuss the sequences. At the end of each session, the radiologist and speech therapist should review the sequences, recording their comments on the suggested form (Table 3.2) (McWilliams-Neeley & Bradley 1964, McWilliams & Bradley 1965). Use of such a pro forma ensures that the relevant areas are covered in compiling a comprehensive report for the client's next clinic visit, where both radiographic and endoscopic sequences should be available for assessment by colleagues.

## Nasendoscopy

It has been recognised for some time that there are several consistent variations in the patterns of non-cleft velopharyngeal closure as shown by normal speakers (Pigott 1969), and that similar variety of function is seen in the groups that present with velopharyngeal incompetence of varying aetiology. Nasendoscopy has been described as 'transnasal endoscopic visualisation of velopharyngeal function during connected speech in the conscious and co-operative patient' (Batchelor 1987) and its routine clinical use has been described (Pigott 1969, Pigott et al 1969, Sommerlad et al 1975, Sommerlad 1981). The interpretation of radiographic images can be notoriously difficult, but the direct endoscopic image of the velopharyngeal valve greatly clarifies the

clinical diagnosis of velopharyngeal incompetence in speech.

### Equipment

Advantages and disadvantages of the necessary equipment together with the techniques involved in its use have been fully described (Pigott 1980) and will not be described in detail here. Depending on the preference of the individual operator, either a rigid or a flexible endoscope can be used. Regardless of the preferred endoscope, the use of a high grade colour camera and video tape recorder are considered to be essential (Fig. 3.14). The patient is seated in a high-backed chair adjacent to the television monitor and wears a body microphone so that his speech can be recorded simultaneously. Local anaesthetic (4% zylocaine) is instilled into the selected nostril using a purpose-made polythene catheter with a cotton wool tip and syringe (Fig. 3.15). Using the *rigid endoscope* (Fig. 3.16) the surgeon looks directly down the endoscope, while when using the *flexible scope* (Fig. 3.17) the operator looks at the monitor rather than directly down the scope to avoid sharing light. For flexible endoscopy the camera is suspended to leave both hands free: the right to control direction of view and orientation axially while the left hand is used to pass the scope along the nostril floor.

It is useful if speech therapist and surgeon can co-operate closely during nasendoscopic sessions, particularly if the therapist has been responsible for other parts of the evaluation protocol. The therapist is often in a good position to select patients for endoscopy, on the basis of their likely co-operation, age and personality. Of all the evaluations described, endoscopy is the most invasive and should ideally be the final assessment attempted.

During recording, the surgeon is usually responsible for the actual endoscopy, while the speech therapist can operate the video tape recorder and elicit the required phonetically-balanced speech sample. As with the radiographic reporting, surgeon and speech therapist can review the sequences together and compile a joint report for case history

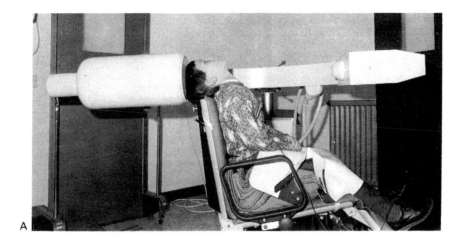

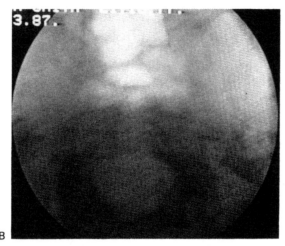

**Fig 3.12** (A) Patient positioned for basal views. (B) Basal view of velopharynx

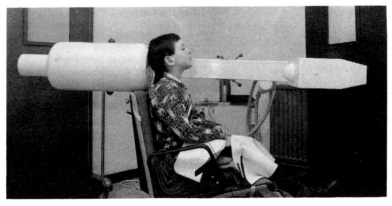

**Fig 3.13** Patient positioned for antero-posterior views

**Table 3.2**   Glasgow Dental Hospital: Video radiographic report

| | |
|---|---|
| Name: | Tape no.: |
| Date of birth: | Lateral: |
| Source of referral: | Basal: |
| Barium: Tongue | Date of sequence: |
|         Nasopharynx | Co-operation: |
| | Dental appliance: |

**Lateral projection at rest**

*1. Soft palate length*

  1. Very long
  2. Moderately long
  3. Average
  4. Moderately short
  5. Very short

*2. Soft palate thickness*

  1. Very thick
  2. Moderately thick
  3. Average
  4. Moderately thin
  5. Very thin

*3. Depth of posterior pharyngeal wall*

  1. Very shallow
  2. Shallow
  3. Normal
  4. Deep
  5. Very deep

*4. Adenoidal mass*

  1. Not present
  2. Small, not at site of closure
  3. Small, at site of closure
  4. Average, not at site of closure
  5. Average, at site of closure
  6. Large, not at site of closure
  7. Large, at site of closure

*5. Post-nasal space*

  1. Appropriate to palate length
  2. Short
  3. Deep

**Movement study**

*6. Prominence of levator eminence*

  1. Very prominent
  2. Readily observable
  3. Observable
  4. Flicker only
  5. Not present

*7. Point of maximum velar lift*

  1. Far anteriorly
  2. Centrally
  3. Posteriorly

*8. Movement of posterior pharyngeal wall*

  1. No movement
  2. Slight movement in direction of closure
  3. Marked movement in direction of closure
  4. Movement present, but above or below the expected site of closure

*9. VP contact*

  1. Total blending
  2. Partial blending
  3. Touch
  4. Close approximation
  5. Moderate opening
  6. Wide opening

*10. Patterns of VP movement*

  1. Very even and consistent with proper timing
  2. Very even and consistent with improper timing
  3. Somewhat consistent
  4. Very inconsistent
  5. Essentially no movement
  6. No movement

**INTRA-ORAL**

Lips at rest: Closed/open
Occlusion
Swallow pattern

Tongue movements: Speech

**Basal projection**

*1. Size of velopharyngeal portals (flap) at rest*

| Right | Left | |
|---|---|---|
| 0 | 0 | No opening |
| 1 | 1 | Tiny |
| 2 | 2 | Small |
| 3 | 3 | Moderate |
| 4 | 4 | Large |

*2. Range of motion of velum and pharynx*

| | Velum | | | Posterior wall | Lateral walls |
|---|---|---|---|---|---|
| | Right | Left | | Right | Left |
| 0. No movement | 0 | 0 | 0 | 0 | 0 |
| 1. Very slight | 1 | 1 | 1 | 1 | 1 |
| 2. Slight | 2 | 2 | 2 | 2 | 2 |
| 3. Moderate | 3 | 3 | 3 | 3 | 3 |
| 4. Substantial | 4 | 4 | 4 | 4 | 4 |
| 5. Extensive | 5 | 5 | 5 | 5 | 5 |
| 6. Extreme | 6 | 6 | 6 | 6 | 6 |

*3. Pattern of motion*

| | Palate | Pharynx |
|---|---|---|
| 1. Very even and consistent with proper timing | 1 | 1 |
| 2. Very even and consistent with improper timing | 2 | 2 |
| 3. Somewhat inconsistent | 3 | 3 |
| 4. Very inconsistent | 4 | 4 |
| 5. Essentially no movement | 5 | 5 |
| 6. No movement | 6 | 6 |

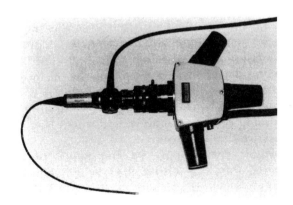

**Fig 3.14** Flexible endoscope attached to colour camera

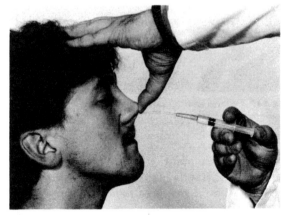

**Fig 3.15** Instillation of local anaesthetic

purposes (Pigott 1980). Speech therapists who are responsible for regular treatment should be especially welcome to participate in these sessions and to contribute their thoughts on future treatment.

*Findings from nasendoscopy*

Endoscopy allows the surgeon to define the dynamics of velopharyngeal closure and to decide if surgery is appropriate. If so, a surgical procedure which will capitalise on

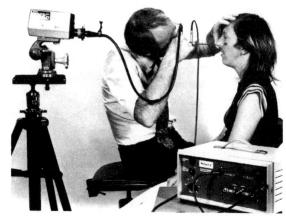

**Fig 3.16** Endoscopy using rigid instrument: examiner uses direct vision

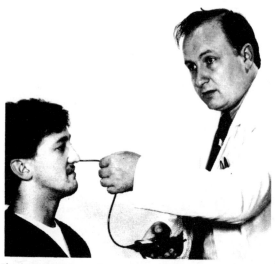

**Fig 3.17** Flexible endoscopy: examiner inserts scope while watching monitor

available movement can be selected. Even more importantly, this investigation can clearly define a group of patients who do not have anatomically-based nasal escape for whom surgery is not appropriate. Where surgery is indicated it is essential that endoscopy should be carried out by the individual surgeon who will then operate on that patient. Many of the patients undergoing these types of assessment will be candidates for long-term care. If they have speech radiographs and endoscopies on repeated occasions, it can be

useful to compile a library of individual video tapes, where sequences are recorded in chronological order, thus allowing more accurate documentation.

Pigott & Makepeace (1975) suggested that it is useful to combine radiography and endoscopy on a simultaneous recording rather than using radiography with a facial view, but Sommerlad (1981) disagreed, stating that, 'Assimilation of each examination individually is difficult enough with the complexity of movement and together the problems are multiplied.' Personal clinical experience would encourage confirmation of Sommerlad's view.

## Summary of objective procedures

The protocol described is desirable for all patients whose speech problems probably include velopharyngeal incompetence giving rise to hypernasality, nasal escape and/or compensatory articulation patterns. Such assessments are routinely carried out by various members of the cleft palate team who have access to these assessments and should be available to any professional who wishes to refer a patient to such a specialised unit for assessment. The case studies which accompany this chapter describe ways in which parts or all of the assessments used critically influenced management and its eventual outcome. Increased understanding and application of the results of these assessments by all those who are involved in the care of patients with speech problems can only increase our understanding of these complex issues and lead to improved patient care.

Pigott (1980) sums up the need for an overall intra-oral rather than velopharyngeal assessment in his statement: 'But the biggest lesson to be learnt from increasingly sophisticated assessment of velopharyngeal function is that intelligibility is almost entirely a function of the tongue not the palate . . . if real progress is to be made towards achieving the eventual goal of improved intelligibility it seems essential that thought must be directed to modifying the faulty habits of the tongue rather than by devising yet more pharyngoplasties.' This statement adds weight to the opinion expressed by Selley (1979) that 'when treating dysarthria the whole of the palato-glossal complex should be treated as one unit'. However, before any treatment can be initiated, a diagnosis must be made on the basis of the assessments described. Use of anemometry and full intra-oral radiographs in conjunction with endoscopy will allow definition of vocal tract behaviour (including tongue function) and enable those responsible to make more informed decisions on future treatment based on objective information.

The case studies which follow are intended to provide examples of the way in which detailed assessment and diagnostic procedures lead to management which is appropriate to the needs of individual cases. Case examples are given not only of cleft palate but include other congenital and acquired velopharyngeal problems.

## CASE STUDIES

**Elizabeth: Cleft of secondary palate** (see Table 3.3)

Elizabeth had a congenital cleft of secondary palate, a type of cleft more commonly found among females. Her mother had been treated for velopharyngeal incompetence (without cleft) at age 20 years, and had undergone a pharyngeal flap procedure at that time. Her speech was acceptable following this procedure, but slight nasal grimacing persisted. Elizabeth's cleft was repaired at 18 months old, in another unit, and prior to that she was spoon-fed, then used a cup. She first had speech therapy when she was 5 and a half years old, on an 'intensive, in-patient basis' in the same unit where palatal surgery had been carried out. Her developmental milestones were achieved normally, but speech was unintelligible to all except her mother at the time of school entry. This creates many obvious problems not least development of reading skills.

The period of intensive speech therapy did not appear to effect any significant progress towards improved intelligibility. It can be tempting to identify psychological or social factors as reasons for poor progress in therapy, and it is vital to establish through objective evaluation whether or not the child has 'the tools for the task', i.e. that velopharyngeal closure is possible in speech and that gross hearing, neurological and intellectual deficits have been excluded. The author had no access to the relevant hospital records at that time of early treatment, but the child's family doctor reported that the surgeons concerned felt they had achieved a satisfactory result from the surgery and that Elizabeth had been discharged from consultant follow-up.

At 7 years, Elizabeth was referred to her local speech therapy service by an educational psychologist because of concern in school. Scores on the RDLS were reported to be age appropriate, but at 7 years and 7 months she was referred to the Regional Plastic Surgery Unit by her local speech therapist for further assessment. At the time of her first visit, she was an outgoing friendly child whose unintelligible conversational speech did not deter her extrovert personality. On intra-oral examination, the soft palate was noted to be short and scarred (Fig. 3.18) and she appeared to be unaware of the correct placement for some sounds, e.g. /f/ /v/. Lip and tongue muscles were flaccid and her apparent inco-ordination led one to query some articulatory dyspraxia. Spontaneous speech was unintelligible with glottal and pharyngeal substitutions, and only the bilabial plosives and all nasal consonants were produced correctly. It seemed logical to assume that such severe intelligibility problems at this age were likely to be attributable to those encountered in dealing with severe intra-oral limitations.

Neither radiography nor nasendoscopy were available in this Unit at that time, but at 8 years, she underwent a palatal re-repair with some effort directed towards creating a more viable muscle sling within the soft palate. Following this, she continued in therapy at a

**Table 3.3**  Case summary: Elizabeth: Cleft of secondary palate

| Age | General management | Speech status & management | Comment |
|---|---|---|---|
| 18 months | Repair of secondary palate cleft | | This cleft most common in females |
| 5 years | | Speech still unintelligible. Period of intensive speech therapy; poor progress attributed to environmental factors, including dual language background | Speech therapy provision was late. All factors need to be considered in the evaluation of progress |
| 7 years | Referral to Regional Plastic Surgery unit. Palate appeared short & scarred | Speech assessment; unintelligible, glottal and pharyngeal substitutions & severe nasal escape | Nasendoscopy & speech radiography would have been valuable, but were not available |
| 8 years | Re-do of palate repair Audiometry—normal | Speech therapy provision near home—poor progress | |
| 8 years & 6 months | Orticochea pharyngoplasty | Delay in provision of speech therapy post-surgery | |
| 9 years & 3 months | Lateral radiographs—no intra-oral tongue contacts. Little movement in velopharyngeal area. Nasendoscopy—poor movement of Orticochea sphincter. Palate flaccid | Best closure on /p, b/ Lack of tongue tip to alveolar contact | Team hypothesised that the poor articulation might be interfering with velopharyngeal function |
| 9 years & 4 months | | Admitted to regional unit for 2 week intensive speech therapy: work on /t, d/ tongue tip & lip work—improved after discharge; continued speech therapy in home locality | Value of providing intensive periods of treatment |
| 9 years & 10 months | Endoscopy: palate still flaccid, but Orticochea sphincter closed consistently on all sounds except pharyngeals | Admitted for further 2 week intensive period of therapy: work on fricatives & affricates which were produced as pharyngeal fricatives | |
| 10 to 11 years | | Local therapist reported persisting difficulties, especially in relation to generalisation of improved speech patterns | Establishment of improved speech patterns may take a very long time |
| 11 years & 9 months | | Further 2 week period of intensive therapy work on stabilisation of fricatives & affricates: improvement | Value of mixture of different modes of intervention |
| 20 years | Lateral radiographs: good tongue & lip movements. Movement of posterior third of tongue eliminated. Endoscopy: active sphincteric action in speech | Good tongue & lip movement in speech Speech standard good | |

local level, but with little lasting improvement in intelligibility.

At 8 years and 5 months an *Orticochea phar-yngoplasty* (Orticochea 1968, Huskie & Jackson 1977, Jackson & Silverton 1977, Lendrum & Dhar 1984) was carried out in an effort to narrow the nasopharyngeal isthmus. *Audi-ometry* was carried out at that time and hearing was reported to be 'excellent'. Following Elizabeth's Orticochea pharyngo-plasty there was a hiatus in speech therapy due to difficulties in arranging local speech

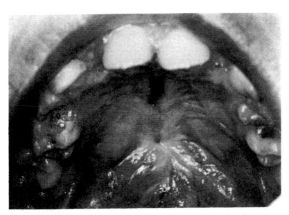

**Fig 3.18** Intra-oral view showing short scarred palate

therapy in her rural setting. In the meantime, endoscopy and speech radiography became available and were carried out when Elizabeth was 9 years and 3 months. Her *lateral radiographs* revealed that there appeared to be no intra-oral tongue contact (except for nasal consonants) and that there was greatly increased movement of the posterior third of the tongue. Her pharyngoplasty could be seen at a low level, but there appeared to be little movement in the velopharyngeal area.

*Nasendoscopy* (using the rigid endoscope) was carried out and reported as follows: 'At rest, at the level of normal velopharyngeal closure, there is an almost oval opening with the long axis situated transversely. The soft palate is notched in the midline and the posterior pharyngeal wall concave forwards. At the lower level of the Orticochea pharyngoplasty, there is a rounded triangular opening. With speech at a higher level there is moderate palatal movement. A fairly large defect remains at this level. Movement with the sounds /p/b/, but palatal movement here appears flaccid, produced by intra-oral air pressure. The levator muscles appear to form a sling somewhere in the middle third of the soft palate, but the levator action is poor. There is no obvious movement of the Orticochea sphincter. This girl's problems seem to be those mainly of articulation defects, which may be interfering with velopharyngeal function.

It is interesting that she obtains the best

closure with sounds /p/ /b/. If articulation improved her velopharyngeal function may well improve. It would be interesting to review her after intensive speech therapy aimed at improving articulation. If surgery is considered, it is difficult to decide on the best operation, but possibly reducing the Orticochea sphincter would be the operation of choice.'

It is worthwhile to consider the statement, 'if articulation improved, her velopharyngeal function may well improve'. Each client must obviously be taken on his own merits, but speech therapists have traditionally taken the stand that good velopharyngeal closure was a necessary prerequisite to achievement of normal articulation, and that it was pointless to try to improve tongue function while the velopharyngeal valve was incompetent. However, the endoscopist was obviously aware of the concept of vocal tract function rather than exclusive velopharyngeal activity, and his ideas helped the speech therapist to realise that therapy, not further surgery, should be the chosen course of action.

At 9 years and 4 months Elizabeth was admitted for *intensive speech therapy* (Huskie 1979) when work was directed towards eliciting and establishing alveolar consonants /t/ /d/. This was helped by making the tongue placement interdental so that the sounds could be seen as well as heard and felt. At the end of a 2-week spell, these sounds were used readily in prepared speech and /k/ /g/ were possible in babbling practice. Great emphasis was placed on improving tongue and lip co-ordination through mirror work and exercises, and all speech work was reinforced by nursing and teaching staff within the hospital.

Elizabeth was discharged home to her local speech therapy service where she continued to work hard. At 9 years and 8 months she was re-admitted to hospital for more intensive work, aimed at stabilising all plosives in spontaneous speech and also working on /s/ /z/ which (contrary to all expectations) were elicited with great ease. At the end of a 2-week period, errors in prepared speech and reading were being spontaneously corrected. At that time, a removable orthodontic appliance was fitted to the maxilla to treat her Class II occlusion; this did not appear to interfere with tongue movements.

As arranged, she was admitted again at 9 years and 10 months when further therapy was aimed to stabilise fricative and affricate sounds, which were most resistant to change. *Endoscopy* was repeated at that time, and although the palate appeared flaccid, the Orticochea sphincter closed consistently on all sounds except fricative and affricate sounds which were still pharyngeal at the time of assessment. A much higher, more active movement was seen for swallowing. It proved singularly difficult to maintain consistent use of fricative and affricate sounds, and her local therapist commented on Elizabeth's difficulties in relation to changes in speech patterns. She was reported to be capable of much clearer speech than she produced spontaneously, but that both her home environment and innate abilities mitigated against any sustained effort.

Further *intensive therapy* was carried out when she was 11 years and 9 months, again aimed at stabilising fricative and affricate sounds. At that time, entry to secondary school was deferred and she returned to Primary 7 to have additional remedial teaching. She made good progress in this setting, but she was distracted from school and speech work by increased home problems. Elizabeth continued to attend the cleft palate clinic for routine review and orthodontic supervision, maintaining good speech and intelligibility. Her treatment is complete, she is now married and has a cleft palate daughter, so the circle is a never-ending one. Elizabeth was seen again recently at 20 years, when radiography and endoscopy were repeated. *Lateral radiography* showed that tongue and lip movements were appropriate for speech and that the movements of the posterior third of the tongue had been entirely eliminated. *Flexible endoscopy* revealed active sphincteric action, closing appropriately, consistently and firmly during speech. It has been suggested earlier that the main aim of palatal closure is to facili-

tate speech, and it follows that the speech therapist should be the best person to evaluate speech and the underlying success of palatal repair. In addition to completing a detailed speech and language assessment, the therapist will require to elicit a sample of speech in clinic, so that the surgeon can hear the standards of speech which are possible. In addition, it is important to investigate any social and psychological factors which may be causative, maintaining or simply co-occurring. In this instance, the family is bilingual (Gaelic and English) but the evidence is that most children are not hampered by a bilingual context. It may seem strange that her mother was apparently not concerned by Elizabeth's poor speech, but it should be remembered that her own speech had been poor until she was an adult, and that expectations for normal speech for her child were perhaps reduced. Finally, at a later stage it became apparent that there had been considerable domestic distress, and under such circumstances it is surprising that her mother coped as well as she did.

### Lesley: Cleft of soft palate with retrognathia
(See Table 3.4)

Lesley was born with a Pierre Robin anomalad (Gorlin et al 1976) and was adopted at 3 weeks of age. She was spoon-fed at that stage, progressing to eating custard and mashed vegetables at about 6 weeks. Her cleft palate repair was undertaken at 16 months. Her mother reported that she was using single words at about 2 years, but her family described early speech development as 'slow'. Pre-school speech therapy was provided and continued until the time she started school, despite only limited improvement. In these early stages of therapy, blowing and sucking work had been carried out, together with auditory discrimination for all sounds. Work on placement for /t/ /d/ /s/ /z/ /ʃ/ /tʃ/ had all been attempted, but there appeared to have been little if any success in achieving any of these sounds. A pharyngeal flap procedure was carried out at 9 years old and revised some 3 years later. When Lesley was 10 years

**Table 3.4**  Case summary: Lesley: Cleft of soft palate with retrognathia

| Age | General management | Speech status & management | Comment |
|---|---|---|---|
| 16 months | Repair of secondary palate cleft | | Possibility of Pierre Robin syndrome |
| 2 years | | Speech & language development slow | |
| 3 years | | Speech therapy provided until school age<br>Limited progress | It is of considerable concern that therapy was provided over an extended period, with little investigation of the reasons for the persisting problems of nasal escape |
| 9 years | Superiorly based pharyngeal flap | | |
| 10 years | | Nasal escape persisted but speech therapy discontinued | |
| 12 years | Revision of previous pharyngoplasty<br>Referral to Regional Plastic Surgery Unit | Velar substitutions. Gross audible nasal emission. Retrognathia persisted and affected speech | Mandibular growth usually catches up by around 5 years |
| | Audiometry showed consistent bilateral hearing loss: post-aural aid worn | Retrognathia persisted & affected speech. Anemometry showed moderate to severe nasal escape | Need for careful consideration of the role of hearing in maintaining speech problem |
| | Lateral radiography: extreme activity of posterior third of tongue. Good palatal lift<br>Nasendoscopy: velopharyngeal area competent for speech | Speech therapy aimed at improving tongue movement arranged in home locality | Importance of identifying appropriate therapy aims |
| 13 years | Radiography: improved tongue function | Anemometry repeated post therapy-reduced nasal air flow | |
| | Endoscopy: poor palate elevation lateral wall movement | Persistent retrognathia interfered with lip closure | The value of the two pharyngoplasties is questionable |
| 15 years | | All sounds possible in spontaneous speech | |

old, her speech therapist commented to the surgeon in charge that the considerable nasal escape was causing great concern, and therapy was suspended until she was referred to the author's clinic for assessment at 12 years old.

When first seen for evaluation in that setting, Lesley was substituting velar for alveolar nasal and plosive sounds, with velar placement for /s/z/tʃ/dʒ/. Persisting *mandibular retrusion* made lip seal difficult, both at rest and for production of bilabial nasals and plosives. Subjectively, audible nasal escape was a prominent feature of speech,

with associated turbulence and friction. *Audiometry* (Fig. 3.19) showed bilateral hearing loss for which she wore a post-aural hearing aid.

*Lateral speech radiographs* revealed extreme activity of the posterior third of the tongue with essentially no tongue tip movement for speech. There appeared to be good palatal lift, but this was limited by the tight, low pharyngeal flap and there seemed to be no forward movement of the posterior pharyngeal wall for speech. However, contrary to expectations, nasendoscopy revealed that the velopharyngeal area was competent for

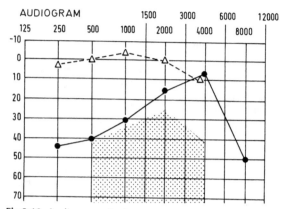

AUDIOGRAM

**Fig 3.19** Audiogram: Lesley at 12 years

speech, thanks to good palatal and lateral wall movement.

On the basis of these subjective and objective evaluations, it seemed more logical to correct the *deviant tongue patterns* than to consider more velopharyngeal surgery. This would be achieved through a planned speech therapy programme, not only to improve tongue placement and resulting intelligibility, but also to reduce the nasal escape caused by the deviant movements of the posterior third of the tongue. Lesley was referred to her local speech therapy service and a programme was devised, in conjunction with the speech therapist concerned, to advance tongue tip placement into an interdental position for /t/ /d/ and, in so doing, compensate for the retrognathia. If the alveolar plosives and nasals could be established successfully, that would act as a basis for work on fricative and affricate sounds. After some 9 months therapy, Lesley's speech had improved considerably, especially as her interest and motivation had increased. The report at that time was as follows: 'Therapy has concentrated on production of alveolar plosives and affricates together with stabilisation of alveolar fricatives. Attendance has been good, but is often affected by appointments elsewhere. Lesley is being encouraged to attend speech therapy alone, or with a friend instead of her mother who still brings her every week. Lesley herself appears willing to do this if allowed. Further weekly therapy is planned but, unfortunately,

more frequent sessions are impossible.' Some 3 months later a further report was received as follows. 'Since my last report, Lesley has continued to make progress with her speech. Alveolar nasal, plosives, fricatives and affricates are now being used appropriately in spontaneous speech, so weekly therapy has been suspended. I propose to see Lesley every 2 months as she is not entirely confident of her speaking ability yet.'

*Nasal anemometry* pre- and post-therapy can be compared to confirm the reduced nasal airflow (Fig. 3.20), while speech radiographs objectively defined her improved tongue action. Bilabial closure, however, continued to be difficult to maintain, due to retrognathia. *Endoscopy* was reported as follows: 'From below there is a broad posterior pharyngeal flap. The port on the left side is small and the port on the right side is large. On making the sound [ah] there is no palatal elevation. There is, however, lateral wall movement and the lateral wall movement on the right side appears to be adequate to obturate the port. From above the lateral ports are well visualised. There is some palate lift which was not apparent from below. There is lateral wall movement but this does not seem to be sufficient to completely obturate the lateral ports. If closure occurs it occurs by palate lift. There is no evidence of a V deformity. The Eustachian cushions were not visualised.'

## Discussion

When Lesley's pre- and post-speech therapy endoscopy recordings were compared, there was no difference in the velopharyngeal action, and if the recordings were played without sound, it would have been impossible to decide their chronological order. The real change was seen in tongue placement which, on the second recording, was now essentially normal, and speech was satisfactory both acoustically and from the resonance balance points of view. The objective evidence proves that speech therapy was entirely responsible for this striking improvement from unintelli-

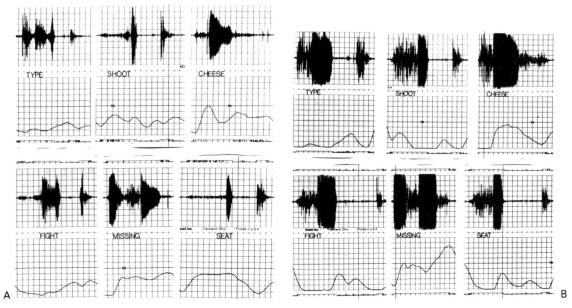

**Fig 3.20** (A) Pre-speech therapy anemometry. (B) Post-speech therapy anemometry

gible to intelligible speech. It is not unreasonable to suggest that the pharyngeal flap did not appear to be contributing to velopharyngeal competence and its low level may have been inhibiting palatal elevation. On that basis, it can be argued that the two pharyngeal flap procedures could have been avoided if accurate evaluation of tongue placement by a speech therapist had led that therapist to realise that the deviant tongue action contributed greatly to the audible nasal escape of air. All therapists involved with such patients have a responsibility in advising surgical colleagues as to the need for more surgery and/or speech therapy, and use of the objective techniques as described here can confirm and augment a speech therapist's clinical judgement.

This case study illustrates the pitfalls of isolated examination of velopharyngeal closure not as an integral part of the vocal tract and as such influenced by the function of other organs. In the early stages of Lesley's treatment, it was rightly recognised that she had nasal escape, but the reasons for this feature were not explored by the professionals involved. A satisfactory speech outcome was

eventually achieved, but it is unfortunate that she was a teenager before appropriate management was instigated.

### Mary: Acquired velopharyngeal palsy (see Table 3.5)

Mary was referred to her local speech therapy service by her family doctor when she was 16, her speech problem being described as follows: 'For 8 months she has spoken in a nasal voice and seems to have a paralysed palate. She has been thoroughly investigated by a neurologist and no physical cause has been found. He thinks she would be helped by speech therapy.' The neurological discharge summary stated that 'the palate moved very poorly and that the gag reflex was reduced but present bilaterally. This young lady was thoroughly investigated for any lesion in the posterior fossa or peripherally. However investigations were in fact entirely negative. Mary was therefore discharged and arrangements should be made for speech therapy to commence as soon as possible. There is no recommended drug therapy.'

She was seen in a local speech therapy

**Table 3.5**  *Case summary: Mary: Acquired velopharyngeal palsy*

| Age | General management | Speech status & management | Comment |
|---|---|---|---|
| 15 years | | Nasal speech noticed at home | |
| 16 years | Neurological assessment negative: found poor palate movement & reduced gag reflex | Referred by GP after neurological examination. Marked hypernasality and escape. Restricted palatal movement on right. Articulation good | |
| 16 years 6 months | | Palatal training device fitted. Evidence of swallowing difficulties & nasal regurgitation | Fitting PTA needs to be preceded by objective evaluation |
| 16 years 8 months | Referred to Regional Plastic Surgery Unit. Lateral radiography & nasendoscopy revealed little levator palati movement, complete paralysis of superior pharyngeal constrictor | Marked nasal escape & associated nasal grimace | |
| | No forward movement of pharyngeal wall. Tongue movements assymetrical. For review in 6 months of monitor progress | | Possibility of progressive neurological disorder noted by team |
| 16 years | Neurological assessment repeated EMI scan normal. Palate weakness considered to be vital in origin | Continued wear of PTA, but very little improvement in speech | |
| 17 years | Reichart pharyngoplasty | Speech unchanged on re-assessment. Dramatic speech improvement following pharyngoplasty; nasal escape much reduced | |
| 18 years | Radiographs & nasendoscopy revealed improved velopharyngeal closure | Minimal hypernasality & nasal escape. Patient happy with improvement | Check at 21 years showed stable position of speech and no new neurological symptoms |

clinic soon afterwards, when it was elicited that hypernasality was first noticed by her father some 12 months previously. Speech was hypernasal throughout interview, and palatal movement was restricted on the right side. Some weeks later, following work on breath direction and palatal exercises, a *palatal training device* was fitted by the orthodontist (Tudor & Selly 1974) (see Chapter 5). There appeared to be a significant functional element in her history, but she had also complained of occasional nasal regurgitation of liquids and food, together with some swallowing difficulties.

Later that year, the local clinician had some discussion with the author about patient selection for palatal training appliances, and the need for careful pre-therapy evaluation was emphasised. As a result of this discussion, Mary was referred to the author's clinic for such evaluation and assessment by the relevant team. *Speech assessment* revealed appropriate tongue and lip placement for speech, but marked nasal escape with associated nasal grimacing during production of plosives, fricatives and affricates. From discussion with Mary and her mother on separate occasions there appeared to be some psychological overlay to the speech problem, but it remained to be seen if this was a true problem or more simply a natural exacerbation of usual parent/child difficulties which arise in adolescence. Mary was understandably very concerned about her speech and progress and it seemed that that anxiety about speech could well be the underlying cause of her behaviour difficulties. From clinical judgement it seemed that the speech problem was a primary factor overlaid by anxiety rather than the reverse.

*Lateral speech radiographs* were carried out with barium coating applied to tongue and nasopharynx. The palate appeared to be of normal length and thickness, while the post-nasal space seemed of normal dimensions. During speech, however, there was no lift or backward movement of the soft palate, and apparently no forward movement of the posterior pharyngeal wall. Tongue movements were appropriate to the sounds attempted. A moderate velopharyngeal gap persisted at all times during speech. Marked nasal grimace associated with vocalisation was seen consistently. *Endoscopy* was reported as follows: 'It was obvious that there was very little levator palati movement and this abnormality appeared symmetrical. There was, however, a complete paralysis of the left superior pharyngeal constrictor muscle, although the right superior pharyngeal constrictor was contracting normally during speech. Tongue movements were asymmetrical, in that the left side of the tongue elevated on making the sound /a/. This may indicate some neuromuscular abnormality in the tongue, but is more likely to be a compensation for the paralysis of the pharyngeal constrictor.

The diagnosis is obscure, but there is definite velopharyngeal incompetence due to paralysis of the left superior pharyngeal constrictor muscle.'

This diagnostic information was discussed and in view of the possibility of progressive neurological disease it was decided to re-assess Mary in 6 months' time to decide if the measurements and/or speech status had deteriorated in the intervening spell, with the option of pharyngoplasty if the condition was static.

*Neurological assessment* was repeated 6 months later when her palatal weakness appeared unchanged from her first visit. Her *EMI scan* was repeated and was again normal, and the cause of her palatal weakness was described as 'obscure' and possibly 'viral' in origin. The speech therapist reported that she continued to wear her palatal trainer, but that there appeared to be no improvement in speech at all, if anything there might have been slight deterioration.

On *speech reassessment* when Mary was 17, the essential features of speech and velopharyngeal function remained unchanged and she underwent *Reichart pharyngoplasty*. Speech was very much improved as a result of this procedure and nasal escape dramatically reduced.

*Radiography* and *nasendoscopy* were repeated at 12 months post-operatively when velopharyngeal closure was very much improved, with only slight lateral gutters remaining, allowing a little nasal escape. Hypernasality and escape were minimal and Mary was delighted with the improvement in intelligibility. She was seen for routine follow-up for some 4 years post-operatively and there was no deterioration in speech status and no new neurological symptoms apparent.

## Discussion

This case study exemplifies why an objective diagnosis should be sought before therapy is embarked upon. In fact, Mary presented with a structural velopharyngeal palsy which was unlikely to respond to traditional speech therapy. It is thought to be inappropriate to fit a palatal training appliance without careful objective evaluation to ensure an accurate diagnosis and that the planned treatment is appropriate. Palatal training appliances may well have a place in the treatment of poor timing and co-ordination in the velopharyngeal area, but it is supremely important to exclude structural problems beforehand, as emphasised by Tudor & Selley (1974). In addition, the possible psychological overlay to this girl's speech problem may have concealed the need to exclude more quantifiable physical problems. It is all too easy to accept a psychological diagnosis and then use that as a reason or excuse not to seek a more definitive basis for the patient's clinical problem. It is vital to keep an open mind when assessing any problem, and to use all available techniques to augment clinical judgement.

### Angela: Hypernasality: an early symptom of myasthenia gravis (see Table 3.6)

Angela, an infant teacher, began to suffer 'laryngitis' at 36 years of age and sought help from her family doctor at that time. Voice problems were so severe that she had to stop teaching because of *dysphonia* and *hypernasality*. These vocal features became associated with foods and fluid leaking nasally; therefore, later that year her general practitioner referred her to an otolaryngologist for his opinion and treatment. His report was as follows: 'Nasal polyp removed. Palate appeared tight and some stretching attempted. Biopsy taken but nothing significant found. There seemed to be some palatal movement and such a degree of tightness that it is thought that there is unlikely to be a neurological basis to this disorder. A poorly conducted tonsillectomy in childhood may be responsible for hypernasality and this may have been exacerbated by recent throat infections.'

**Table 3.6** Case summary: Angela: Hypernasality an early symptom of myasthenia gravis

| Age | General management | Speech status & management | Comment |
|---|---|---|---|
| 36 years | Seen by GP for laryngitis | Laryngitis & hypernasality forced patient to stop work as a teacher | |
| | GP referred for ENT opinion; 'palate stretching' & removal of polyp carried out | ENT referred for speech therapy. PTA fitted. Therapy programme included work on breath direction, blowing exercises & relaxation | |
| | | Speech & swallowing difficulties persisted. Longer loop fitted to PTA which produced marked improvement | Patient on holiday reported dizzy spells, walking difficulties, worried by bright sun light |
| | | Increased swallowing problems. Speech becoming more nasal even with extended PTA | |
| | Lateral & basal radiographs, showed loop acted as palatal lift. Limited palatal movement. Lack of facial expression & droopy eyelids noted | | |
| | Nasendoscopy identified progressive palatal fatigue on repeated movements | | Possibility of neurological factors noted at this point |
| 37 years | Neurological opinion sought: myasthenia gravis diagnosed | | Myasthenia gravis most common in women with onset in 3rd decade. Muscles supplied by cranial nerves usually first affected |
| 38 years | Thymectomy performed later in year. Radiographs & nasendoscopy showed normal velopharyngeal function | Normal speech restored after thymectomy, patient able to resume teaching post | Thymectomy may bring about remission of the disease |

Angela was then referred by the otolaryngologist to a local speech therapist who decided to fit a *palatal training appliance* onto the patient's existing upper partial denture, having first sought approval from the otolaryngologist concerned. A plan of therapy was made (Curle 1979), beginning with establishing control of breath direction without vocalisation, onto vocalisation of vowels, monosyllabic and polysyllabic words, simple phrases, sibilants and blends, finally introducing nasals and blends. In the early stages of therapy, blowing exercises and relaxation were carried out; then blowing work had to be discontinued when speech became more hypernasal and swallowing became more difficult. Regular therapy was provided and proceeded according to plan. After about 2 months it was decided to fit a longer loop, which made a dramatic difference to Angela's speech, even to the point of denasalisation. The therapist noted: 'Patient delighted with new training loop, but we both feel it is functioning as a palatal lift. When this is removed, there is no significant improvement in hypernasality compared to initial interview. Resonance and intelligibility deteriorate markedly. However, she is not willing to do without it as communication is difficult and patient is going on holiday.' On that August holiday in France, Angela reported that sun and light annoyed her, she had several episodes of dizziness, felt her legs very weak and she also reported that cutting bread was difficult. In addition to these new symptoms, increased hypernasality over prolonged periods of speaking rendered conversational speech virtually unintelligible. In late August she also reported some weight loss which she attributed to her swallowing difficulties. Anxiety was increasing greatly and the possibility of a psychological basis to the disorder was discussed by patient and therapist, but the patient did not think that her speech problems were related to anxiety.

Angela was then referred to the author's clinic for further investigations, when her speech was mildly hypernasal with her palatal training appliance, but grossly so without it,

to the verge of unintelligibility over more than a few sentences. On *intra-oral examination*, tongue and lip movements were appropriate, but sluggish palatal lift was noted on repeated /a:/ sounds. *Lateral* and *basal speech radiographs* with barium coating to nasopharynx and tongue were carried out both with and without her palatal training appliance in place. This loop appeared to act only as a palatal lift, and there appeared to be only very limited palatal movements without it. She appeared to achieve touch patterns of velopharyngeal contact, and there was extreme effort in maintaining any vestige of movement approaching closure. It was noticeable from the facial view that she lacked much facial expression and that her eyelids seemed droopy. *Basal views* revealed an oval velopharyngeal orifice, and any movement towards closure was palatal with little if any contribution from lateral and posterior pharyngeal walls.

*Nasendoscopy* carried out some weeks later was reported as follows: 'On examination, wearing her plate, she has an almost completely flattened palate which moves little on the first sound and then rapidly fatigues. There is a striking feature of fatigue of the movements on repetition. Easy instrumentation through right nostril without plate revealed a large patulous ovoid velopharyngeal aperture which closed a little with the first sound and not at all thereafter. With the lift device in place she achieved a pharyngoplasty-like situation with two largish triangular lateral ports. Again these closed a little initially, but rapidly became incompetent. I suspect there is an underlying neurological cause for this problem and am therefore referring the patient to a neurologist for his opinion.'

While awaiting hospital admission for investigations Angela reported weakness when peeling potatoes and in hand co-ordination for knitting. She reported that these skills would deteriorate, she would rest, then function would be restored. She was puzzled and worried by this aspect and again began to think she was imagining her symptoms. Following an out-patient appointment, Angela was admitted to hospital in the care of the neurologists and, among other results, the following were received: 'Following a Tensilon test there was an unequivocal improvement in this girl's diplopia on upward gaze and in the quality of her speech, despite the administration of only a small dose of Tensilon (2 mg). This test and the history confirms the diagnosis of *myasthenia gravis*. The question of thymectomy has been raised with her and will be carried out in the New Year.' *Thymectomy* was carried out as planned and she was discharged from hospital some 6 weeks later and made a good recovery from this surgery—so much so that she was able to return to her teaching post 6 months later.

*Speech radiography* and *nasendoscopy* were repeated one year post-thymectomy and reported as follows:

'*Problem:* This patient presented with nasal escape of unknown aetiology which was suggested nasendoscopically to be myasthenia gravis. She was referred to a neurologist who confirmed the diagnosis and arranged appropriate treatment (in her case thymectomy).

*Nasendoscopy:* Easy instrumentation through left nostril. Good view obtained of dynamic high palatal lift and good lateral pharyngeal wall movement. In short, a normal examination. The lateral and basal speech X-rays also show good dynamic closure of her velum.

*Opinion:* The neurological therapy has solved her problem. She has therefore been discharged from plastic surgery follow-up.'

Her resonance balance in speech was normal and there was no audible nasal escape. She was able to cope with a strenuous teaching day and have no voice problems. It was gratifying to have been involved in the management of such a patient.

## Discussion

This lady was referred quickly for further assessment by an alert speech clinician who realised at an early stage that there was more to Angela's problems than was obvious initially. Both speech radiographs and nasendoscopy were critical to this diagnosis, but the endoscopic view which demonstrated graphically the tiring and deterioration in palatal function was especially impressive. The facial view combined with radiography is sometimes described as superfluous, but features of facial appearance are often more obvious on a television monitor than in one-to-one contact. Her characteristic myasthenic facies were much more apparent when we reviewed her recordings than when she had been interviewed in clinic.

These case studies demonstrate the importance of reaching an appropriate diagnosis early in treatment and exemplify the importance and benefits of the application of available resources in solving complex clinical problems. General practitioners, otolaryngologists and paediatricians may be among the first medical staff to see clients who have speech and language problems at an early stage and therefore need to be aware of the available speech therapy resources and also of the relevant diagnostic evaluations. It is the responsibility of speech therapists to inform other medical specialities of the services they can provide and also the additional evaluations to which they have access; then patients like Mary and Angela might have more appropriate treatment much earlier.

## FUTURE DEVELOPMENTS

### Ultra-sound

Intra-oral anatomy and physiology is usually investigated by a combination of air flow studies, video fluoroscopy (multiview), nasendoscopy and occasionally ultrasound. Ultrasound has some advantages over conventional radiography because it appears to be free of risk, but has not been fully applied to head and neck studies because of technical problems and subsequent difficulties in the interpretation of results. A transducer placed on the patient's neck pulses an ultrasound beam toward the pharyngeal wall and the beam is deflected back to the transducer when it reaches the interface between the mucosa of the pharyngeal wall and the air in the pharynx (Skolnick et al 1975). Skolnick (1984) has described the major limitations of the technique as follows:

1. The ability of ultrasound to detect lateral pharyngeal wall motion is crucially dependent upon the transducer orientation to these walls. Slight differences of beam orientation to the lateral walls can result in significantly different degrees of pharyngeal wall movement.
2. Ultrasound imaging is highly dependent on operator skill.
3. Ultrasound does not relate velar or flap level to region of maximum lateral pharyngeal wall movement.
4. The ultrasound does not always image the same portion of the lateral pharyngeal walls as does frontal video fluoroscopy. Therefore two modalities may not record the same extent of pharyngeal wall movement. Skolnick concluded that at present ultrasound could not replace frontal video fluoroscopy for evaluation of lateral pharyngeal wall movement.

**Computerised tomography**

Honjo et al (1984) have described the use of CT scan and endoscopy to evaluate velopharyngeal closure, stating that this combination could help to decide a retronasal choice of treatment for cleft palates. Computerised tomographic apparatus was combined with a flexible Olympus endoscope. However, David & Bagnall (1984) in reviewing this work suggest that the use of CT scanning is a natural progression into new technology, but that its objectivity can be questioned. Speech is dynamic and actions of the velopharyngeal valve cannot be isolated to specific events; and a phoneme cannot be isolated from its phonological context. Fricative and plosive consonants require higher and tighter closure if air is not to leak nasally, since these sounds require greater intra-oral air pressure. The closure of the valve varies in height for the characteristic formants that distinguish one vowel from another. It is suggested that a

tomogram of phonation must delineate what the patient is phonating. When comparison is made between the velopharyngeal valve at rest and when phonating, the cuts must be at precisely the same level, and this does not appear to be the case from the illustrations in the original. Bagnall suggests that use of the rigid endoscope would obviate problems when the 'dead angle' of the palate 'obscures the view and appearance of ineffective closure at the periphery of the valve'.

The changes in management resulting from this technique are not described, and it is indicated that the inability to observe the valve during running speech and doubtful reliability of the view obtained are major disadvantages precluding its use. These reviewing authors suggest that rigid nasendoscopy combined with lateral video fluoroscopy on a split screen with synchronised sound should be the assessment of choice.

**Xeroradiography**

Berry et al (1982) have described the combination of xeroradiography and electrolaryngography to provide quantifiable visual information on soft tissue changes associated with voice disorders, and it has been suggested that these techniques can be applied to the treatment of patients who present with apparent velopharyngeal incompetence where an abnormal mode of vocal fold vibration may be detected by the electrolaryngograph (MacCurtain & Sell 1985). Xeroradiography in this instance revealed deviation in the vocal tract postures, and the information from the two sources of electrolaryngography and xeroradiography was essential in planning therapy.

Xeroradiography has a 'characteristic clarity of soft tissue detail obtained at low cost in X-ray dose: even individual muscle groups can be detected'. However, it must be said that xeroradiography is a still technique and that is a major disadvantage compared to the moving images produced by video fluoroscopy. It would be an ideal situation if the soft tissue clarity could be combined with a moving image—perhaps that may be possible in the future.

## Nasopharyngoscopy: a therapeutic tool

### Velopharyngeal insufficiency

Speech therapists are aware that normal speech patterns can be changed to include features of cleft palate speech, particularly nasal escape and hypernasality. It would appear that the converse should be true and early work by Shelton et al (1975) describes use of an oral panendoscope in the study of voluntary velopharyngeal movements. The use of an oral panendoscope obviously limits intra-oral movements, but these have been largely overcome by the nasopharyngoscope which allows unhindered intra-oral movements and spontaneous speech.

Hoch et al (1986) suggest that use of a nasendoscope may allow modification of velopharyngeal valve action, much as one would correct oral articulatory patterns in selected cases. Some six types of velopharyngeal insufficiency are described, together with the criteria for patient selection, prior to a therapy programme. Several advantages to this approach are outlined, the most important being that surgery to correct velopharyngeal incompetence may be avoided, or that it may be possible to use a less obstructive pharyngeal flap if movement of the lateral walls is increased. A small number of sessions will indicate whether or not biofeedback therapy is likely to be successful.

It is suggested that if the concept of speech therapy (conventional and biofeedback) prior to surgery can be accepted by more clinicians, some answers to difficult questions concerning cleft speech may be forthcoming. These include why some subjects develop compensatory articulation patterns while others do not. Does it take longer periods of therapy to improve articulation pre-operatively than post-operatively? The recommended therapeutic approaches are controversial in their timing and order, but if surgery can be modified or perhaps prevented, surely the programme should be explored.

Witzel et al (1987) describe use of the nasopharyngoscope after pharyngeal flap surgery for five adults in an effort to improve velopharyngeal closure in connected speech. It is suggested that children gain more benefit from pharyngeal flap surgery than adults, and that use of biofeedback therapy in the adult group may help them to capitalise on their surgery to gain maximum benefit.

### Dysphonia

Bagnall (1984) describes use of a nasopharyngoscope in voice therapy as a biofeedback tool (Fig. 3.21). This approach to voice therapy is very much in its infancy, but it is thought that the combination of visual and auditory dimensions will be beneficial to patients and an exciting concept for voice therapists. Bagnall states that the technique does not supplant examination of the patient by the otolaryngologist, but that it does allow the voice therapist to explore the physiology of the larynx in order to plan a treatment programme. The technique presents itself as an opportunity of working with the patient to change his vocal technique, as demonstrated by the image from the fibrescope.

Bagnall states that 'voice therapy now has an additional dimension' and further reports of the effects of this technique are awaited with interest.

## ACKNOWLEDGEMENTS

Considerable gratitude is due to a number of plastic surgeons who have encouraged my early interest in cleft palate and taught me to co-operate as a team member. Chief among these are I. T. Jackson, B. C. Sommerlad, D. A. McGrouther and A. G. Batchelor, all consultant plastic surgeons. Dr W. N. Mason and his radiographic staff at Glasgow Dental Hospital and School have co-operated more than fully in developing and refining the techniques of speech radiography that have been described, while R. E. Ellis and F. C. Flack

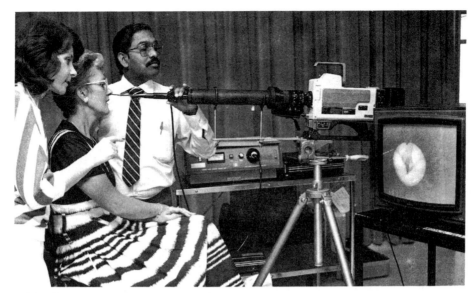

**Fig 3.21** Use of flexible endoscopy

have been generous in sharing their scientific knowledge in medical physics.

I am indebted to my speech therapy colleagues, G. M. Baker, J. R. Michie, M. MacDonnell and L. M. Vallance for their initiative in referring the clients in the case studies to me and for their later help in management and preparation of the case studies.

Joy Stackhouse gave permission for publication of her checklist for Examination of Oral Structure and Function, which provided

guidelines for that section of the text, while Alison Bagnall gave kind permission for the publication of Figure 3.27.

Grateful thanks are due to the Medical Photography and Illustration Departments of Canniesburn Hospital and Dental Hospital and School, both of Glasgow, for their help in the preparation of illustrations.

Perhaps most importantly, Evelyn McNaught must be thanked for her patient, humorous secretarial assistance.

## REFERENCES

Antony J F K 1980 Aerodynamics and phonetic analysis. In: Edwards M, Watson A C H (eds) Advances in the management of cleft palate. Churchill Livingstone, Edinburgh

Bagnall A D 1984 Show me your Voice. Australian Association of Speech and Hearing Conference Proceedings Beyond 1984

Batchelor A G 1987 Personal communication

Berry R J, Epstein R, Fourcin A J, Freeman M, MacCurtain F, Noscoe N 1982 An objective analysis of voice disorder: part one. British Journal of Disorders of Communication 17: 67

Curle H J 1979 Therapeutic methods for the incompetent soft palate. In: Ellis R E, Flack F C (eds) Diagnosis and treatment of palato-glossal malfunction. College of Speech Therapists, London

David D J, Bagnall A D 1984 The evaluation of velopharyngeal closure by C T scan and endoscopy. Discussion. Plastic and Reconstructive Surgery 74: 626.

Ellis R E 1979 The Exeter nasal anemometry system. In: Ellis R E, Flack F C (eds) Diagnosis and treatment of palatoglossal malfunction. College of Speech Therapists, London

Gorlin R J, Pindborg J J, Cohen M M 1976 Syndromes of the head & neck. McGraw-Hill, New York

Hoch L, Golding-Kushner K, Siegel-Sadewitz V L, Shprintzen R J 1986 Speech therapy. Seminars in Speech and Language 7: 3. Thieme Inc, New York

Honjo I, Mitoma T, Ushiro K et al 1984 Evaluation of velopharyngeal closure by CT scan and endoscopy. Plastic and Reconstructive Surgery 74: 621

Huskie C F, Jackson I T 1977 The sphincter

pharyngoplasty; a new approach to the problems of velopharyngeal incompetence. British Journal of Disorders of Communication 9: 45

Huskie C F 1979 Intensive therapy—Glasgow experience. In: Ellis R E, Flack F C (eds) Diagnosis and treatment of palato-glossal malfunction. College of Speech Therapists, London.

Jackson I T, Silverton J S 1977 The sphincter pharyngoplasty as a secondary procedure in cleft palates. Plastic & Reconstructive Surgery 59, 4: 518

Lendrum J, Dhar B K 1984 The orticochea dynamic pharyngoplasty. British Journal of Plastic Surgery 37: 160

MacCurtain F, Sell D 1985 New measurement techniques in velopharyngeal incompetence. Paper presented at Fifth International Congress on Cleft Palate and Related Craniofacial Anomalies, Monte Carlo

McWilliams Neeley B J, Bradley D P 1964 A rating scale for evaluation of video tape recorded x-ray studies. Cleft Palate Journal 1: 88

McWilliams B J, Bradley D P 1965 Ratings of velopharyngeal closure during blowing and speech. Cleft Palate Journal. 2: 46

Morley M E 1958 Cleft palate and speech. Churchill Livingstone, Edinburgh

Orticochea M 1968 Construction of a dynamic muscle sphincter in cleft palates. Plastic & Reconstructive Surgery 41: 323

Pigott R W 1969 Nasendoscopic appearance of the normal palato pharyngeal valve. Plastic & Reconstructive Surgery 43: 19

Pigott R W, Benson J F, White F D 1969 Nasendoscopy in the diagnosis of velopharyngeal incompetence. Plastic & Reconstructive Surgery 43: 141

Pigott R W, Makepeace A R W 1975 Technique of recording nasal pharyngoscopy. British Journal of Plastic Surgery 28: 26

Pigott R W 1980 Assessment of velopharyngeal function. In: Edwards M, Watson A C H (eds) Advances in the management of cleft palate. Churchill Livingstone, Edinburgh

Russell V J 1980 A cautionary tale—in praise of anemometry. College of Speech Therapists Bulletin, No. 342, 8

Selley W G 1979 Dental and technical aids, In: Ellis R E, Flack F C (eds) Diagnosis and treatment of palato glossal malfunction. College of Speech Therapists, London

Shelton R L, Paesani A, McClelland K D, Bradfield S S 1975 Panendoscopic feedback in the study of voluntary velopharyngeal movements. Journal of Speech and Hearing Disorders 40: 232

Skolnick M L, Shprintzen R, McCall G 1975 Patterns of velopharyngeal closure in subjects with repaired cleft palate and normal speech: a multi-view video fluoroscopic analysis. Cleft Palate Journal 12: 369

Skolnick M L 1986 Simultaneous ultrasonic and video fluoroscopic evaluation of lateral nasopharyngeal wall motion during speech. Proceedings of the British Craniofacial Society, Manchester Univ Press.

Sommerlad B C, Hackett M E J, Watson J 1975 A simplified method of recording in nasal pharyngoscopy. British Journal of Plastic Surgery 23: 34

Sommerlad B C 1981 Nasendoscopy. In: Jackson I T (ed) Recent Advances in Plastic Surgery, Vol 2. Churchill Livingstone, Edinburgh

Stackhouse J 1981 Checklist for examination of oral structure and function. Unpublished student hand-out, Birmingham Polytechnic

Stuffins G M 1984 Tongue tip movement patterns in the unilateral cleft lip and palate child related to pre-surgical orthodontic treatment. Proceedings XIX Congress of International Association of Logopaedics and Phoniatrics. College of Speech Therapists, London

Tudor C, Selley W G 1974 A palatal training appliance and a visual aid for use in the treatment of hypernasal speech. British Journal of Disorders of Communication 9: 117

Van Demark D R 1974 Assessment of velopharyngeal competency for children with cleft palates. Cleft Palate Journal 11: 310

Veau V 1931 Division palatine. Masson, Paris

Warren D W 1967 Nasal emission of air and velopharyngeal function. Cleft Palate Journal 4: 148

Warren D W 1976 Aerodynamics of speech production. Contemporary issues in experimental phonetics. In: Lass J N (ed) Academic Press, New York

Witzel M A, Tobe J, Salyer K E 1987 The use of nasopharyngoscopy biofeedback therapy in the correction of inconsistent velopharyngeal closure. Paper presented at 14th annual meeting of the Society for Ear, Nose and Throat Advances in Children. Philadelphia, USA

Introduction
Principles of intervention
  Timing of therapy
    Case study: Anna; timing of therapy
  Frequency of therapy
    Case study: Tom; frequency of therapy

Type of intervention
  Therapy for articulation
    Consonants in isolation
    Integration of consonants into single
    words and sentences
    Generalisation into everyday speech
    Case study: Susan; generalisation into
    everyday speech
  Therapy for hypernasality and nasal emission
    Case study: Stephen; therapy for phoneme
    specific nasal emission
  Therapy for articulation problems associated
  with malocclusion
    Case study: Helen; malocclusion

# 4

# Approaches to the treatment of speech problems

## L. Albery

## INTRODUCTION

The aim of this chapter is to help the student speech therapist or practising clinician to understand the rationale behind differing approaches to therapy for children and adults with cleft palate, to suggest practical methods of carrying out remediation and, with case history examples, to see the speech therapy role within the wider scheme of general management of the cleft palate client.

Over the years a number of speech therapists have written about therapy procedures for clients with cleft palate, but while much research has been directed to the evaluation of velopharyngeal function for speech, the empirical research literature on therapy for clients with cleft palate is scanty (McWilliams et al 1984). This reflects the difficulty of measuring speech changes in evaluating different therapies, given the heterogeneous nature of the population and the multiplicity of variables. Notwithstanding, appropriate speech therapy intervention is of vital importance to the child with cleft palate, and articulation therapy in particular is a key speech therapy service for those clients with cleft palate who have articulation difficulties. If a cleft palate repair has not resulted in velopharyngeal sufficiency, secondary surgery in the form of a pharyngoplasty can set the scene for improvement in articulation and makes a vital contribution, but it is speech therapy which can directly improve articulation and communication skills. For 70% to 95% of children with cleft palate (McWilliams et al 1984), their primary palate repair gives them velopharyngeal sufficiency for speech so that they do not require secondary surgery.

Many children with cleft palate never require speech therapy intervention, although estimates vary and probably around 50% require some speech therapy intervention from a speech therapist at some time. Successful surgery and effective speech therapy go hand in hand. If significant velopharyngeal insufficiency persists following primary repair to the palate there may be nothing a speech therapist can do to improve articulation to any significant extent. If, on the other hand, there is velopharyngeal sufficiency for speech, there is no gross collapse of the alveolar arch, and disturbance to maxillo-facial growth is minimised, it is much easier for the speech therapist to effect speech changes. Thus it is vitally important for surgeons and speech therapists to liaise closely in the management of children and adults with cleft palate.

## PRINCIPLES OF INTERVENTION

In any treatment programme for speech the following principles should be considered:

1. Check that auditory discrimination skills and recognition of a child or adult's own errors are adequate.
2. It is usual to follow the normal sequence of phonetic/phonological development; so, for example, it would be normal to tackle the plosive group of sounds before the fricative and affricate groups.
3. Use as many sensory approaches as possible, that is, auditory, visual, tactile and to this end, whenever appropriate, introduce biofeedback help, for example, a palatal training appliance and visual speech aid, tape recording of the client's speech, the nasal anemometer, electropalatography (see Ch. 6).

4. With older children and adults, help them to achieve as much insight and understanding as possible into their problem and therapy aims. Prepared tapework and diagrams may be useful.
5. Parents need explanations about the mechanisms involved so that they are more able to help their children.
6. Motivation is important to maintain at all times so use progress charts, rating charts, sticker stamps etc.
7. If you suspect consistent velopharyngeal insufficiency, producing nasal escape and/or hypernasality, refer on for further investigation, with a view to surgery if necessary. The evidence for blowing and sucking exercises per se in improving velopharyngeal function for speech is lacking, so do not expect to improve palate function for speech using these exercises.

### Timing of therapy

As a very general rule, the earlier articulation therapy is initiated, the more quickly a successful result will be achieved. This is provided that language is at an appropriate level for the child's age. It is surprising how many 3-year-olds, for example, will co-operate and concentrate for articulation work, provided it is fun and there are plenty of 'rewards' such as stickers and stars. However, not all pre-school children will respond positively to direct articulation work and the therapist may have to wait until they are ready. The same principles of articulation therapy apply to the pre-school age group as to any other. It is important to check language levels before embarking on any articulation therapy (see Ch. 2).

Some therapists (for example, Henningsson 1984, from Stockholm) intervene with direct articulation therapy at a very early age, that is, between 1 and 2 years. If, when Henningsson assesses a toddler's speech, she hears a preponderance of glottal stops, she will teach the mother to use negative reinforcement, i.e. turning her head away when a string of glottals is produced. The necessity for this type of intervention depends on a variety of factors. The children Heningsson is treating in this way have their palates repaired at 1 year plus and it is likely that more of those children show a preponderance of glottal stops in their articulation than children who have their palates repaired before they are a year old.

The work by Dorf & Curtin (1982) shows that children with later palate repair develop compensatory articulation. Therefore, probably less children who undergo early palate repair require speech therapy intervention than those whose palate repairs are delayed.

Another factor which affects timing and duration of therapy is the need for secondary surgery such as a pharyngoplasty. There is one school of thought (Shprintzen 1983) which states that articulation therapy should be completed pre-pharyngoplasty. This is mainly because if a child is using, for example, a glottal stop articulation pattern, the velopharynx may not be moving as well as it might and articulation therapy may be the catalyst for achieving better movement and a less radical pharyngoplasty may be needed. This has been clearly shown by Henningsson (1986).

Another school of thought states that it is pointless trying to change articulation in the face of gross velopharyngeal insufficiency, and indeed many experienced therapists feel that there are some children who must have a pharyngoplasty before they have a chance to alter their articulation patterns. Perhaps it is wise to be flexible and to steer a course between the two extremes of thought. If, for example, one is presented with a 3-year-old with nasalised vowel sounds and glottal stops and no oral consonants, one would certainly wish to try a period of 3 to 6 months of diagnostic therapy before committing that child to surgery. There are some children who present with consistent moderate or gross nasal escape and hypernasality with the associated compensatory articulation patterns who do seem to improve through articulation therapy. In these cases improvement of articulation automatically appears to trigger the palate to move appropriately, and complete velopharyngeal closure is seen on X-ray. In other cases, the velopharyngeal isthmus comes nearer to closure with good articulation but never closes (except during swallowing), so these cases still require a pharyngoplasty, but perhaps a smaller one than would have been thought previously. It would appear that children are being referred earlier and earlier who have nasal escape and hypernasality and associated articulatory problems; they need to be monitored very carefully and a fine balance achieved between knowing when to stop therapy and when to ask for surgery. However, diagnostic therapy should be short term, that is, if the child is co-operative not longer than 6 months. The aim should be to get one or two correctly articulated consonants such as /p,b/ so that the potential for speech progress can be evaluated. If a young child can manage the /p,b/ and put them into single words, without nasal escape or hypernasality, then that is a very good sign that they will also be able to do this for other plosives and then onto fricatives. If, on the other hand, a co-operative child can produce the /p,b/ but there is still a lot of associated nasal escape, this is a bad sign and points to the need for surgery.

Anna, a case of pharyngeal disproportion, illustrates the timing of therapy. The case is summarised in Table 4.1.

### Case study—Anna: Timing of therapy

Anna, aged 7, was referred for therapy to a specialist unit from her home locality. She was the eldest of three children. Her parents were extremely anxious about Anna's speech. Anna had presented to her local regional plastic surgery unit at age 4, with hypernasality. She had previously undergone a pharyngoplasty, but speech had remained the same. At age 6 she underwent a second pharyngoplasty for pharyngeal disproportion but speech still did not change and this was put down to 'habit'.

On assessment at age 7 there was moderate to gross hypernasality and a glottal and pharyngeal articulation pattern. Given that she had had two pharyngoplasties, it was felt that intensive therapy was indicated, although

**Table 4.1**  Case summary: Anna: Pharyngeal disproportion

| Age | General management | Speech status & management | Comment |
|---|---|---|---|
| 4 years | | Hypernasal speech developed, with nasalised vowel sounds, glottal stops, pharyngeal fricatives | It is important that clinicians identify signs of velopharyngeal problems early on in a child's speech development. Anna's problems should have been picked up before 4 years |
| 5 years | Pharyngeal flap for pharyngeal disproportion | No improvement, re-referred to plastic surgery | |
| 6 years & 6 months | Different second pharyngoplasty using cartilage graft | Post-pharyngoplasty only minimal improvement. Local speech therapist & surgeon felt there must be a habit factor | Do not assume that pharyngoplasty has worked. Use nasendoscopy facilities |
| 7 years | Referred to specialist unit for intensive speech therapy course | Moderate to gross hypernasality. Glottal & pharyngeal articulation | The nasality was *not* habit |
| | Nasendoscopy showed a large velopharyngeal gap remaining | Decided to continue with speech therapy for rest of course. Articulation improved with 'nose-holding'. Discharged | |
| 7 years & 6 months | Readmitted for Honig pharyngoplasty | Immediately post-op speech was hyponasal. Anna had 'forgotten' her improved articulation | At last, a good result, but was there any point in articulation work pre-operatively? |
| | Continued with local speech therapy | | |
| 8 years | Nasendoscopy showed good closure of velopharyngeal isthmus | Speech dramatically better with some reminders necessary for generalisation. Discharged | Note the importance of the pharyngoplasty being 'tailor made' to the individual's velopharyngeal problems |

there was not much hope about the outcome.

Anna worked very hard, and using conventional articulation therapy at the end of 3 weeks all consonants in isolation and single words were achieved, but only with nose holding. This seemed to be the only way Anna could obtain sufficient intra-oral air pressure for consonant production. Nasendoscopy and lateral and basal X-rays were done at this point, which revealed a big velopharyngeal gap, and no real sign of any previous pharyngoplasty. Anna was therefore sent home and readmitted 3 months later for a Honig pharyngoplasty. This is a combined pushback of the palate, and a superiorly-based pharyngeal flap.

In the meantime, without speech therapy, Anna 'forgot' all the 'new' consonant sounds, and had to relearn them with her local speech therapist. However, she made good progress (without nose holding!) and when last seen, 6 months later, had almost generalised the sounds into her everyday speech.

## Frequency of therapy

It is evident when working with cleft palate children, as with all speech-impaired children, that each individual's management programme has to be tailored to meet the individual's specific needs. For a proportion of children with deviant speech arising from cleft palate or associated velopharyngeal disorders, conventional weekly therapy fails to facilitate acceptable speech. This is despite successful surgical correction of velopharyngeal insufficiency, either at a primary palate repair or secondarily in the form of a pharyngoplasty. In the United States over the past 20 years, intensive speech therapy courses have been set up, initially to provide speech therapy for children with cleft palate who come from rural areas and who otherwise might not receive speech therapy (Bzoch 1979). In the U.K. some intensive programmes have also been developed (Albery & Enderby 1984, Huskie 1979).

At Frenchay Hospital, Bristol, in the U.K., 46 children with deviant articulation secondary to cleft palate or other velopharyngeal disorders took part in a controlled trial to gauge the efficacy of intensive speech therapy. Subjects were randomly allocated either to attend a 6-week intensive course of speech therapy or to continue with their conventional weekly therapy. Results indicate a significant improvement in articulation for those children receiving intensive help immediately post-course as compared with a very slight improvement seen in the speech of the control group (Albery & Enderby 1984). This improvement achieved by children on the

course was maintained throughout the 2 year follow-up period and, although the articulation of the control group continued to improve, at the end of the 2 year follow-up period, the children on the course had better articulation scores.

A child with 'glottal stop' articulation, phoneme-specific nasality or articulation problems which have plateauxed, seems to benefit most from intensive therapy, that is, twice a day for a period of up to 6 weeks dependent upon need. Sometimes intensive therapy on a daily basis in a group or individually can be provided locally for a cleft palate child. This involves least disruption to family and school life. However, sometimes it is essential to bring a child in for intensive therapy into a specialist unit, where they can stay from Monday to Friday and be part of a group of children with similar speech problems. Children below the age of 6 may not be mature enough to cope with being away from home, so for them twice weekly therapy with good back-up from home may be adequate. It is not always easy, under present constraints, to be able to offer flexible arrangements in

**Table 4.2** Case summary: Tom: Sub-mucous cleft

| Age | General management | Speech status & management | Comment |
| --- | --- | --- | --- |
| 3 years | Referred to plastic surgeon out of region. Repair of sub-mucous cleft | Nasal escape, hypernasality, glottal articulation | Sub-mucous cleft often have worse speech than children with overt cleft, due to late referral & operation |
| 8 years | | Weekly/review speech therapy locally | It would have been more cost effective had intensive therapy been available locally |
| 8 years | Referred to specialist unit for intensive speech therapy | On assessment reluctant to communicate. Generally unintelligible. Glottal & pharyngeal articulation | Note the value of intensive provision to break long-standing habits |
| | Seen twice a week for 6 weeks | Articulation improved. All consonants correct at single word level apart from /tʃ, dʒ/. More work needed on generalisation | |
| | | Discharged with recommendation that weekly therapy should continue locally | |

terms of frequency of therapy, but it should be remembered that it is possible that 6 weeks of intensive therapy may achieve much more than several years on a weekly basis. It is not necessary for one therapist to be responsible for all the intensive therapy and it can work quite well for two or more therapists to be involved in the treatment of one child. The case study of Tom, who had a sub-mucous cleft, and the period of intensive help he received, are summarised in Table 4.2.

*Case study—Tom: Frequency of therapy*

Tom had a sub-mucous cleft not diagnosed until he was 3 years of age; this was then operated on. He presented at the specialist unit at 8 years, meanwhile having had 4 years of weekly therapy and monitoring. His parents were concerned about him and did not have a very high opinion of speech therapy or their son, who they felt was lazy and did not 'try'. He was referred for a 6 week course of intensive speech therapy really in desperation.

On examination at referral, speech was within acceptable limits for resonance, but was characterised by effortful tense articulation. Articulation consisted mainly of glottal stops and pharyngeal fricatives. In careful speech /p, b, k, g/ were correct. In Tom's case, years of conventional therapy prior to an intensive course had not achieved an adequate result and therefore has to be questioned as an appropriate approach. Extended periods of unproductive or minimally productive intervention may lead to lack of motivation in the child, family and therapist. There may be overconsciousness about speech and consequently poor communication. In financial terms it would be difficult to support the approach.

When Tom joined the intensive programme he was not keen to speak, not surprisingly, as it was difficult to understand him; and he had adopted a head-down posture with little eye contact. We commenced work with /p, b/ with which he had already had some success. We then tried /t/ which proved difficult, so we left it and tried /f, v/ which proved a

success and was put into sentences. Having got the idea of friction we turned to /s/ which, with the aid of diagrams and explanations before we attempted it, came surprisingly easily. Tom was delighted and this had all been achieved by the end of the first week. We then went back to /t/ which Tom achieved after 'tongue-tapping' exercises (see Table 4.3). The rest of the plosives and fricatives were achieved by the end of 6 weeks, at least at single word level. We did not have time for the affricates /tʃ, dʒ/, nor for much generalisation work.

Our experience has shown that a 6-week course of intensive therapy is particularly appropriate for breaking the strong habit factors associated with inappropriate glottal and pharyngeal realisation of consonants.

## TYPE OF INTERVENTION

### Therapy for articulation

Speech therapists make their biggest contribution to the speech problems resulting from cleft palate in the treatment of articulation problems. There is much current debate about phonology and phonetics and where cleft palate speech disorders belong (see Chs. 1 and 2). It is clear, however, that as cleft palate subjects have a structural disorder of the vocal tract they most often exhibit phonetic speech disturbances, although that is not to say that they may not exhibit phonological problems as well.

A comprehensive speech assessment should clarify what are phonetic and what are phonological disturbances and should point the way to appropriate remediation. Assuming that most of the difficulties experienced are of a phonetic nature, it is appropriate to use an articulation therapy approach, focussing on production of the different consonant sounds. Before the speech therapist starts, she should check that auditory discrimination and recognition are adequate and, particularly with young children, it is usually best to follow the normal sequence of phonological development. The principles outlined at the beginning

**Table 4.3** Elicitation of plosives, fricatives and affricates in isolation

| Consonant | Common difficulties | Techniques |
|---|---|---|
| /p/ | May be glottal, glottalised or imploded | The ability to achieve a lip seal should be checked. To get forward airstream, lips should be closed, blow up cheeks with air then release to move a paper tissue held in front of mouth. If /p/ is substituted by a glottal the tissue won't move |
| /b/ | Glottal, glottalised, imploded | Can be more difficult to obtain than /p/, but if you obtain /p/ first, describe /b/ as a noisy version of /p/ perhaps getting the child to feel the vibration from your larynx. Avoid excess tension and forcing |
| /t/ | Glottal, glottalised, velarised, palatalised | An important consonant to obtain as it can lead on to other alveolar or palato-alveolar consonants. Sometimes very resistant to change. Try: (a) Just lifting tongue tip to alveolar ridge & back down. (b) Increase sensory awareness of tongue tip and alveolar. (c) On a breath out (to inhibit glottal) gentle 'tongue-tapping' making a non aspirated /t/. (d) When (c) is consistent go on to aspirated /t/ |
| /d/ | Glottal, glottalised, velarised, palatalised | A noisy /t/ as /b/ is to /p/. Avoid tension & forcing which will precipitate hard glottal attack |
| /k/ | Glottal, glottalised, uvular | Difficult one to obtain. Try imitation of a 'gun' noise for children 'k, k, k, k'. If old enough, explain with pictures how the tongue lifts at the back to hit the soft palate. Hold front of tongue down with spatula while back is lifting up. Use mirror |
| /g/ | Glottal, glottalised, uvular | A noisy /k/. Avoid forcing & tension |
| /f/ | Glottal, glottalised | Visual feedback is helpful. As for /p/, moving a tissue or feeling the airstream on the back of the client's hand when producing /f/ |
| /v/ | As for /f/ | Noisy /f/. Avoid forcing & tension. Feel vibration on larynx & buzz on lips |
| /θ/ð/ | Many children produce /f, v/ in place of these consonants normally, so children with cleft palate may experience some difficulties as with /f, v/ viz glottal, glottalised. | Easy to imitate using a mirror, also as for /f/ making sure airstream is forward by feeling it on back of hand. Normally these sounds are very late to develop, so may be left until last. Sometimes interdentals may be elicited as a springboard for achieving the post-alveolar fricatives |
| /s/ | Glottal, glottalised, palatalised , velarised, pharyngealised | If /t/ can be produced, try imitating a very long /t/ making it into a fricative. If /θ/ can be produced, move tongue behind teeth & continue forward airstream. If /ʃ/ with tongue further forward and lips spread. It is better to have one of these consonants to work from. Blowing down a straw positioned centrally in mouth to produce bubbles in water may help to get the airstream central and forward and the resulting sound can then be refined |
| /z/ | As for /s/ | A noisy /s/. Feel vibration of larynx & buzz of tongue tip. Be careful not to force as tension may precipitate glottal |
| /ʃ/ | As for /s/ | Usually easier to obtain after /s/. Produce /s/ with lips rounded & placing tongue further back |
| /ʒ/ | As for /ʃ/ | Noisy /ʃ/. Feel vibration of larynx |
| /tʃ/ | Glottal, glottalised, velarised | Should get /t/ & /ʃ/ first. For children, noise a train makes, 'ch, ch, etc'. May have to break it down to /t, ʃ/ then bring them together quickly. This & /dʒ/ usually the final consonants to obtain |
| /dʒ/ | As for /t/ | A noisy /t/ |

of this chapter should all be considered. An articulation programme should follow three main stages: (1) consonants in isolation; (2) integration into words and sentences; and (3) generalisation into everyday speech.

## 1. Consonants in isolation

This is the level at which most children with cleft palate 'fail' if they have a problem, and a speech assessment for this group of children must include the testing of each consonant in isolation. Generally, auditory discrimination is good provided hearing is reasonable, and except for very young children they are often aware of their 'errors'. Thus it is important to place the therapeutic emphasis on achieving correct production of consonants. If most of the plosive, fricative and affricate consonants are in need of remediation, it is best to begin with 'easy to imitate' consonants first, for example, the bilabials /p, b/ and the labio-dental /f, v/. The unvoiced one of each pair of consonants should be attempted first. It is unusual for the approximants or nasals to be affected in cleft palate speech. Table 4.3 provides suggestions as to how to elicit plosives, fricatives or affricates in isolation. If the stimulus of hearing the therapist's correct production of a consonant in isolation is insuf-ficient for the child or adult to produce it correctly in imitation, use any visual or tactile aids to help, e.g. mirrors, diagrams of correct tongue placement, tissues, or paper animals that move in front of the mouth when breath direction is forward. The same technique may not work for all children.

*Failure to achieve consonants in isolation.* There may be a small group of children with velopharyngeal sufficiency who seem totally resistant to any of these techniques. There may be sensory, occlusal, motivational or learning problems. For them, electropalatog-raphy (see Ch. 6) may be very useful at a suitable age. For consonants such as /t/ or /s/, it may be worth trying a small acrylic dental plate with a ridge or ridges to guide correct tongue placement. A dentist or orthodontist may be willing to take impressions of the client and have the plate made up. These procedures are discussed further in Chapter 5.

It is interesting that even children with gross velopharyngeal insufficiency may be able to learn the correct production of all consonants in isolation, but it is certainly difficult for them and may be only possible while holding their nose to block nasal escape of air.

## 2. Integration of consonants into single words and sentences

This should be a relatively straightforward phase of therapy. Sometimes babbling-type practice with /CV, VCV/ combinations may be useful, e.g. 'ta, ta, ta, ta', and 'ata, ata, ata', but this is sometimes unnecessary. Sometimes the newly acquired consonant, e.g. /t/, has to be separated from the rest of a word. It is easier to commence with practice of final sounds first, e.g. [hat], then go on to initial /t/, e.g. [top]. The single words practised should be at an appropriate level for the child or adult, and similarly the sentences. In very young children nursery rhymes may be an initial substitute for sentences.

## 3. Generalisation into everyday speech

This is a crucial stage; it is useless if a child shows improvement in a clinic situation, then does not use that speech at home or at school. While parents need always to be involved, teachers and friends should be advised regarding ways of encouraging improved patterns to be used in everyday speech without subjecting the child to undue pressure to do this. At this stage it is useful for the therapist to visit the child's school to talk to the teacher, showing the teacher the sounds that the child is capable of producing. A teacher can then often help the child to remember these sounds, particularly during one-to-one reading practice, rather than pulling a child up for forgetting a sound in front of the whole of the class. Parents at home can have a chart system with stars for each time a child remembers the correct sound, or they may find it appropriate to have a period each day, perhaps the hour before the child goes to bed, when correct speech is insisted upon. This period can then gradually be extended.

Depending upon motivation and such factors as intelligence, hearing and support from parents and teachers, this last stage of therapy can vary considerably in length from child to child. It is possible often to place a child under review during this phase, monitoring carefully that the child's use of the correct consonants is becoming more frequent, and that parents, teachers and child are happy with progress.

The case study which follows is an example of a child receiving articulation therapy following pharyngoplasty at 5 years of age. Table 4.4 summarises Susan's management.

## Case study—Susan: Generalisation into everyday speech

This 5-year-old girl with a soft palate cleft was the youngest child of a family of four, the other children being all into their teens. Being a pretty, sweet child, Susan was very much 'babied' by the rest of the family. Her soft palate was repaired rather late at 2 years of age with a conventional two flap repair. From an oral view the soft palate seemed mobile, although short.

The first main speech and language assessment was undertaken at 3 years of age. Language was found to be delayed; expression at 2 year level, although comprehension was within normal limits. Her parents were unaware of any language difficulty or hearing problem. ENT examination revealed bilateral middle ear effusions; grommets were therefore inserted. Language levels improved, but

**Table 4.4** Case summary: Susan: Soft palate cleft

| Age | General management | Speech status & management | Comment |
|---|---|---|---|
| 0–2 years | ENT observation. Middle ear effusion. No action | | Late palate repair is detrimental to both hearing & speech development. Surgically the repair may not have been possible earlier |
| 2 years | Palate repair. No complications | 'Quiet' toddler. No words yet | Language is already delayed |
| 3 years | Grommets inserted | Language delayed (expression at 2 year level). Speech therapy commenced | Would early ENT intervention (myringotomy grommets) have prevented language delay? |
| 4 years | Hearing levels normal | Language near normal but speech nasal & glottal | |
| 4 years & 6 months | Videofluoroscopic assessment of velopharyngeal sufficiency. Large velopharyngeal gap | | At 4 & a half years some children may be too immature for nasendoscopy |
| 5 years | Honig pharyngoplasty | Post-op speech hyponasal. Therapy twice a week commenced for articulation. Phonetic inventory consisted of glottal stops & pharyngeal fricatives | Hyponasality immediately post-op is usual |
| 5 years & 6 months | Repeat videofluoroscopy showed complete closure of the velopharyngeal gap | 75% accuracy in consonant production in spontaneous speech. Put on review | |
| 6 years | | Discharged with good speech | |

speech sounded nasal and there was a preponderance of glottal stops. /p/ was elicited, but was accompanied by nasal emission.

Videofluoroscopy was undertaken at age 4, Susan being too immature for nasendoscopy. X-rays showed a large velopharyngeal gap throughout speech, even on correctly articulated /p/.

A Honig pharyngoplasty was performed. Immediately post-pharyngoplasty, resonance was very hyponasal, but much less so after 3 weeks, when therapy commenced. Susan's speech status at the beginning of therapy was as follows: in spontaneous speech /p, b, t, d, k, g, f, v, tʃ, dʒ/ were replaced by glottal stops. /s, z, ʃ, ʒ/ were produced as pharyngeal fricatives. Before surgery only /p/ could be elicited correctly.

The first speech therapy session involved checking Susan's auditory discrimination and recognition, which were fine. The production of /p, b/ in isolation and into single word level was worked on and achieved, initially and finally. In the second session, 2 days later, Susan achieved production of /t, d/, having to resort to 'tongue-tapping' to inhibit glottalisation. Susan received help twice a week (using techniques as specified in Table 4.3), usually introducing two or more 'new' sounds at each session. At the end of 4 months, she was able to produce all sounds in isolation, single words, and sentence level in a structured situation. Mother reported marked improvement in everyday speech. Susan was then seen once a fortnight for 6 weeks until she was put on review. Although her mother had not recognised any speech or hearing problem when Susan was 3, she certainly did accept that when Susan commenced therapy at 5, her speech was very poor. At that time her mother was extremely supportive in Susan's therapy; if she had not been so diligent, such rapid progress could not have been achieved.

It will be noted that Susan suffered hearing impairment from an early age. This could have been a factor contributing to the delay in her language development, although, as the delay was mainly in her expressive language, it is possible that she was restricting her language output because of her poor speech. It is essential that middle ear problems are identified and treated as early as possible.

From the discussion in Chapter 1, the reader will be aware that many cleft palate children of pre-school and school age suffer from fluctuating conductive hearing loss. Whilst the hearing loss may not be the major factor in the child's articulation difficulties, if a child's hearing is down, it may not be the best time to benefit from speech therapy, unless the child is receiving amplification from a hearing aid. It is often better to wait for ENT intervention or, if this is not planned, a period should be identified when hearing may be at its optimum, to give speech therapy its best chance.

There is much debate among ENT specialists about the timing and type of intervention for middle ear effusions, surgeons tending to adopt either an aggressive or conservative stance. Although grommets generally provide at least some months of improved hearing, the long-term effects of scarring of the ear-drum are not fully known (McWilliams et al 1984a). For the development of communication it is critical for children to be able to hear well during the first few years of life so that they have every opportunity to understand and acquire speech and language.

### Therapy for hypernasality and nasal emission

Hypernasality and nasal emission usually occur directly as a result of velopharyngeal insufficiency, but the presence of a fistula in the hard or soft palate can complicate the diagnosis and must always be taken into account. It is possible that a fistula, if it is large enough and in a certain position, may affect speech in this way, though sometimes to make an accurate diagnosis a fistula has to be blocked with dental wax or chewing gum to assess if there is still nasal escape and hypernasality. If there is, then a child or adult should undergo nasendoscopy and lateral X-rays to look at the functioning of the velopharyngeal isthmus.

Other factors which can affect perceived nasality can include the degree of mouth opening and tongue height during speech, the posture of the head and also the loudness. The louder a child with velopharyngeal insufficiency speaks, the higher the perception of nasal escape and/or hypernasality. If any of the above features are found in assessment, therapy should aim to modify them. For example, a change in the degree of mouth opening used by an individual may have a marked effect in reducing hypernasality. Consistent and persistent hypernasality and nasal escape which is rated as more than slight is best treated by surgery or, in some cases, by a palatal training appliance and/or visual speech aid. These approaches are discussed elsewhere in this volume.

Inconsistent nasal escape, for example a client with 'phoneme-specific nasality' (usually /s/ and /z/ signalled by a nasal snort alone, denoted /$n^F$/), is best treated with intensive speech therapy as it is sometimes a difficult habit to break. A technique which should produce success with children who direct the airstream nasally rather than orally for /s/ and /z/, is to work from a pressure consonant they can produce orally, for example /t/, and ask them to prolong the sound. Alternatively, one can ask them to move their tongue forward from /ʃ/ or backwards from /h/. As long as the child does not realise in the first instance that he is being asked to produce an /s/, and it just 'happens' using one of the above techniques, rapid progress can usually be made.

Visual aids to help therapy for nasality include, for first choice, the Exeter Biofeedback nasal anemometer, or, if funds do not permit, a Sea-Scape monitor. The Sea-Scape (CC. Publications Inc 1984) is an instant monitoring device which provides an assessment of nasal emission (not hypernasal resonance). It consists of a small clear plastic cylinder with an attached flexible tube, with a nose piece, which inserts just inside the nostril. Nasal emission causes a foam float at the bottom of the plastic cylinder to move upwards. For auditory feedback, a tape-recording and playback of a client's speech can be helpful. Slight or variable degrees of hypernasality and nasal escape may be controlled in this way, although reduction of nasality in single words alone is not enough, and therapy should be continued until the control of nasal escape and hypernasality is possible in continuous speech.

The case study of Stephen, which follows, is an example of a phoneme specific nasality. His management is summarised in Table 4.5.

**Table 4.5** Case summary: Stephen: Phoneme-specific nasality

| Age | General management | Speech status & management | Comment |
|---|---|---|---|
| 5 years | School concerned about lack of intelligibility | Therapy locally once a week. No progress | Intensive therapy is more appropriate for this speech problem |
| | History of ear infections & variable hearing loss | | |
| 6 years | Referred to Regional Plastic Surgery Unit for assessment & ?surgery ?therapy. Nasendoscopy showed minimal palate lift except for /s, z, ʃ, ʒ, tʃ, dʒ/ | Language normal /s, z, ʃ, ʒ, tʃ, dʒ/ signalled by nasal fricatives & affricates. 4 weeks of intensive therapy | We don't know why some children have this specific problem in the absence of any 'clefting'. Surgery is not appropriate. The role of hearing needs consideration |
| | Nasendoscopy showed palate lifting well for all sounds in careful speech | Stephen discharged with good speech, albeit with occasional 'slips'. Telephone contact maintained with mother | It is important to maintain contact until generalisation is well advanced |

*Case study — Stephen: Therapy for phoneme specific nasal emission*

Stephen was referred at age 6 by his local speech therapist because of failure to respond to therapy. He came from a caring, fun loving family who had only recently become concerned about his speech. He had had no surgery but had a history of ear infections and associated variable hearing loss.

Stephen presented with 'phoneme-specific nasality', so that /s, z, ʃ, ʒ, tʃ, dʒ/ were replaced by a nasal fricative. He underwent nasendoscopy which showed complete closure for all sounds except the above. It was decided to tackle this problem by intensive speech therapy; Stephen therefore came into hospital for 4 weeks from Monday to Friday.

On session one, /s/ was elicited from a prolonged /t/ and then he attempted to put it into single words. This proved difficult because Stephen produced [snᶠi] for [si]. The Exeter Biofeedback nasal anemometer was introduced to give Stephen visual feedback to help him inhibit the intrusive nasal fricative. This was successful; once this was achieved, therapy for /z/, then /ʃ, ʒ/ and finally /tʃ, dʒ/ were moved through quickly. These last two were rather effortful for Stephen. At the end of 4 weeks Stephen was generalising well. Following the intensive period of supervision, telephone contact was maintained with his mother to check that progress continued.

Nasendoscopy post-therapy showed that Stephen's palate was lifting well for all sounds during careful speech.

### Therapy for articulation problems associated with malocclusion

Dental-occlusal hazards to speech have been outlined in Chapter 1 of this volume. Orthodontists tend to be involved very early in a cleft palate child's life to provide feeding plates or carry out pre-surgical treatment. Towards adolescence they become involved in the management of cases with malocclusion.

Narrow collapsed alveolar arches, missing or misaligned teeth, and malocclusion, usually Class III, may individually or in combination, have some effect upon articulation. A number of studies have looked at the influence of dentition in non-cleft children (Weinberg 1968, Fymbo 1936, Snow 1961, Bankson and Byrne 1962). They suggest that missing teeth can affect some children's articulation of /s/ and /z/. Starr (1979) studying 6 to 11-year-old cleft children felt that missing or misaligned dental deviations seldom impose severe problems in articulation, but when they occur in conjunction with velopharyngeal insufficiency or hearing loss, or low IQ, or poor familial standard for speech, their potential effect is greatly enhanced. The same seems to be true for the presence of a collapsed alveolar arch or a Class III malocclusion which restricts tongue space within the maxilla. Although good articulation can exist in the presence of these abnormalities, they do predispose children to speech difficulties, particularly for sounds such as /s, z/ which may be lateralised or palatalised.

Some clinicians consider that speech therapy is inadvisable during a course of active orthodontics, perhaps where the maxillary arch is being expanded or teeth are being 'moved', and it is best to wait until treatment is complete. Other therapists may feel that during a phase of active orthodontics a patient's oral sensory awareness is heightened and it may well be a good time to capitalise on this and to do articulation work. The age at which active orthodontics usually begins, i.e. early adolescence, is not usually the time of optimum motivation for speech therapy, so if therapy has not been completed by age 10 it is often best to wait until clients are motivated to seek help, which they sometimes do later in their teens.

The following case study is of Helen who has a class III malocclusion; her management is summarised in Table 4.6.

*Case study—Helen: Malocclusion*

Helen, aged 7, had a history of a unilateral complete cleft lip and palate. She had the lip repaired at 3 months of age, and the palate at 6 months of age. She had a supportive family and when assessed at 3 years of age, language levels were above average and phonology and

**Table 4.6** Case summary: Helen: Unilateral complete cleft with Class III malocclusion

| Age | General management | Speech status & management | Comment |
|---|---|---|---|
| 3 months | Lip repair<br>Monitored by ENT<br>Middle ear effusions | | |
| 6 months | Palate repair | | Early palate repair appears to produce better speech results |
| 3 years | | Normal language. Good articulation apart from palatal lateral /s/. i.e. /ʃᵉ/. Velopharyngeal sufficiency. No intervention | Clinical impressions are that palatal/lateral /s/ is more common than glottal stop articulation in unilateral and bilateral clefts |
| 4 years | Myringotomy & grommets | | |
| 5 years | *Oral examination.* Already in Class III malocclusion. Moderately collapsed alveolar arch | Articulation still slightly impaired by /ʃᵉ/. Therapy once a week for 2 months, poor progress | This therapy is quite difficult because the distinction between /s/ and /ʃᵉ/ is so fine |
| 5 years 6 months | | /s/ good in single words, but poor in continuous speech. Decided to review | |
| 6 years | | Perfect /s/ in continuous speech | So, what part did therapy play? |

articulation were normal, apart from a palatal/ lateral/ s/, i.e. [ʃᵉ]. At this stage we decided not to intervene as intelligibility was not affected. Oral examination revealed a slightly collapsed alveolar arch and already a Class III malocclusion. At age 5 the [ʂˤ] was still present, so a short trial course of therapy was implemented. Helen could produce a good /s/ in isolation and in single words, but had great difficulty maintaining it in continuous speech. After 2 months of therapy without much progress, intervention was discontinued. At this time consideration was given to the fact that the malocclusion and narrow arch were making it too difficult to produce a perfect /s/ all the time. One year later, when reviewed, Helen was consistently producing a perfect /s/. The reason for this history was not clear. Some of the therapy that Helen had received had included auditory as well as production work and it was difficult to know why there was no carry over earlier on. Perhaps we should have made the therapy more intensive or continued it for longer. We could perhaps have used electropalatography for a case like Helen, but this was not avail-

able at the time and she may have been too young. In the end, it could well have been that speech therapy was able to 'tune her in' to the correct sounds but that spontaneous maturation and the sudden realisation that she could, and should, make the effort to sound as good as possible, may have given her the final push to use the correct /s/ at all times.

Ideally, children with a cleft palate should have achieved good enough speech not to draw comment from their peers by the time they are starting school, but this is not always possible. Reasons may include inadequate density of therapy pre-school, an unsupportive family background, lack of co-operation and motivation in therapy sessions, low IQ or poor hearing, or persistent problems with the structure of the vocal tract. The type, intensity and timing of intervention is also related to progress and requires careful evaluation. However, there is no age limit for 'normal' speech to be achieved. Hypernasality and nasal escape can be eliminated with an appropriate pharyngoplasty at any age, and articulation can be permanently changed, provided the client is motivated.

# REFERENCES

Albery E, Enderby P 1984 Intensive speech therapy for cleft palate children. British Journal of Disorders of Communication 19: 115

Bankson N W, Bryne M C 1962 The relationship between missing teeth and selected consonant sounds. Journal of Speech and Hearing Disorders 27: 341

Bzoch K R 1979 Advantages of intensive summer training programs. In: Bzoch K R (ed) Communicative disorders related to cleft lip and palate. Little Brown, Boston

Dorf D S, Curtin J W 1982 Early cleft palate repair and speech outcome. Plastic and Reconstructive Surgery 70: 74

Fymbo L H 1936. The relation of malocclusion of the teeth to defects of speech. Archives of Speech 1: 204

Heningsson G 1981 Personal communication at Workshop on Cleft. Montefiore Hospital, The Bronx, New York

Henningsson G 1986 Velopharyngeal movement patterns in patients alternating between oral and glottal articulation: a clinical and cineradiographical study. Cleft Palate Journal 23: 1

Huskie C F 1979 The Glasgow experience. In: Ellis R, Flack F C (eds) Palatoglossal malfunction. College of Speech Therapists, London.

McWilliams B J, Morris H L, Shelton R L 1984a Cleft Palate Speech B C Decker Inc. C V Mosby, St Louis

McWilliams B J, Morris H L, Shelton R L 1984b Otological and audiological disorders. In: Cleft palate speech: B C Decker Inc. C V Mosby, St Louis

Shprintzen R 1983 Paper given to Cranio-Facial Society International Meeting, Birmingham, England

Snow K 1961 Articulation proficiency in relation to certain dental abnormalities. Journal of Speech and Hearing Disorders 26: 209

Starr C D 1979 Dental and occlusal hazards to normal speech production. In: Bzoch K R (ed) Communicative disorders related to cleft lip and palate. Little Brown, Boston

Weinberg 1968 A cephalometric study of normal and defective /s/ articulation and variations in incisor dentition. Journal of Speech and Hearing Research 11: 288

Introduction
Interdisciplinary co-operation
Theoretical basis for tongue and palate training
appliances
    Indications for use of palatal appliances

Report of palatal training appliance study
    Assessment indications for training appliance
    use
    Criteria for selection of patients
    Sequence of case management
    Speech results in a study of 26 patients using
    PTA
    Speech therapy with PTA

Case studies
    Mandy: cleft of soft and hard palate and
    tongue tie
    Brian: congenital velopharyngeal
    incompetence
    Roy: Pierre Robin syndrome

Obturators
    Use of obturators in unrepaired cleft palate
        Selection of cases and criteria for use of
        obturators in unrepaired clefts
        Guidelines for therapy in cases of
        unrepaired cleft palate
    Obturation of residual fistulae
        Method of testing nasal emission through
        oronasal fistula

Palate and tongue training appliances
    Design of a palatal training appliance
    Criteria for selection of cases for PTA
    Guidelines for therapy with PTA

Aids to visual feedback for hypernasality and
nasal emission
    'N' indicator
    Nasal anemometer training model
    Mirror detail reflector
    Visual speech aid
    Suppliers of equipment

# 5

# The use of appliances in the treatment of speech problems in cleft palate

*G. M. Stuffins*

## INTRODUCTION

The speech clinician in general practice will occasionally encounter a child who appears unable to produce an acoustically satisfactory oro-nasal resonance balance in spontaneous speech. The clinical aetiology may include repaired palatal or sub-mucous cleft, but in some cases the resonatory deviance may be apparently idiopathic. The clinical speech picture may also include phonetic and/or phonological difficulties. These difficulties may be related to placement of the articulators, manner of production, consistent production or problems with sequencing speech sounds at the rate and complexity required for normal intelligible speech.

If it emerges that the expected changes in patterns cannot be achieved through a conventional therapeutic approach, advice should be sought at an early stage from a colleague who has specialist experience in this area. This colleague may well be a member of the Regional cleft palate team, who will be able to assess and advise in these cases. The timing of this decision will be subject to intrinsic factors in each case, but early referral is never a disadvantage. This permits the possibility of intervention at an earlier stage in neuromuscular development and also results in economical use of therapeutic resources and client time. If after investigation by the team, as described by Huskie in Chapter 3, it is decided that no surgery is appropriate, then alternative approaches must be found. One of these is the use of a palatal training appliance which has been shown to be effective in a number of cases.

## INTERDISCIPLINARY CO-OPERATION

The initiation of treatment using tongue and palate training aids can only be established with the full co-operation of all the disciplines involved. The orthodontist or dentist, the dental technicians and speech therapist should establish good communication between themselves and agree on a clear idea of the aims and problems involved. The speech therapist is generally the first member of this group to recognise the need for alternative approaches for patients who have failed to respond to the usual approaches offered in speech therapy. At this point a clinician in general practice may seek advice from speech therapists who have experience of this approach and further reading can be undertaken. References to papers are included at the end of this chapter.

The orthodontist involved with the Regional cleft palate team or a dentist working as a clinical assistant with that unit could be approached with a request for a meeting to discuss the possibility of making a palate training aid for a specific case. Good documentation, based on a detailed analysis of speech, is essential and should include a history of lack of progress. If the specialists to be approached have not used this type of appliance before, it is important to avert any obstructions, caused by feelings of threat, about entering into an area of unknown procedures. It is helpful to present a full intelligible report of the patient's control of oral musculature and observed speech difficulties at this time, together with copies of articles describing the plate, its uses and apparent benefits. However it is important to remember that there may be very sound reasons why the appliance is not appropriate in a particular case and these should be recognised by everyone concerned including the child and parents.

## THEORETICAL BASIS FOR TONGUE AND PALATE TRAINING APPLIANCES

The speech problems associated with cleft palate patients involve movement and placement of tongue and oro-pharynx. These are often viewed as two separate areas of function but should be seen as part of a moving dynamic whole. The inter-relationship of both the motor and sensory aspects of this complex neuromuscular structure must be recognised. While the motor aspects of speech dysfunction can be assessed using a variety of observational and objective scientific techniques, the sensory aspects, though vitally important, are often omitted from consideration. Oral anaesthesia affecting the sensory nerves during dental treatment is a common experience which should serve as a useful basis for understanding these issues.

Good sensory feedback of tactile, kinaesthetic and proprioceptive information is clearly of great importance in both feeding and speech as is demonstrated by the difficulty in carrying out those functions with half the tongue and lips anaesthetised on a temporary basis by dental injections.

Dixon (1962) demonstrated that the proprioceptors are largely in the tongue tip area, while Grossman (1964) showed that the tongue tip had the ability to distinguish shape in the mouth. Hochberg & Kabcenell (1967) reported that cleft subjects have an inferior sensory ability to distinguish shape in the mouth and that the introduction of a prosthetic appliance in these cases enabled the tongue to differentiate changes of shape more readily in these cleft individuals. McDonald & Aungst (1970) viewed the speech-producing system as resulting from a closed cycle servo-system under continuous modulation in which tactile, proprioceptive and auditory senses provide feedback. Collected papers describing oral sensation and perception are presented in published symposia (Bosma 1967 & 1970).

Attempts to improve the speech function of subjects following operative procedures for cleft palate, brain damage from injury or disease, and idiopathic palatal malfunction, have been described by Gibbons & Bloomer (1958), Gonzales & Aronson (1970) and Thompson (1985). The prosthetic appliances described in most of these studies are aimed at providing physical support to a soft palate which is unable to function in the normal way.

An attempt to improve the sensory feedback to the tongue and soft palate motivated Selley to design and describe *the palatal training appliance* (Tudor & Selley 1974). This is a thin acrylic plate with raised ridges following the shape of the alveolar ridge, a central ridge and a posterior ridge. It is a removable appliance retained by Adam's cribs incorporating a 'U'-shaped wire loop processed securely into the posterior edge (see Fig. 5.1). The features of this plate provide feedback in three stages:

1. The anterior ridges provide good targets to focus tongue tip placement.
2. The ridges on the lateral, central and posterior edges of the plate give the blade of the tongue feedback about its shape and contacts.
3. The wire loop gives sensory feedback to the soft palate about its position at rest and during movement.

Selley (1979) has suggested from his subsequent observation of a large number of cases using this appliance that the loop not only provides surface sensation information to the soft palate but also assists in inhibiting the posterior bunching movement of the palatoglossus muscle. This allows the levator palati muscles to work more effectively in raising the soft palate posteriorly to contact the pharyngeal wall. Excessive movement of the dorsum of the tongue is a frequently observed feature of oral movement during videofluoroscopic examination of cases of incompetent velopharyngeal closure, as described by Huskie in

Chapter 3. The construction of the palatal training appliance is shown in Figures 5.1 to 5.4. A modification of this plate design by Tudor & Selley (1974) *is the visual speech aid*, in which electrodes are substituted for the wire loop and the soft palate forms a connection between the two exposed ends when at rest. This completes an electrical circuit which is attached by wire from the anterior part of the plate to a metal box. The

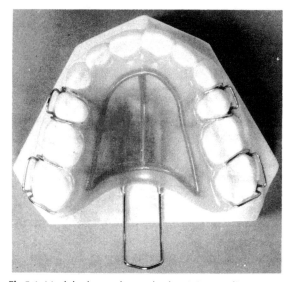

**Fig 5.1** Model of complete palatal training appliance

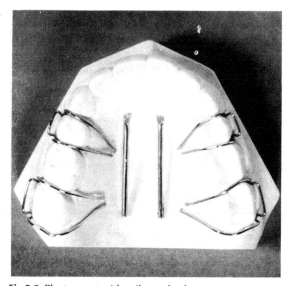

**Fig 5.2** Plaster cast with cribs and tubes

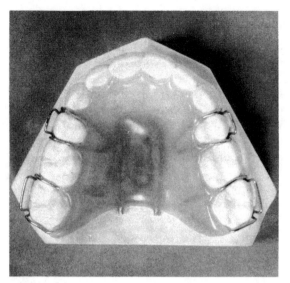

**Fig 5.3** Acrylic base plate

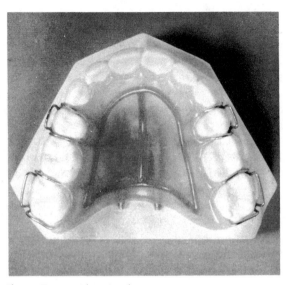

**Fig 5.4** Target ridges in place

box is so designed that a bulb lights up when the soft palate completes the circuit and thus gives visual feedback to the patient of soft palate position. This appliance can only be used in practice as an additional aid to the wearing of a palatal training appliance. A full illustrated description is given by Tudor & Selley (1974).

### Indications for use of palatal appliances

Patients with apparently normal oral structures or post-operative cleft palate subjects with persistent hypernasality, audible air emission and phonetic problems who fail to make expected progress may be worthy of consideration for this approach. Evidence of slow, inaccurate or inconsistent tongue and velar movements are also good indicators.

Careful assessment should be carried out of all aspects of oral function, speech, language and hearing before a decision is taken to proceed with this type of intervention. Assessment should include observational and objective recordings of soft palate function, using videofluoroscopy, nasendoscopy and nasal anemometry, as described in Chapter 3. The use of a *mirrored surface detail reflector* (see Fig. 5.5) may also be valuable in providing

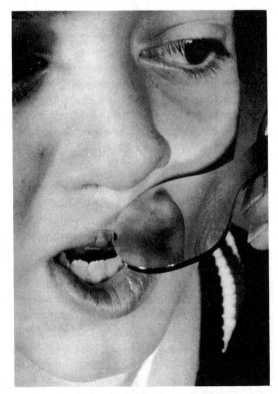

**Fig 5.5** Nasal air emission shown on a reflector

evidence of nasal air emission. It is important to gather evidence of air emission on single sounds, words and longer phrases carefully designed to show competence on the whole range of speech sounds.

When the assessment results are reviewed objectively, it may be clear that nasopharyngeal disproportion exists to such an extent that no amount of effort on the patient's part would result in velopharyngeal closure. In such cases a palatal training appliance would be contra-indicated and further consultations regarding possible pharyngeal surgery should be initiated.

## REPORT OF PALATAL TRAINING APPLIANCE STUDY

### Assessment indications for training appliance use

A study of 26 patients treated by the author and an orthodontist showed the following indications from assessment:

1. Incompetent soft palate movement
2. Hypernasality
3. Audible nasal emission
4. Inconsistent soft palate movement
5. Inconsistent tongue placement
6. Sound sequencing difficulties
7. Presence of fistulae in some cases.

In 2 of the 26 cases hypernasality and nasal air emission were the only presenting symptoms; in the rest, the symptoms were mixed and in 9 cases there were severe problems including inconsistent, inaccurate and slow tongue and lip placement, combined with palate involvement which indicated a neuromuscular disorder.

### Age range of patients treated with a palatal training appliance

Table 5.1 shows that 19 of the patients were between 3 and a half years old and 12 years old. They were all subjects with post-operative cleft palate problems or idiopathic velopha-

**Table 5.1** Age range of patients treated with palatal training appliance

Total patients: 26
Age range between $3\frac{1}{2}$ years–62 years

| | |
|---|---|
| $3\frac{1}{2}$ years–7 years | 8 patients |
| 8 years–12 years | 11 patients |
| 15 years–19 years | 5 patients |
| Over 30 years | 2 patients |

ryngeal problems. The patient of 3 and a half years is illustrated as a case study and indicates the advantages of early intervention to maximise the use of the developing neuromuscular system, but he would normally be considered young for fitting a PTA. The patients over 12 years included all the acquired problems of disease or injury.

### Vocal tract anomalies and sex distribution

Table 5.2 shows that in the first group of patients shown, 9 of the 11 with incompetent velopharyngeal closure had severe speech problems which were part of the whole oral malfunction for speech and not separate problems. This type of speech difficulty is characterised by inconsistent placement of tongue, lips and palate which suggests an underlying neuromuscular problem. Intelligibility was severely affected in 5 of the 9 cases.

**Table 5.2** Vocal tract anomalies and sex distribution

| | Total | Male | Female |
|---|---|---|---|
| 1. Incompetent soft palate | | | |
|   a. with severe speech problem | 9 | 7 | 2 |
|   b. excessive nasal resonance | 2 | 1 | 1 |
| 2. a. repaired submucous cleft | 1 | 1 | — |
|   b. unrepaired submucous cleft | 1 | 1 | — |
| 3. Repaired cleft palate | 5 | 4 | 1 |
|   a. with fistula present | 4 | 2 | 2 |
| 4. Nerve disease or injury | 4 | — | 4 |
| Totals | 26 | 16 | 10 |

*Referral source of patients*

1. Referred by speech therapist                17
2. Referred by plastic surgeons                 5
3. Referred by orthodontist                      2

The reason for referral was generally a failure to develop adequate velopharyngeal closure despite prolonged speech therapy and corrective surgery.

The four cases shown in Table 5.2 in group 4, nerve disease or injury, had lost their ability for velopharyngeal closure following the development of an acquired neurological disorder or head injury. These included:

1. Multiple sclerosis
2. Road traffic accident
3. Post-operative brain tumour
4. Motor neurone disease

## Criteria for selection of patients

In addition to positive assessment indications, there are other criteria which should be considered before embarking on this treatment programme:

1. Good oral hygiene
2. Acceptable occlusion
3. Adequate retention available
4. Positive assessment indications
5. Commitment to complete treatment
6. Regular speech therapy available
7. Age appropriate for co-operation
8. Co-operation for dental impressions.

The first three points are concerned with intra-oral conditions in the patient, any one of which could rule out the use of an acrylic plate. The patient's and parents' commitment to treatment and regular speech therapy in the locality are of equally vital importance. Success in using this type of intervention relies entirely on the training of new speech patterns in the presence of the acrylic plate, which enables the patient to make use of improved sensory information about position and movement of the oral musculature. The plate has seldom been found to produce improvements without simultaneous training taking place.

## Sequence of case management

It is important that the patient should be seen by the professionals involved on a joint clinic basis. The opportunities for joint learning and the avoidance of misunderstanding cannot be overstated. The patient and parents find it very reassuring and reinforcing to see two professionals in accord about the approach to treatment. Close liaison between the speech therapist member of the team and the local speech therapist is very important and should be frequent, supportive and amicable. Where possible, the local speech therapist should be encouraged to visit the joint clinics with the patient. It is important for all members of the team to recognise the value of intermittent breaks in the treatment regime for assimilation of newly learnt skills and for the recovery of motivation in the patient and his parents.

In summary, the sequence of case management includes:

1. Joint clinic with orthodontist and speech therapist
2. Dental extractions if necessary
3. Dental impressions taken
4. Plate fitted and worn during the day and night (or in accordance with the orthodontist's advice)
5. 3 weeks after fitting, the wire loop is attached
6. Plan and monitor treatment with local speech therapist
7. Review at joint clinic at 2–3 month intervals
8. Joint decision to remove the plate when maximum improvement has been achieved and maintained
9. Gradual removal of the plate for increasing fixed periods during the day, monitoring maintenance of speech improvement and retaining the fit of the plate.

For the purposes of this study, the plate was worn both day and night and only taken out for cleaning after meals. Night time wear is a matter for the orthodontist's advice in each case. 3 weeks were allowed between inserting the appliance and the addition of the wire loop to let the patient get used to the plate.

It is important that the speech therapist is present at the joint clinic when the loop is fitted to advise on both its length and shape. It should extend to the point of maximum soft palate lift and not exert any pressure against the palate which could result in ulceration. The effectiveness of this treatment relies on the soft palate resting very lightly on the wire loop which does not act as a palatal lift (Selley 1979). There is usually no speech therapy intervention during the 3 weeks of accommodation to the wearing of the plate.

*Time period of plate retention*

The length of time that patients have worn these plates varied very considerably. The time periods required by this group of 26 cases to complete treatment wearing a palatal training appliance is shown in Table 5.3. This shows that 18 of the 26 patients completed treatment in one year, while the remaining 8 took considerably longer owing to their severe speech problems.

There have been very few difficulties in the toleration and retention of these plates. One patient, illustrated in a case study later in this chapter, was very reluctant to relinquish her plate at the end of treatment. There has been one case of allergy to the acrylic material of the plate and in this case treatment had to be discontinued. In general, those who completed treatment within 1 year achieved very good results but it does not follow that the longer retention time indicated progressively poorer results. The remaining case study patient

**Table 5.3** Plate retention time periods. 26 patients retained their plates between 3 months–3½ years

| | |
|---|---|
| 3 months—5 patients | 1½ years—3 patients |
| 6 months—5 patients | 2 years—1 patient |
| 9 months—4 patients | 2½ years—3 patients |
| 1 year —4 patients | 3½ years—1 patient |
| Total: 18 patients | 8 patients |

began wearing his plate at the age of 3 and a half years, retained it for a further 3 and a half years and achieved unpredictably good results during that time. His original speech patterns at the age of 3 and a half years consisted of nasalised vowels, while at the end of treatment his articulation patterns were normal for place and manner, he was quite intelligible and retained a minor degree of hypernasality which could be regarded as within normal limits. There is no doubt that early intervention in this case afforded the opportunity of working with a child in the early stages of speech development and establishment of neuro muscular co-ordination and memory patterns for this complex communication activity.

**Speech results in a study of 26 patients using the palatal training appliance**

Table 5.4 shows the speech results in 26 cases broadly categorised. It shows that 11 patients in the total of 26 achieved normal speech and resonance, i.e. 42%, and 8 patients made major improvements, i.e. 30%. This consti-

**Table 5.4** Speech results in a study of 26 patients using the palatal training appliance

| | Normal speech | Major improvement | Minor improvement | Nil change | Total |
|---|---|---|---|---|---|
| Incompetent soft palate | 7 | 3 | 2 | 1 | 13 |
| Repaired cleft palate | 3 | 4 | 2 | — | 9 |
| Nerve disorder | 1 | 1 | — | 2 | 4 |
| Total | 11 | 8 | 4 | 3 | 26 |
| Percentage | 42% | 30% | 15% | 13% | 100% |

tutes 72% of the patients in a group who had previously had a very poor prognosis as there were no indications for reconstructive surgery and prolonged speech therapy had failed to yield adequate results. The palatal training appliance has much to recommend it in cases such as those illustrated in the case studies. It is neither expensive nor life-threatening and offers hope to the patient of improvement which would normally be lacking in such an unpromising situation.

## Speech therapy with the palatal training appliance

Changes in speech patterns are greatly assisted by the patient wearing a plate but are not affected unless the patient is trained to use the sensory feedback from the different parts of the plate against his tongue and soft palate. Changes in vegetative patterns of swallowing and a decrease in drooling problems associated with improved swallowing have been noted in patients across the complete age range from neonates to elderly stroke patients by Selley (1979).

Speech therapy should be directed at improving speed and accuracy of articulation placement and reduction of hypernasality and nasal air emission. Auditory, visual and tactile sensory channels should be used to give maximum feedback to the patient about his performance. Tape-recording with immediate playback and longitudinal recording for comparison week by week are very effective. Nasal air emission can be shown on a mirror-surfaced detail reflector (see Fig. 5.5), particularly if the patient can see the misting on the reflector in a large mirror at the same time. This is particularly useful for home practice.

Other feedback methods include the *Exeter Nasal Anemometer* clinical feedback device described by Ellis (1979). This gives the patient immediate visual feedback of nasal air escape on a needle swing meter. This works in exactly the same way as the Exeter Nasal Anemometer, described and illustrated in Chapter 3, but is a smaller piece of equipment which

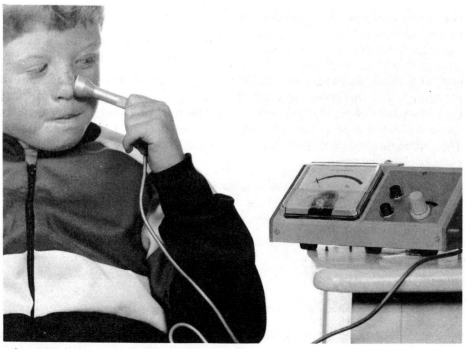

**Fig 5.6** Use of an 'N' indicator. Note needle stationary on 'p'

does not have a recording facility. The 'N' *indicator* also gives immediate feedback on a needle swing meter, but uses a microphone placed against the side of the nose in the alar area to transfer sound vibration of air passing through the nose to the meter (see Fig. 5.6).

*The electropalatograph* is also a visual feedback device, described in Chapter 6, which gives detailed visual feedback to tongue positioning during the production of speech sounds. It can be used in both assessment and intervention programmes as illustrated in depth in Chapter 6.

Self-monitoring and discrimination are a vital part of changes in speech patterns. Tactile feedback from the tongue and soft palate is increased by the acrylic plate with alveolar ridges and wire loop. Patients report that during treatment they can feel and make use of the sensations from the plate. Reference to studies of oral sensation and perception is made earlier in this chapter.

The patient can be helped to change the muscle synergisms of his speech by consciously incorporating sensory information into his strategies for change, which with much practice can be transferred to the automatic level of activity. Methods of therapy will be described in a later section of this chapter.

## CASE STUDIES

### Mandy: Cleft of soft and hard palate and tongue tie (see Table 5.5)

*Medical history*

This child was born with a wide cleft of the soft palate and posterior third of the hard palate and this was accompanied by a tongue tie. Surgery was delayed because she failed to thrive and had low haemoglobin but also because the width of the palate presented surgical problems.

Her failure to thrive probably had psychosocial elements as her mother left her father to live with another man in the first few months of her life. Surgery to repair the palate and release the tongue tie took place at the age of 5 years. This late repair and the arrival of four more subsequent children created a situation where the child's needs for communication development were seriously neglected. At the age of 7 years 4 months, her soft palate was noted to be tight and movement was very restricted.

A hearing test at this time showed normal function.

*Speech and language development*

Assessment at 7 years showed very restricted and immature expressive language development and articulation which was both deviant and immature. Mandy was a withdrawn child with a poor personal image and low status in the family situation. Attempts to remediate these problems were unsuccessful owing to non-attendance for therapy. Successive assessments at school showed minimal changes in word and sound production. On entry to secondary school at the age of 12 years 1 month, the remedial teaching department took immediate steps to attempt remediation by referring to speech therapy again and offering involvement in daily practice of a treatment programme. The work on improvement of tongue tip placement for alveolar sounds began to take immediate effect.

At 12 years 6 months, a palatal training appliance was fitted, but the addition of a training wire loop was postponed until 5 months later. Progress was rapid at this stage and while intelligibility improved, so did motivation, self-confidence and communication skills generally.

This continued until the plate was finally withdrawn at the age of 14 years 2 months. At this stage, the soft palate was noted to be moving much more than at the beginning of treatment and speech was now completely intelligible. Follow-up continued until school leaving age at 16 years with no deterioration noted.

**Table 5.5** Case summary: Mandy: Cleft hard and soft palate

| Age | Medical and surgical management | Speech and language |
|---|---|---|
| Birth | Wide cleft of soft palate and posterior 1/3 hard palate and tongue tie | |
| 4 months | Failure to thrive. Low haemoglobin. Surgery delayed because of width of cleft and low haemoglobin | |
| 1 year & 6 months | Low haemoglobin treated with iron supplement | |
| 5 years | Surgery to repair wide palatal cleft and tongue tie released | |
| 7 years & 4 months | Soft palate tight but seen to move a little. Audiometry normal | Referred by health visitor for speech therapy. Expressive language very restricted and immature. Articulation deviant and immature. No velar sounds. Voiceless laryngeal fricative most frequent initial sound. Nasals and glottal stops very evident. Nasal air escape and nasality observed |
| 8 years & 7 months | | Persistent non-attendance for therapy. Assessed in school. Minimal change in word and sound production |
| 10 years & 6 months | | Continued non-attendance for therapy. Reassessment shows some friction appearing labio-dentally. Bilabial plosion work. Fronting of velars. Voiceless laryngeal. Friction and stops still evident |
| 12 years & 1 month | Soft palate tight wide dental arch. Minimal scarring of velum. Little movement seen on videofluoroscopy. | Entered secondary school. Urgent referral from the remedial teaching department. Began weekly therapy with daily practice with remedial teacher. Work on alveolar plosion |
| 12 years & 3 months | Orthodontic consultant to consider fitting PTA | Regular speech therapy. IQ and attainment tests below normal so has most lessons in the remedial department |
| 12 years & 4 months | Hearing tested—within normal limits. Two teeth extracted prior to taking dental impressions for PTA | Lip and tongue tip placement improving in speech and accuracy for plosion. Fricative sounds affected by laryngeal friction habit and nasal air escape |
| 12 years & 6 months | Acrylic plate fitted but dental hygiene poor. Postpone fitting training wire loop | Work on velar plosion progressing well. Very quiet girl, little spontaneous speech in clinic or school. Only one friend |
| 12 years & 11 months | Training wire loop fitted | |
| 13 years & 2 months | Palate moving much more but space between velum and pharyngeal wall still apparent. Refer back to plastic surgeon for opinion on pharyngoplasty | |
| 13 years & 6 months | Plastic surgeon does not recommend pharyngoplasty because palate cleft had been wide and difficult to close | Speech much more intelligible. Weekly speech therapy and regular daily practice with teacher. Alveolar friction and velar plosives now being assimilated into speech. Affricates being used in medial and final positions. Nasal air escape still evident on alveolar plosives and fricatives. |
| 13 years & 8 months | Began withdrawal of PTA. Wearing only at night | Speech completely intelligible. Most articulation correct for place and manner. Nasal air emission much reduced. Confidence much increased. Will take part in class drama activities |
| 13 years & 10 months | Should now cease wearing PTA | Speech within normal limits with no deterioration |
| 13 years & 11 months | Still wearing plate against advice | |
| 14 years & 2 months | Persuaded to part with plate. Occlusion good | Speech continues well. Regular treatment ceased |
| 16 years | Discharged | Following reports from school find speech acceptable. Discharged |

*Points to note in Mandy's case*

1. Wide cleft
2. Late repair
3. Psycho-social factors in the family background
4. Palate movement very restricted
5. Severe speech and language delay and disorder
6. Very late remediation intervention
7. Speed of improvement using the palatal training appliance
8. Great value of daily practice programme conducted by a remedial teacher.

**Brian: Congenital velopharyngeal incompetence** (see Table 5.6)

*Medical History*

There was no observable overt clefting in this case but the mother noted failure to babble normally in the first year. Her concern about Brian's poor development of speech motivated her to pursue a solution through a number of channels. Hearing was found to be normal and an ENT consultant, suspecting palate malfunction, referred Brian to a plastic surgeon. Videofluoroscopy and nasendoscopy showed an immobile soft palate of adequate length. No surgery was deemed to be advisable and a palatal training appliance was recommended.

*Speech and language development*

At the age of 3 years 1 month, his speech consisted of nasal consonants and nasal vowels which did not include any bilabial sounds. His language and interpersonal communication appeared to be developing well, but intelligibility was so poor that frustration on the part of mother and child was quite marked. The fitting of a palatal training appliance presented some problems as the shape of teeth in the first dentition tends to be conical and does not lend itself to secure clasping. It was for this reason of security of retention that it was agreed that a wire loop would not be fitted at this time as it would have added extra weight and leverage at the posterior part of the plate. The local speech therapist began work in liaison with the team at the Regional Centre and changes began to take place very quickly.

Within 2 months of the plate being fitted, spontaneous bilabial babble was observed by the mother. New sounds were added to his repertoire quite quickly and gradually began to appear in spontaneous speech. Brian and his parents were very keen to make changes and worked very hard. Although the family moved and changed speech therapist, improvement continued and the training wire loop was finally fitted at the age of 6 years 3 months. This was at first uncomfortable and caused some retching but Brian persevered with wearing it for increasingly long periods. Fricative sounds proved to be quite difficult to acquire.

At the age of 7 years, hearing tests showed that there was fluid congestion of the middle ear. At this stage, the final fricatives /s/ and /z/ were being acquired. An ENT surgeon was sufficiently concerned about the hearing problem to plan both insertion of grommets and adenoidectomy. After strenuous resistance to the removal of adenoids by the parents and other professionals involved, because of the anticipated loss of adequate palatal closure, a minimal lateral adenoidectomy was performed. At this time, nasendoscopy showed much improved palate movement with a residual small gap in velopharyngeal closure. Videofluoroscopy confirmed this finding.

Speech continues to be intelligible but Brian still needs to use a little effort to maintain accurate articulation, particularly of alveolar fricatives.

*Points to note in Brian's case*

1. Early observation of failure to develop speech normally by mother
2. Very severe speech problems with apparently normal language development
3. Early referral for intervention
4. Parents and child very committed to treatment programme
5. Early fitting of palatal training appliance

**Table 5.6**  Case summary: Brian: Congenital velopharyngeal incompetence

| Age | Medical and surgical management | Speech and language |
|---|---|---|
| 1 year | | Mother observed failure to babble normally |
| 2 years | Audiometry normal | Mother concerned that words attempted were only vowels and nasals. No other sounds heard |
| 2 years & 4 months | ENT consultation suspected palate malfunction | |
| 3 years & 1 month | Plastic surgery consultation | Inconsistent nasal consonants and nasal vowels observed. Language quite well developed. Intelligibility poor |
| 3 years & 3 months | Videofluoroscopy and nasendoscopy showed immobile soft palate of adequate length. No surgery advised. PTA recommended | |
| 3 years & 6 months | Joint clinic with orthodontist for PTA consideration. Impressions and plate fitted. Training wire loop not added at this time for safety reasons | Began speech therapy at local clinic. Liaison between therapist and plastic unit set up. Speech still unintelligible. No bilabial sounds or alveolar or velar placements. Nasal vowels & nasal consonants only. No lip closure |
| 3 years & 8 months | | Began bilabial babble spontaneously on /p/. Variety of other sounds appeared |
| 3 years & 9 months | | New sounds appearing rapidly /g, k, b/ |
| 3 years & 11 months | | /l, w, f, j/ acquired in babble sequence |
| 4 years | | Alveolar plosives /d, t/ appearing. Works very well with practice. Parents very keen & work hard |
| 5 years & 6 months | New plate fitted | Continued speech therapy |
| 5 years & 11 months | | Family moved to a new area |
| 6 years & 3 months | Wire training loop finally fitted to plate uncomfortable but persevered, wearing for longer and longer periods | New speech therapist contacted and work began on alveolar friction sounds |
| 6 years & 8 months | | Acquired /tʃ, dʒ/ then /ð, θ, ʃ/ |
| 7 years | Hearing tests showing middle fluid congestion | Finally managed /s, z/ with much difficulty |
| 7 years & 3 months | Plate withdrawal begun | |
| 7 years & 6 months | Hearing loss fluctuating but up to 60 dB bilaterally. ENT surgeon plans to insert grommets and remove adenoids.<br><br>Plate withdrawal complete | Adenoidectomy strenuously resisted by parents, speech therapists and plastic surgeons. Speech within normal limits. Effort needed to maintain correct place and manner of articulation |
| 7 years & 9 months | Minimal lateral adenoidectomy performed. Nasendoscopy showed much improved palate movement with still a small velopharyngeal gap. Videofluoroscopy confirmed this finding | Speech continues to be intelligible. Effort still required to keep up accurate articulation, particularly on alveolar fricatives. Speech therapy review only now |
| 8 years | | Speech continues to be intelligible. To follow up for 2 more years. |

6. Rapid changes at the outset of treatment, particularly with bilabial sounds
7. Difficulty with acquisition of alveolar fricative sounds
8. Hearing problems giving rise to a possible adenoidectomy
9. Minimal lateral adenoidectomy performed without serious consequences to speech function.

### Roy: Pierre Robin syndrome (see Table 5.7)

*Medical history*

This child was born with Pierre Robin syndrome which involved a wide cleft of the soft and hard palate. His tongue tip was sutured to his lower lip to prevent choking and this situation remained until he was 11 months old. Palate repair was postponed until he was 3 years 8 months because of the surgical difficulties involved. The repair was carried out with a procedure which left a large fistula at the junction of the hard and soft palate. It subsequently appeared that the surgical technique had been both complicated and innovative but had resulted in no muscle fusion and much scarring.

*Speech and language development*

Roy's parents were concerned about future speech development and his attempts at vocalising at the age of 11 months, but were not offered access to a speech therapist.

At 5 years 3 months, speech therapy assessment revealed a sound system restricted to nasal vowels and glottal stops with some tongue tip placement for liquid sounds. The tongue tip was blunted following its 11 month tethering period and no movement was observable in the soft palate.

Hearing problems were noted associated with enlarged glands and tonsils. Speech remediation attempts produced poor results despite the commitment of his parents.

Tonsillectomy was performed at 7 years and the ear infections reduced. However, there was active caries and few permanent teeth. Videofluoroscopy at the age of 8 years 10 months showed that the palate was of reasonable length but totally immobile. Speech therapy attempted at this time produced little progress.

In order to modify the velopharyngeal incompetence, consideration was given to both a Gillies Fry operation, which involves detaching the soft palate from the hard palate and filling the resulting gap with an obturator attached to an acrylic plate, and also a Hynes pharyngoplasty to tighten the muscles of the pharynx. In view of the immobility of the soft palate and the scarring, it was considered inadvisable to interfere surgically in this case.

At the age of 14 years 11 months, the orthodontist suggested fitting a palatal training appliance which would act as an obturator for the existing fistula, provide targets for tongue tip placement and also possibly improve soft palate movement. The plate also provided an opportunity to do some simultaneous orthodontic correction.

At the time of fitting the palatal training appliance, speech assessment showed hypernasality, glottal stopping of plosives and tongue thrusting for alveolar fricatives combined with lateralising of affricates. It was interesting to note that his mother's speech, while quite intelligible and clear, did include some inconsistent glottal stopping for velar plosives. Examination revealed no overt or submucous clefting in her case. Speech therapy began with the full co-operation of Roy and his family. He reported that he found the ridges extremely helpful in correcting his tongue tip placements and appreciated the obturation of the fistula.

Speech intelligibility improved considerably and the soft palate began to show some movement. The plate was finally withdrawn at the age of 16 years 6 months after he had left school and had begun work on a youth opportunity programme.

His speech at that time was quite intelligible but retained a minor degree of nasality.

**Table 5.7** Case summary: Roy : Pierre Robin syndrome

| Age | Medical and surgical management | Speech and language |
| --- | --- | --- |
| Birth | Pierre-Robin syndrome. Wide palate cleft of soft and hard palate. Tongue tip sutured to lower lip to prevent tongue blocking airway. | |
| 11 months | Palate cleft too wide to repair. Tongue tip released from lower lip | Vocalising and attempting tongue protrusion. Parents concerned about future speech development |
| 1 year & 11 months | Palate cleft still too wide for repair | Parents ask for speech therapy. Surgeon explained it would not help |
| 3 years & 8 months | Palate repaired with unusual procedure because of width. Fistula at junction of hard palate & soft palate | |
| 4 years | Fistula causing nasal regurgitation of fluids | |
| 4 years & 3 months | Oral surgeon for consideration of obturator. Not possible. Teeth carious and wrong shape for clasping. Plan Gillies-Fry later | |
| 5 years & 3 months | | Speech therapy assessment. Sound system restricted to nasal vowels and glottal stops with some tongue tip placement for liquids. Tongue tip blunted |
| 5 years & 5 months | Hearing problems. Enlarged glands and tonsils | Speech therapy attempted with poor results despite commitment of parents |
| 6 years | ENT consultation for tonsillectomy | |
| 7 years | Tonsillectomy. Ear infections reduce. Active caries—few permanent teeth | |
| 8 years & 10 months | Palate of reasonable length but totally immobile. Pharynx average depth. Fistula between hard and soft palate causes little problem. Proposed: Gillies-Fry operation. As palate immobile retropositioning would not produce results | Speech therapy attempted with little progress. Bilabial placement and tongue tip to alveolar placement is accompanied by glottal stopping and friction in double articulation |
| 10 years & 5 months | Videofluoroscopy showed soft palate short and immobile. Plan: Hynes pharyngoplasty to tighten up pharynx | |
| 11 years & 4 months | Examination under anaesthetic for Hynes pharyngoplasty. Palate very scarred and immobile soft palate not advisable to split to get access. Gillies-Fry not recommended because of immobility of soft palate | |
| 11 years & 5 months | | Speech language and audio assessment. Intelligibility poor. Comprehension of language below normal. Hearing difficulty at 12 feet, quiet voice. Expressive language normal but restricted. Tongue & lip movement fair. Pharyngeal sound substitutions for /t, d, k, g/ Tongue thrusting on /L, s, ʃ/ with nasal air emission and nasality |
| 12 years & 11 months | Plastic surgeon discussed situation with Roy and his father. No surgical help to be offered | Speech assessment showed nasality, glottal stopping of plosives, tongue thrusting for alveolar fricatives and lateralising of affricates. Speech therapy begun aimed at using the ridges in the alveolar area of appliance to target tongue tip placement |
| 14 years & 11 months | Orthodontist suggested PTA to also act as obturator and orthodontic appliance | |

**Table 5.7**   (contd)

| Age | Medical and surgical management | Speech and language |
|---|---|---|
| 15 years & 2 months | PTA fitted | |
| 15 years & 5 months | Plate continues to fit well and act as an orthodontic appliance as well | Roy finds the ridge helpful in correcting his tongue tip placement. He works well. Now finds that speech sounds distorted without the plate |
| 16 years & 3 months | Soft palate showing some movement. Plate withdrawal began | Speech much improved though there is still evidence of minor nasality. Tongue accurate for alveolar placement nearly normal. Intelligibility approaching normal |
| 16 years & 6 months | Plate withdrawn completely | Speech continues to be intelligible. Roy now finds communication an enjoyable and rewarding experience |

*Points to note in Roy's case*

1. The late repair of the soft palate
2. Speech therapy advice not offered when requested by the parents
3. Innovative surgical procedure with poor functional results
4. Speech therapy producing no progress in the early school years
5. Difficulty with decisions about secondary surgical intervention
6. Late fitting of palatal training appliance which acted as an obturator and orthodontic appliance
7. Patient reports using the sensory feedback of the ridges and loop to correct articulation placements
8. Rapid speech improvements including some changes in soft palate movement to produce adequate speech results.

OBTURATORS

The effect on speech of defects in the hard and soft palates has been recognised for centuries. The need to restore the oral cavity to as near normal shape and function as possible motivated physicians to design obturators for palatal clefts as early as the 16th century.

The clefts that concerned them were usually those acquired through injury or disease. Materials such as wax, sponge and, in some cases, leather or silver, were used to plug the opening in the palate (Platt 1947).

A silver obturator worn by a character in a farce by Feydeau, 'Un Fils a la Patte', is used as a pivot for the classic theme of mistaken identity. The character's speech is so transformed when wearing the obturator that he is indistinguishable from his identical twin.

The frequent loss of the plate during the action of the play changes the character from a confident, articulate person, to a diffident, unintelligible one.

The importance of normalising the intra-oral space in respect of future speech development is reported in a study of congenital unilateral cleft subjects treated with pre-surgical orthodontic appliances from birth. (Stuffins 1983). It appears from this study that cases treated in this way are significantly more likely to develop normal tongue tip movement patterns in relation to the alveolar ridge in later speech development.

The pre-surgical appliances are described by Huddart (1961).

**Use of obturators in unrepaired cleft palate**

Even though there have been considerable advances in surgical technique, there are still some cases of cleft palate which cannot be repaired either through insufficiency of tissue or difficulty with surgical access. Two of the case studies in this chapter illustrate these difficulties, see Table 5.5 and 5.7.

In cases where the palatal cleft has to remain unrepaired for a considerable time, consideration should be given to fitting an obturator. The advantages to the patient, both in feeding and the development of tongue movement behaviour, in addition to the modification of voice tone, are quite evident.

At some centres when pre-surgical orthodontic treatment is employed, the appliance is not worn following lip repair at approximately 6 months. At other centres, a small acrylic plate is stapled to the hard palate in the interim period between lip repair and palate repair some months later.

In older patients where palate repair has to be delayed (see Fig. 5.7), the design of an obturator should follow certain principles. A thin acrylic plate with a smooth oral surface clasped to the teeth with Adam's cribs (see Fig. 5.8) does not provide nasopharyngeal closure or sensory feedback to the tongue surface for accurate placement in speech in the alveolar area. The addition of ridges as shown in Figure 5.4 would provide targets for tongue placement. The need to provide maximum occlusion of the nasopharyngeal area indicates the design of an extension into this area (see Fig. 5.9). This has the advantage of reducing nasal air flow during speech and providing a target for the lateral and posterior pharyngeal walls to make some attempt at closure. In young patients, the sensitivity of the borders of the unrepaired cleft palate and posterior pharyngeal wall necessitates that small additions to an obturator should be made at intervals of time (see Fig. 5.10). This allows for reduction in sensitivity and some keratinization to develop.

The shape of the teeth for clasping in the first dentition can create a difficulty with retention. However, the cleft palate team in Ljubljana (Oblak & Kozelj 1987) have overcome this problem successfully by using dental plate paste fixative in very young children. In a few cases, poor oral hygiene and, more rarely, allergy to acrylic materials make the provision of an obturator inadvisable.

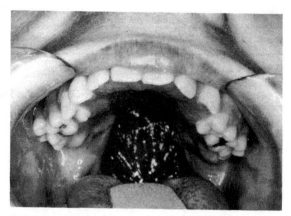

**Fig 5.7** Unrepaired cleft of hard and soft palate

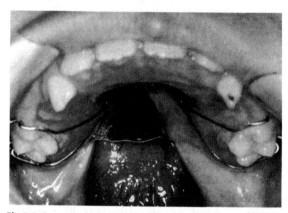

**Fig 5.8** Smooth surfaced obturator, hard palate area only

Cases treated in this way have shown perceptible changes in voice tone and unexpected improvements in confidence with oral communication based on the increased social acceptability of their voice tone.

A further design modification in an obturator for an unrepaired cleft is shown in Figure 5.11 with a large, solid, vertical extension into the nasal cavity.

This patient showed marked improvement in speech but complained of nasal congestion.

*Selection of cases and criteria for use of obturators in unrepaired clefts*

1. Co-operation of the patient for dental impressions

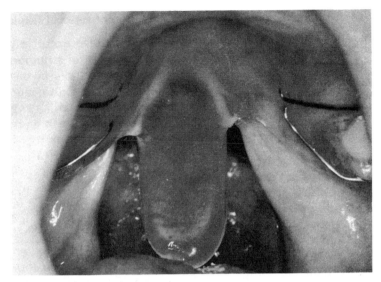

**Fig 5.9** Extension of obturator into the nasopharynx

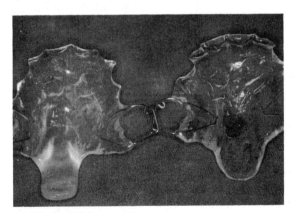

**Fig 5.10** Additions to obturator at intervals of time

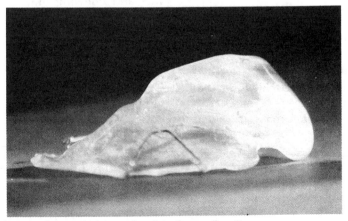

**Fig 5.11** Obturator with large, solid, vertical extension into the nasal cavity

2. Commitment of the patient and parents to treatment
3. Adequate opportunity for dental clasping and secure retention
4. Good oral hygiene
5. Absence of allergy to acrylic materials.

*Guidelines for therapy in cases of unrepaired cleft palate*

When a cleft of the palate has remained unrepaired since birth, inevitably speech patterns will have developed using closure and friction movements in the laryngeal and pharyngeal areas.

Experience has shown that these are extremely difficult to change and any changes achieved frequently include double articulation using the posterior and anterior parts of the oral cavity simultaneously. Expectations of speech improvements will naturally be very limited, both on the part of the patient and the speech therapist.

The long-term aim of speech therapy treatment should be to improve intelligibility through modification of the acoustic effect of sound production rather than to expect normal articulatory placements. Work on making alveolar tongue placements and bilabial movements can produce satisfactory visual and acoustic changes in speech output. Therapy programmes should be conducted at the non-word level for a considerable time to overcome established word concepts.

Sensory feedback from the tongue against the plate, visual feedback of facial movements in a mirror and auditory feedback using a tape recorder, are helpful in establishing correct articulation placements. The use of rhythm and associated physical activities, including mime, are useful in practice schemes to establish new skills at the automatic production level. Frequent tape-recording for longitudinal study of changes is essential and very reinforcing for both patient and therapist.

The overall length of treatment should be determined by both the therapist and the patient and is often best undertaken in short stages with rest periods giving time for assimilation and renewal of motivation at intervals.

## Obturation of residual fistulae

Residual fistulae occur in post-operative cleft palate patients for a number of reasons. Some surgical procedures involve leaving the hard palate unrepaired in order to take advantage of maximum maxillary growth as in the Schweckendiek technique. This technique produces a long, narrow fistula which is left unrepaired in some cases until the age of 12 or 13 years. In other cases, shortage of tissue has created the necessity of leaving a hard palate fistula whilst attempting to create adequate soft palate length and musculature mobility.

A study by Stengelhofen & Foster (1979) of the effects of residual oronasal fistulae on speech, concluded that there was no evidence that there was a direct relationship between the size of the fistula and the amount of nasal air emission.

Observations showed that the function of the tongue and its ability to occlude the fistula during speech was a major factor. It was noted that in subjects with a Class III occlusion, where the tongue occupies the mandibular space as a result of maxillary contraction, there was a greater tendency towards nasal air emission through the fistula (see Ch. 1).

In order to determine the extent of nasal air emission through the fistula, it is necessary to provide temporary obturation for testing procedures. Bless (1980) describes methods using a variety of materials including dental wax and chewing gum. Both these materials are quite suitable for use in the clinic; sugar-free chewing gum is easier to use and is often very acceptable to the child, although the parents usually have some reservations.

*Method of testing nasal air emission through oronasal fistula*

Dental wax can be moulded by hand to form a temporary plug, while chewing gum can be chewed and moulded by the patient to occlude the fistula. Speech testing can then take place using visual indication of nasal air escape—either a detailed reflector shown in Figure 5.5 or the 'N' indicator shown in Figure

5.6 or the nasal anemometer described by Huskie in Chapter 3. A speech test should be constructed to demonstrate velopharyngeal closure on all speech sounds both in isolation, in CV nonsense sequences and in phrases using the same consonant repeatedly.

*Example protocol*

1. 'p'
2. 'pu'
3. 'pu' 'pu' 'pu' 'pu'
4. paper
5. paper poppy
6. play with a paper poppy.

Using this type of protocol, it is possible to detect a number of features in the subject's speech abilities:

1. The difference between the amount of nasal emission both with and without the fistula occluded
2. The adequacy of velopharyngeal closure
3. Whether closure breaks down at the successive stages of articulation complexity
4. The difference nasal air emission makes between voiced and unvoiced sounds
5. The consistency of articulation placement
6. Auditory memory for sound and word sequences
7. Whether velopharyngeal closure can only be achieved with considerable effort on single sounds in non-word utterances.

It is clearly very important to omit any nasal consonants from the test procedure and to detect the difference between the subject's nasal air emission during speech production and on breathing out at the conclusion of each attempt.

Detailed observations during this test procedure should be made and the conclusions drawn should give indications for future management.

In cases where there is nasal air emission only with the fistula open, this would indicate a need for either surgical closure or obturation. In cases where nasal air emission is evident throughout the test, further investigation should be carried out using either nasendoscopy or videofluoroscopy as described by Huskie in Chapter 3. Where there is

evidence of velopharyngeal closure with effort or inconsistent closure, consideration should be given to the use of a palatal training appliance which would provide obturation for the fistula as well as training opportunities for palate function.

## PALATE AND TONGUE TRAINING APPLIANCES

Prosthetic aids to speech production have been described by Gibbons & Bloomer (1958) and Gonzalez & Aronson (1970). These appliances were designed to assist subjects with functional velopharyngeal closure problems, either by lifting an inert palate to make contact with the posterior pharyngeal wall or, in the case of a short soft palate, a combination of lift and obturation of the remaining palatopharyngeal space.

Developments and modifications of these plates to provide a facility for training inadequate soft palate movement have been made by a number of authorities.

A selected review of palatal training procedures was undertaken by Ruscello (1982). This paper describes a number of velopharyngeal training procedures and discusses disagreements between different authorities.

A palatal training appliance described by Tudor & Selley (1974) has been used by the author in a study of 26 patients which is reported earlier in this chapter. As can be seen in Table 5.4, 40% of patients treated with this procedure achieved normal speech. A remaining 32% made considerable improvement both in velopharyngeal closure and improved articulation placements. The role of removable orthodontic appliances of this type in the investigation and management of patients with hypernasal speech has been described by Thompson et al (1985).

### Design of a palatal training appliance

The construction of a palatal training appliance is illustrated in Figures 5.1 to 5.4. A thin acrylic plate is made, retained by Adam's cribs and incorporating steel tubes used to secure a 'U'-

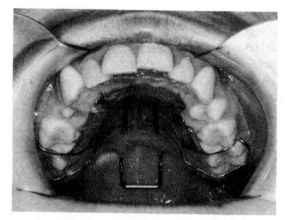

Fig 5.12 Palatal training appliance in position

shaped wire loop which is added during the fitting of the appliance. Another feature of the plate is the addition of ridges to provide tongue localisation aids which should have fairly sharp edges. These ridges follow the shape of the alveolar ridge, mark the posterior border of the plate and the full length of the plate in a central position.

The plate is worn for at least 3 weeks before the training wire is added to allow the patient to adjust to it. In a joint session with the orthodontist and speech therapist, the training wire is inserted into the steel tubes and fixed with cold cure acrylic. The length and angle of the wire loop should be adjusted to each patient's needs so that the loop reaches to the point of maximum soft palate lift and does not exert any pressure on the soft palate at rest (see Fig. 5.12).

In practice, where the soft palate is immobile or in a state of tension during examination, difficulties may be experienced in making these fine adjustments. Stimulating the gag reflex can be helpful in estimating the length of the loop, and the relaxation following this reflex could show undue pressure of the loop against the soft palate.

### Criteria for selection of cases for PTA

A thorough assessment of speech, language, hearing and oral function as described in Chapter 3 should be carried out before any

management decisions are made. The following criteria may be useful in a decision to proceed with a palatal training appliance.

1. Evidence from objective assessment of adequate palate length
2. Evidence of insufficiency of soft palate movement
3. Nasal air emission and hypernasality
4. Intermittent and inconsistent velopharyngeal closure during speech
5. Soft palate closure possible during single sound production with breakdown in spontaneous speech
6. Evidence of mistiming of soft palate closure during speech
7. Clinical observation of speech patterns which are inaccurate, inconsistent or deviant
8. Evidence of difficulty in sequencing speech sounds as in articulatory dyspraxia.

As can be seen from the last two criteria, a training plate can be used to modify speech patterns where there is no palatal function involvement. In these cases, the training wire loop may not be needed although it provides valuable tactile feedback to the posterior part of the tongue during speech.

The criteria listed above need not all coexist in each case. Only two or three positive assessment indicators are necessary to make a decision about proceeding with an appliance.

Other criteria concerned with oral hygiene and co-operation are as follows:

1. Good oral hygiene
2. Acceptable occlusion
3. Adequate retention available
4. Commitment to complete treatment
5. Regular speech therapy available.

This plate has also been found to be effective in case of speech difficulties of a dysarthric type and associated problems of saliva control in stroke patients (Selley 1979).

### Guidelines for therapy with PTA

Subjects considered suitable for the use of a palatal training appliance will have previous experience of unsuccessful speech therapy. The speech therapist will therefore need to use an unusual amount of energy, enthusiasm, ingenuity and encouragement to motivate the patient and overcome his earlier negative experiences. The fitting of the plate itself and the co-operation between the local speech therapist, the team in the orthodontic department, the parents and the child provide a good basis for a new start in therapy. Parents and child are reassured by the presence of a physical assistance to speech production in the mouth.

The sensory feedback to the tongue and soft palate of the training features, the ridges and loop, on the plate should be used consciously to maximum effect. In addition to this feedback, visual biofeedback using the detail reflector (Fig. 5.5), the 'N' indicator (Fig. 5.6), or the nasal anemometer clinical training model, similar to the assessment model described in Chapter 3, should be used regularly in therapy and practice sessions. *Auditory feedback* using a tape recorder for immediate playback and longitudinal progress recording, is also essential.

The subject needs every assistance with *all sensory feedback channels* to make changes in speech behaviour and monitor the assimilation of those changes into spontaneous speech.

A therapy programme should be devised working initially on *improved articulation realisations of individual speech sounds*, starting with those that the subject finds easiest to produce.

Success at this stage relies on a great deal of *repetition*, and motivation can only be maintained with adequate reinforcement techniques. *Reinforcement* should not rely on therapist approval for sound production attempts. A variety of techniques are available, using simple equipment which may include glove puppets, coloured light reinforcers, physical activities such as posting small objects and noise-making with musical instruments. Progress is greatly assisted by depersonalising reinforcement.

The use of rhythmic movement and miming activities can be used to great effect from the early stages in treatment through to the *assimilation of new speech patterns into spontaneous utterance*. New articulation skills should be well established at the single sound and sequences in rapid repetition before attempting the word level.

*Auditory discrimination exercises* involving cognitive dissonance can be played as a family game with much benefit as the patient is always right in pointing out the mispronunciations of the other players. The game should be carefully structured so that the patient's own speech difficulties are not mocked and that it is conducted as an auditory exercise not requiring production.

When some speed and accuracy is established in the production of speech sounds, an *alternation exercise* can be introduced to contrast the old and new sound realisations in juxtaposition.

Visual and auditory feedback using the equipment already referred to provide valuable reinforcement of this activity.

Where the patient shows evidence of difficulty with accurate tongue movement and placement combined with poor sound sequencing ability, it may be advisable to do an assessment for articulatory dyspraxia, e.g. the Nuffield Dyspraxia Programme.

These patients are frequently helped to achieve improved speech sounds as a basis for the therapy programme. Once the secure establishment of speech sounds in rapid non-word sequences has taken place, progress to the *word level* should be quite straightforward. The need to do adequate work at the non-word level cannot be over-emphasised. The strength of the old word production patterns is so great that even in quite young patients, work directed at this level is likely to be unsuccessful. It is important for the child, parents and therapist to be fully aware that only when new muscle synergisms for sound sequence production have been established, is it possible to break into the established speech and language structure.

From the single word level through gradual *increase in phrase length by one word at a time*, a carefully planned and structured treatment programme should continue. As has been suggested earlier, it may be advisable to arrange breaks in regular therapy attendance to establish assimilation and recovery of motivation. During the period of treatment, the patient will return to the team for checks on the fit of the plate and continued oral hygiene. These occasions are useful for liaison with the local speech therapist, when progress reports and advice can be exchanged.

When maximum progress has been achieved with the agreement of the team, the patient, and the therapist involved, a planned programme of *withdrawal of the plate* can begin. At first, a period of 2 hours each day, usually after school hours, can be established as a time when the plate is not worn. The plate should be kept in water during these periods to prevent shrinkage. These intervals of time may be lengthened over about 3 months until the plate is only worn at night to maintain the fit. Continued observation and recording of speech accuracy will determine whether there is any deterioration without the benefit of the plate.

The case summaries, Tables 5.5, 5.6 and 5.7, illustrate the length of time required for plate withdrawal. When this is complete, the patient is discharged from the care of the team but the local therapist should continue to monitor the maintenance of adequate speech patterns over a period of 2 years post-treatment.

## AIDS TO VISUAL FEEDBACK FOR HYPERNASALITY AND NASAL EMISSION

### 'N' indicator

The nasal indicator was designed mainly for use in training nasalisation and denasalisation in children with hearing difficulties. The indicator has a swing needle meter and a red and green lamp which give visual biofeedback. A small contact microphone is held with light pressure against the soft part of the nose. This detects sound vibrations which are amplified and the intensity of the vibration is shown by the deflection of the pointer.

In Figure 5.6, the subject is producing a plosive /p/ which produces no needle movement, while in Figure 5.13, the subject produces the nasal consonant /m/ and needle movement is noted. It is possible to adjust the sensitivity of the indicator to different levels of vocal output in each subject. The red lamp indicates when the level of nasalisation is above 50% of the full scale. The green light indicates that the signal is below the level that corresponds to 50% of the full scale and is activated when non-nasalised vowels are produced. This is a potent indication of incomplete velopharyngeal closure on vowel sounds in normal speech and a vitally important point to be observed during therapy. This device clearly has great value in the *treatment of hypernasality nasal air emission* and, if used with a patient, should be made available for both therapy sessions and home practice, as the establishment of an association between visual feedback and the speech production movement cannot be done on a part-time basis. Initial reservations about the expense of using this device in this way should be set against the need to make intervention as short and as effective as possible for patients with sensory feedback difficulties. Detailed instructions are included with the device which is battery-operated and easily portable.

### Nasal anemometer training model

This is a smaller, portable version of the clinical assessment model as described in Chapter 3. It registers nasal air emission through a face mask to produce deflection of a swing needle meter. The constraint in using this equipment is that it responds to air movement in the room as well as nasal air emission. It therefore requires more care in the provision of therapy and practice accommodation. Draughts from windows, doors and air-ducted central heating will render the meter readings inaccurate.

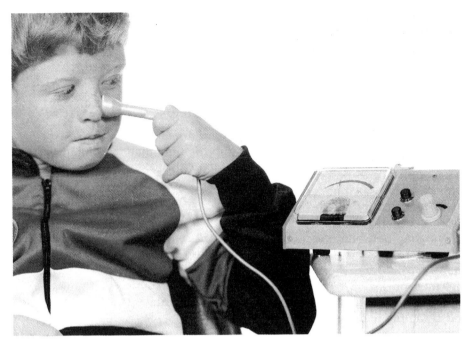

**Fig 5.13** 'N' indicator. Note needle deflection on 'm'

### Mirror detail reflector

This is shown in Figure 5.5 and is a simple, cheap and portable treatment aid. It was designed to reflect the lingual and hidden dental areas in the mouth. It gives immediate visual feedback of nasal air emission by misting on the mirrored reflecting surface when held under the nose as illustrated. During assessment it can be held by the speech therapist and gradually slid under the nostrils from right to left to show nasal air flow on given sound productions. A test protocol for this procedure is given earlier in the chapter. It is possible to detect nasal air flow from each nostril in this way. Where there is air flow on one side only, this can indicate leakage through an anterior fistula, blockage of one nasal passage or asymmetrical closure of the soft palate. It is possible to distinguish between air flow that is diffuse or focussed in a small area, differences between the amount of air flow from either nostril and on different sound productions. The reflector can be used in assessment and is an invaluable aid in practice sessions. It is important to ensure that the reflecting surface is not handled, as if it becomes warm or covered in finger prints, it ceases to be effective. Practice is required to determine whether air flow is being observed on the patient's sound production attempts or simply by breathing out either at the beginning or end of the speech task.

### Visual speech aid

This is a development from the palatal training appliance described by Tudor & Selley (1974) and illustrated in the same paper. The training wire in the visual speech aid is replaced by two electrodes insulated by plastic sheathing except for the terminal ends. The electrodes are connected by insulated wire to the external visual speech aid control box containing a 6 volt battery and a small lamp. The operating principle is that the soft palate rests on the ends of the electrodes, thus completing the electrical circuit which illuminates the lamp. The circuit is broken by the soft palate lifting, the light goes out and the patient therefore has visual feedback of his palatal movement. The plate is intended for use in practice only, and is used on a regular daily basis in addition to the wearing of a palatal training appliance as described earlier.

Great care must be taken to ensure that accurate visual feedback of palate movement is gained from using this device by ensuring that saliva stringing between the two electrodes is cleared frequently. Indications for using this device would be where the palatal training appliance on its own produces very limited, or no improvement at all.

A detailed description of the construction and use of this appliance is given in the paper by Tudor & Selley (1974). By monitoring palatal movement the visual speech aid can be used in the treatment of resonatory, nasal emission and articulatory problems.

## ACKNOWLEDGEMENTS

I would like to express my thanks to Mr A. G. Huddart, Consultant Orthodontist at the West Midlands Regional Plastic and Jaw Surgery Unit, for his support, advice and encouragement in the instigation of the use of palatal training appliances at the Unit. My thanks also go to Mr P. Smith and his staff at the Dental Laboratory, Wordsley Hospital, for their help in constructing these appliances. The illustrations were provided by Mr Tony Coote and his staff at the Medical Photography Department, Wordsley Hospital, to whom I am very grateful.

## SUPPLIERS OF EQUIPMENT DESCRIBED

*'N'indicator*
SCI Instruments Limited
39 Hinton Way
Great Shelford
Cambridgeshire CB2 5AX

*Nasal anemometer*
Bio Instrumentation Limited
Holm Croft
School Road
Silverton
Near Exeter EX5 4JH

*Detail reflector*
Floxite Company Inc.
Rainbow Boulevard
Niagara Falls
New York State 14303 U.S.A.

*Visual speech aid*
Bio Instrumentation Limited
Holm Croft
School Road
Silverton
Near Exeter EX5 4JH

*Nuffield Centre dyspraxia programme*
The Nuffield Hearing and Speech Centre
Royal National Throat, Nose and Ear Hospital,
Grays Inn Road
London WC1

# REFERENCES

Bless D M, Ewanowski S J, Dibbell D G 1980 A technique for temporary obturation of fistulae. Cleft Palate Journal 17: 297

Bosma 1967 Symposium in oral sensation and perception. Papers by Henkin and Banks, Rutherford and McCall; Shelton, Arndt and Hetherington. Charles C Thomas, Springfield, Illinois

Bosma 1970 2nd Symposium in oral sensation and perception. Papers by Arndt, Gaver, Shelton, Crary and Chisum; Elbert and Shelton; McDonald and Aungst. Charles C Thomas, Springfield, Illinois

Dixon A D 1962 The position, incidence and origin of sensory nerve termination in oral mucous membrane. Archives of Oral Biology 7: 39

Ellis R E 1979 The Exeter Nasal Anemometer. In Ellis R E, Flack F C (eds) 1979 Diagnosis and treatment of palato-glossal malfunction. The College of Speech Therapists, London.

Gibbons P, Bloomer 1958. A supportive type of prosthetic speech aid. Journal of Prosthetic Dentistry 8: 362

Gonzalez J B, Aronson A E 1970 Palatal lift prosthesis for treatment of anatomic and neurologic palatopharyngeal insufficiency. Cleft Palate Journal 7: 91

Grossman R C 1964 Methods of evaluation of oral surface sensation. Journal of Dental Restoration 43: 301

Hochberg I, Kabcenell J 1967 Oral stereognosis in normal and cleft palate individuals. Cleft Palate Journal 4: 47

Huddart A G 1961 Presurgical dental orthopaedics, Transactions of the British Society for the Study of Orthodontics 107

McDonald E T, Aungst L F 1970 2nd Symposium in oral sensation and perception. Bosma J (ed). Charles C Thomas, Springfield, Illinois

Oblak P, Kozelj V 1987 Personal communication

Platt J H 1947 The history and principles of obturator design. Journal of Speech Disorders 12: 111

Ruscello D M 1982 A selected review of palatal training procedures. Cleft Palate Journal 19: 181

Selley W G 1979 Dental and technical aids for the treatment of patients suffering from velopharyngeal disorders. In: Ellis R, Flack F C (eds) Diagnosis and treatment of palatoglossal malfunction. College of Speech Therapists, London

Stengelhofen J, Foster T D 1979 An investigation into the effects of residual oronasal fistula in repaired cleft palate. Proceedings of the 8th National Conference of College of Speech Therapists, London

Stuffins G M 1983 Tongue tip movement patterns in the unilateral cleft lip and palate child related to presurgical orthodontic treatment. Proceedings of the 19th Congress of International Association of Logopedics and Phoniatrics 1: 215

Thompson R, Ferguson J W, Barton M 1985 The role of removable orthodontic appliances in the investigation and management of patients with hypernasal speech. British Journal of Orthodontics 12: 70

Tudor C, Selley W G 1974 A palatal training appliance and visual speech aid for use in treatment of hypernasal speech. British Journal of Disorders of Communications 9: 2: 117

Introduction
Instrumentation for articulatory analysis

Case studies
    Carl 10 years
        Medical history
        Speech and hearing
        Speech findings before using EPG
        Personality and educational ability
    Tim 8 years
        Medical history
        Speech and hearing
        Speech findings before using EPG
        Personality and educational ability

Instrumental assessment
    Pressure/flow measurements
        Assessment of oral/nasal air flow patterns
        Assessment of intra-oral pressure
        Co-ordination between tongue and
        velopharyngeal mechanism
    Measurements of voicing
    Measurements of tongue-palate contact
        The electropalatograph
    Results of EPG investigations
        EPG patterns for Carl
        EPG patterns for Tim
    Discussion of EPG results
    Possible reasons for persisting speech
    problems

Therapeutic intervention
    Reasons for limited success in therapy

The use of visual feedback in therapy
    Therapy for Carl and Tim
        Intervention for Carl
        Intervention for Tim
    Results of therapy for Carl and Tim
        Results of intervention with Carl
        Results of intervention with Tim
    Conclusion

# 6

# Instrumental articulatory phonetics in assessment and remediation: case studies with the electropalatograph

*W. Hardcastle    R. Morgan Barry
M. Nunn*

In this chapter we examine articulatory problems that occur in two cleft palate children who present with normal velopharyngeal function. A detailed auditory-based phonetic analysis is made of the children's speech, and their tongue activity is recorded by the instrumental technique of Electropalatography (EPG). In the final section of the chapter we describe how EPG was used as a visual feedback tool in the treatment of the children's articulatory problems. Although the main aim of this chapter is to illustrate the potential use of EPG with cleft palate children, the technique has proven to be a valuable clinical tool in work with other client groups, e.g. dysarthric and dyspraxic speakers (see Hardcastle et al 1985). Some clinicians are now using EPG in contexts such as language units as well as in hospitals, and there are indications that it will become more widely available in the future. It is to be hoped that the procedural guidelines in this chapter will be of relevance to all client groups where articulatory abnormalities are the primary presenting symptoms.

# INTRODUCTION

From discussion in earlier chapters it is apparent that, despite surgical intervention, a number of cleft palate speakers nevertheless suffer various degrees of speech impairment. In many cases the nature of the impairment can be directly attributed to inefficient functioning of the velopharyngeal mechanism. In this instance, unwanted escape of air into the nasal cavity may lead to a disorder in normal oral/nasal acoustic coupling, resulting in a subjectively perceived hypernasal voice quality. Or there may be abnormal nasal emission of air accompanying the production of obstruent sounds, i.e. those sounds such as stops, fricatives and affricates involving a close articulatory stricture in the oral tract and subsequent build-up in intra-oral pressure. For stops, any such leakage of air through the nasal cavity during the closure phase will mean difficulty in achieving the required oral pressure necessary for their characteristic energy burst at release. For fricatives, the leakage may prevent a sufficiently high rate of air flow through the narrowed articulatory constriction for the production of turbulent air. In both cases the sound produced will be acoustically affected by the presence of nasal flow. More radical effects on articulatory gestures result if the speaker with velopharyngeal insufficiency attempts compensatory strategies such as blocking off the nasal cavity by raising the back of the tongue during anterior obstruent production or substituting a glottal stop or simultaneous glottal and articulatory closure for oral stops (Bzoch 1965, Henningsson & Isberg 1986). Other compensatory gestures mentioned in the literature include retracting the root of the tongue towards the back wall of the pharynx (e.g. Trost 1981), replacing anterior oral stops by mid-dorsum palatal stops and producing posterior nasal fricatives sometimes with audible nasal air emission for /s/, /ʃ/ etc. (Trost 1981). Various prosodic effects also have been noted. These include abnormal temporal co-ordination between the oral articulators and velopharyngeal mechanism (Warren et al 1985), timing problems such as general slowing down of rate, increased duration of closure phases for obstruents, abnormal voice qualities etc. As discussed in Chapter 1, many of the prosodic abnormalities can be attributed to hearing problems which often accompany cleft palate or to a variety of organic complications that may occur.

However, abnormal articulatory patterns may persist in post-operative cleft palate cases even when there is no evidence of velopharyngeal incompetency. It has in fact been estimated that about 35% of post-operative cleft palate speakers with perceptually normal nasal resonance show deviant lingual articulation, although this figure is lower if they attained adequacy prior to mastering the lingual consonants (see Lawrence & Philips 1975). A variety of abnormal articulatory patterns may occur, including a general tendency for lingual place targets to be shifted posteriorly (Lawrence & Philips 1975), and for extensive palatal contact by the tongue dorsum with release of air laterally. The abnormal articulations are generally regarded as persistent and relatively resistant to conventional therapy (Bzoch 1971, Green 1960, Van Demark 1974). However, although it is important clinically to identify the nature of such misarticulations, there have been relatively few attempts in the literature to describe them in detail. Most descriptions are based on perceptual judgements by trained listeners. However, subjective impressions are notoriously unreliable and give no precise indication of the nature of the abnormality. For such a description objective investigative procedures are necessary.

# INSTRUMENTATION FOR ARTICULATORY ANALYSIS

There is unfortunately a relative lack of suitable instrumentation for examining details of articulatory organs. X-ray techniques, electromyography, ultrasonics, magnetometers and photodetectors have been used but all have their limitations. They have recently been reviewed by Hardcastle (1985). *Conventional X-ray* techniques are limited by the potential damage to soft tissue by exposure to radiation, although recent significant advances in technology, for example in the development of the *computerised X-ray microbeam system* (see Kiritani et al 1975), have resulted in the development of new, relatively safe applications. In the X-ray microbeam system movements of individual lead pellets attached to specific articulatory structures are tracked by computer-generated X-ray pulses with special interactive software providing time-varying and two-dimensional plots of these pellets simultaneously with the acoustic signal trace. At the present time, however, the facility is extremely expensive and is available only at the Universities of Tokyo and Wisconsin. *Electromyography*, using either surface or hooked-wire electrodes inserted into muscles, provides useful information on electrical potentials associated with muscle activity, but there are difficulties in interpretation of dynamic patterns of activity in articulatory organs and in locating individual muscles. A system using *magnetometers* is also a relatively non-invasive technique potentially valuable for providing information on tongue activity during speech. The magnetometer system uses alternating magnetic fields to track articulatory activity. Articulatory movements may be tracked in the midsagittal plane by using two transmitter coils placed on the subject's head, and two receiver coils mounted in the same orientation as the transmitters straddling the mid-line of the tongue surface (Perkell & Cohen 1985) The system, however, is still in the experimental stage and some problems of calibration and interpretation exist. The image from *ultrasonic* investigation also is difficult to interpret in terms of dynamic tongue patterns in relation to fixed structures such as the hard palate. In recent years the technique of *Electropalatography* (EPG) which records spatio-temporal details of tongue contacts with the hard palate has emerged as a safe and reliable technique for obtaining relatively, large amounts of data on the dynamics of lingual articulation. The procedure will be described in detail later in the chapter. It has been used to investigate lingual activity in Japanese cleft palate cases with normal velopharyngeal function and has revealed two main classes of articulatory abnormality: a palatalised substitution for dental and alveolar sounds such as /s/, /t/, etc. in which contact between the posterior aspect of the dorsal surface of the tongue and the posterior border of the hard palate occurred; and a lateral misarticulation involving extensive central-palatal articulation with lateral release of air, similar perceptually to a lateral fricative substitution. For a full description see Michi et al (1986). In the present study EPG forms the basis of our investigation into articulatory abnormalities in two cleft palate children both of whom were judged to have normal velopharyngeal function. Results of the EPG analysis are compared with auditorily-based transcriptions. The use of the technique in providing visual displays of tongue-palate contact for use in the remediation of these children's articulatory problems will also be explored. The cases of two children will now be described; this will provide descriptions of the procedures used as well as detailed analysis of their speech before and after intervention. The case studies are intended to show how theoretical knowledge and the use of instrumentation can be brought together to resolve entrenched speech problems in cleft palate cases. The principles involved may be relevant to other client groups.

## CASE STUDIES

**Carl: 10 years** (see Table 6.1)

*Medical history*

At birth, Carl presented with a left unilateral sub-cutaneous cleft of the lip and a left wide post-alveolar cleft, but with the arch intact. A 4-flap V-Y operation was carried out at 7 months to close the soft palate leaving the hard palate unrepaired. At 3 years it was noticed that there was occasional nasal escape of food, due probably to the unrepaired hard

**Table 6.1** Summary of case study: Carl 10 years

| Age | Medical condition and surgery | Speech/language |
|---|---|---|
| birth | L.unilateral sub-cutaneous cleft lip + L.wide post-alveolar cleft. Arch intact | |
| 7 months | 4-flap V–Y operation to close soft palate only | |
| 2 years & 6 months | Hearing investigated; found depressed, grommets rejected | Referred for speech therapy. Assessed for language: comprehension/expression found to be delayed. Articulation assessment: alveolar sounds found defective |
| 3 years | Nasal escape of food noted | |
| 3 years & 6 months | Hearing re-assessed, grommets re-inserted | |
| 4 years & 6 months | Hearing fluctuating around 40–50 dB loss, grommets inserted | Continued to be assessed and observed. Advice on management given |
| 5 years | Surgery on lip, local operations to close anterior hard palate fistula | Language now age appropriate. Normal school entry |
| 6 years | Continued to have nasal escape of food | Regular speech therapy to improve alveolar sounds |
| 7 years | Nasendoscopy attempted inconclusive result | |
| 7 years & 6 months | Further surgery to close fistula | Continued regular therapy with intermittent breaks |
| 8 years | | Continued work on improvement of alveolar sounds |
| 10 years | | Accepted for the investigation using EPG visual feedback technique |

palate. At 5 years, further surgery was carried out on the lip, together with an operation to close the fistula. This, however, was only partially successful; food continued to escape down the nose and at 7 years nasendoscopy was attempted to determine whether this was due to a remaining fistula, or via an inadequate velopharyngeal sphincter. The results were inconclusive, and it was decided that a second attempt should be made to close the fistula. This was done at 7 years and 6 months by the flap closure method and was successful. No further nasal emission was noted.

## Speech and hearing

Carl was referred for speech therapy at 2 years, and kept under observation while investigations into his hearing ability were carried out. This was found to be depressed, and grommets were inserted at 2 years and 6 months and 3 years and 6 months, and removed at 4 years and 6 months. His hearing, rejected at 4 years and 6 months. His hearing, 40–50 db loss in both ears across all frequencies.

Initial speech therapy assessment found his language to be slightly delayed. The following articulation difficulties were found:
— alveolar stops /t, d, n/ were palatalised
— fricatives /s, z, ʃ/ were lateralised and 'diffuse'
— affricates /tʃ, dʒ/ were deviant (but it was not specified in what way)

He had normal velopharyngeal function and adequate oral pressure for the normal production of oral stops.

Therapy was carried out at intervals between 6 years and 10 years along the following lines:
— improvement of alveolar placement for /t, d, n/
— work on /θ, ð/ so that when these became consolidated tongue retraction could be demonstrated to achieve /s, z/
— improvement of /ʃ, ʒ, tʃ, dʒ/.

Progress was made with the alveolar stops,

but articulation of these was not consistent. The fricatives became less lateral, but remained diffuse and sometimes palatalised. Affricates continued to be deviant.

Amount of therapy given:
— management and assessment up to 6 years
— 6-months regular therapy from 7 years and 4 months to 7 years and 10 months
— further regular treatment from 8 years and 2 months to 8 years and 6 months
— ongoing therapy from 9 years and 3 months to the present study.

*Speech findings before using EPG*

Assessments carried out both subjectively and instrumentally confirmed the impression that Carl had:
— normal and adequate velopharyngeal function
— oral and nasal resonance within normal limits
— reasonably intelligible articulation, but with the fricatives /s, ʃ, z, ʒ/ and affricates /tʃ, dʒ/ palatalised or lateral or both.

*Personality and educational ability*

Carl was an emotionally stable child, co-operative and willing to take part in the experimental use of the visual feedback technique. He was of average ability and coped well in school.

**Tim: 8 years** (see Table 6.2)

*Medical history*

Tim had a bi-lateral cleft: the right-sided cleft was complete, involving lip, alveolus and palate; the left-side comprised a pre-alveolar cleft only. At 5 months, repair was carried out on the right cleft lip, and at 8 months, a rotation advancement repair of the left pre-alveolar cleft. At 11 months a V-Y closure using two Veau-type flaps was performed on the soft palate, leaving the anterior hard palate unrepaired. At 5–6 years, the anterior fistula was closed by rotation of a left-sided muco-periosteal flap. The upper arch form prior to any surgery was described as 'a good arch relationship' and it was felt that pre-

**Table 6.2**  Case study: Tim 8 years: Summary of medical and speech-language history

| Age | Medical condition and surgery | Speech/language |
|---|---|---|
| birth | Bi-lateral cleft: R.complete; L-pre-alveolar only | |
| 5 months | Repair of R. cleft lip | |
| 8 months | Rotation-advancement repair of L. pre-alveolar cleft | |
| 11 months | V–Y closure of soft palate only | |
| 2 years & 6 months | Hearing investigated, found depressed grommets inserted | |
| 2.9 years | | Speech assessment: no velar sounds, no fricatives, some nasal escape |
| 3 years | Hearing still depressed, grommets re-inserted | Advice on management, kept under observation |
| 4 years & 4 months | | Regular therapy to improve rate and rhythm of speech and speech work. Velars now established; work on alveolar sounds |
| 5 years & 6 months | Maxillary hypoplasia and type III malocclusion noted. Orthodontic treatment deferred. Closure of anterior hard palate fistula | Continued intermittent therapy |
| 8 years | | Acceptance for the investigation using EPG visual feedback technique |

surgical orthodontics was not required at that stage.

## Speech and hearing

Assessments were carried out from the age of 2 years and 3 months, when grommets were inserted, and informal assessment revealed that his language development was age-appropriate and his speech reasonably intelligible. Examination at 2 years and 9 months found that there were no velar sounds and little use of sibilants together with noticeable nasal escape.

Early intervention consisted of advice on management. His hearing continued to be depressed, and grommets were re-inserted at 3 years. At 4 years and 4 months Tim began regular therapy, which aimed to:
— slow down rate of utterance and improve pace and rhythm (very rapid speech was a family trait)
— improve placement of palatalised alveolar stops /t, d, n/
— improve fricatives /s, z, ʃ, ʒ/ and affricates /tʃ, dʒ/.

Therapy continued with intermittent breaks for 4 years, during which time improvement was effected on his production of /t/d/n/ and on his rate and rhythm of utterance, with great benefit to intelligibility. The fricatives, however, remained both diffuse and retracted.

Amount of therapy given:
— advice on management from 2 years and 9 months to 4 years
— 8 months regular therapy from 4 years and 4 months to 5 years
— intermittent therapy from 5 years to the period to be described here.

## Speech findings before using EPG

On assessment at the beginning of the study, Tim was found to have:
— normal velopharyngeal function
— diffuse and palatalised fricatives.

## Personality and educational ability

Tim was of good average ability and coped well in school. He was lively and co-operative in clinic and very much enjoyed the interaction with the computer for the visual feedback therapy sessions.

As indicated in the above case summaries, both children therefore presented with ongoing difficulties of articulation that affected mainly the fricative and affricate systems, reducing both intelligibility and acceptability. It was this area that the instrumental phonetic techniques sought to investigate diagnostically, with a view to providing therapeutic intervention. The various measurements carried out will now be discussed in detail.

## INSTRUMENTAL ASSESSMENT

### 1. Pressure/flow measurements

Both children were judged by the therapists to have normal resonance with no indication of velopharyngeal insufficiency. This judgement was essentially confirmed by measurements of intra-oral pressure and oral/nasal flow during the production of obstruent sounds. Intra-oral pressure was measured by a *pressure transducing system* (type Manophone, F-J Electronics) from an open catheter tube placed just inside the lips. Oral and nasal air flow were recorded by a *pneumotach system* using a specially constructed rubber mask with an air-tight seal round the face and a rubber partition fitted inside just below the nose (see Hardcastle & Morgan 1982). The partition enabled air flow from the mouth to be recorded separately from the nose. The measuring procedures used and the main results are as follows:

### Assessment of oral/nasal air flow patterns

Oral/nasal flow patterns were recorded during production of three short sentences:
— Bobby bought a beer at the pub (containing oral stops, no nasals)
— Marmalade the musical mouse (mixture of oral obstruents and nasals)
— 'Safety first' says Tufty (mainly fricatives, no nasals).

When compared to normal children's production of the same sentences the two cleft palate children showed no evidence of abnormal nasal flow during the oral stops which would have been expected in the event of velopharyngeal insufficiency.

### Assessment of intra-oral pressure

Oral pressure was measured during production of bilabial stops and labio-dental fricatives in three words, 'papa, buffer and bumper'. The cleft palate children achieved generally normal intra-oral pressure (i.e. 8–10 cm $H_2O$) on these items. However their values for the /f/ in 'buffer' were slightly lower than the norm for children of their age.

### Co-ordination between tongue and velopharyngeal mechanism

This was assessed indirectly from the patterns of oral/nasal air flow during production of nasal-stop sequences such as occur in the words 'hunter, camper, band, tamper'. Observation of the patterns of oral and nasal flow during production of these words by a normal child shows the following sequence (see Fig. 6.1a for 'hunter'): the nasal flow trace rises rapidly during the nasal consonant, reaching a maximum at a point coinciding with the drop in amplitude of the acoustic wave-form. The nasal trace sharply decreases and reaches zero just before the rapid rise in the oral flow trace signalling the onset of the oral release. Both cleft palate children exhibited generally lower peak values for the nasal flow than two normal children matched for age; they had no evidence of a rapid rise in nasal flow (rather a plateau-shaped configuration) and a much more gradual slope at the end of the acoustic signal before the release of the oral stops (see Fig. 6.1b for 'hunter'). These abnormal patterns of nasal flow are probably a reflection of a relatively more sluggish operation of the velopharyngeal mechanism which would be expected from these subjects. In addition, there was evidence of oscillation of the soft palate during the closure for Carl. This is perhaps reminiscent of the 'nasal flutter' phenomenon noted in the X-ray data of Trost (1981). In neither cleft palate case, however, was there any perceptual evidence of abnormal nasal emission during the oral stop.

### 2. Measurements of voicing

In addition to the pressure/flow measurements, various other relevant parameters relating to voicing and segmental duration were assessed. These included Voice Onset Time (VOT) for initial stops (measured from oscillograms as the time from release of initial stop to onset of vocal fold vibration) and relative vowel duration before phonologically voiced/voiceless stops in words such as pin, bin, curl, girl, dart, tart (for VOT) and seat, seed, back, bag, cup, cub (for vowel duration).

The cleft palate children were within normal limits on all these measures.

### 3. Measurements of tongue-palate contact

### The electropalatograph

Details of the timing and location of tongue contacts with the hard palate were recorded by the technique of electropalatography (EPG). In the Reading system (see Hardcastle 1984, Hardcastle et al 1987), each subject wears a thin acrylic plate, custom-made from a plaster impression of the upper palate and teeth and extending from the alveolar ridge to the junction between the hard and soft palates. Embedded in the surface of the plate are 62 silver electrodes arranged according to a pre-determined schema based on anatomical landmarks such as the front incisors and the junction between hard and soft palates. In spite of surgical intervention, these landmarks were discernible for the cleft-palate children and enabled the electrodes to be placed so that comparison could be made between these and normal subjects (for a fuller description of the rationale behind this schema see Hardcastle 1984). Figure 6.2 shows the artificial palates constructed for Carl and Tim and for a normal child.

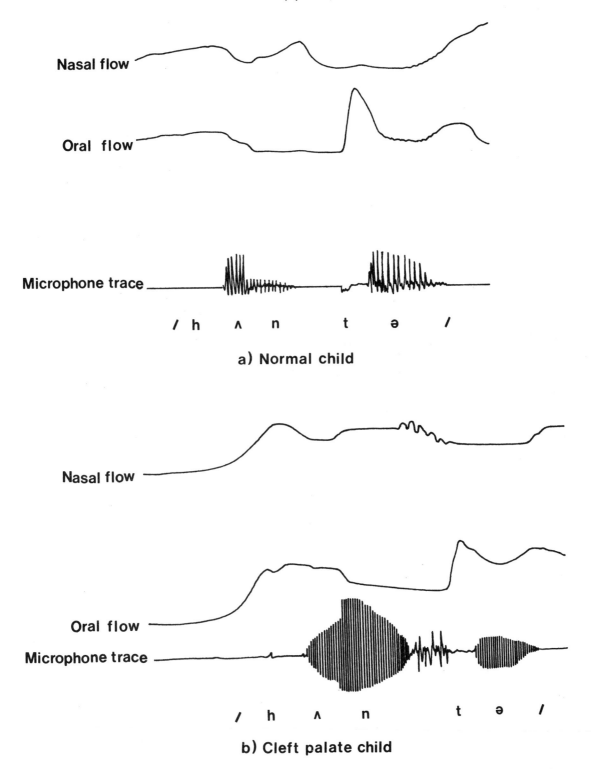

**Fig 6.1** Oral and nasal air flow and acoustic signal trace during production of the word 'hunter' by: (A) a normal child; (B) a cleft-palate subject

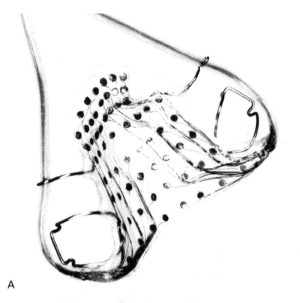

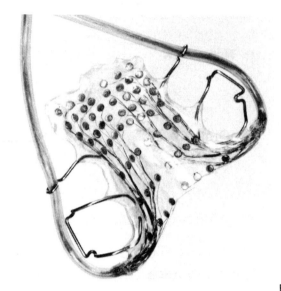

A

B

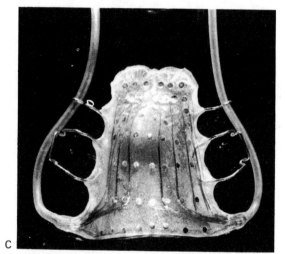

C

**Fig 6.2** Artificial palates for: (A) Carl (B) Tim (C) a normal child

In the normal operation of the system, when contact occurs between the tongue and any of the electrodes, a signal is conducted via lead-out wires to an external processing unit which enables the patterns of contact to be displayed on the VDU of a microcomputer (see technical details in Jones 1984). Figures 6.3 and 6.4 show the various components of the system and the system in operation respectively.

Permanent records of the tongue palate contacts can be obtained in the form of a computer print-out such as in Figure 6.5. This print-out shows the tongue palate contacts that occur during production of the word 'KitKat' by a normal speaker. In this form of print-out, patterns of contact are shown as small palate diagrams 10 ms apart which can be read from left to right like a cine-film. The display both on the VDU and in the print-out shows a schematic representation of the electrodes as places on the plate. Figure 6.6 shows an enlarged single palate diagram with articulatory zones marked according to conventional phonetic place descriptions.

Each subject was provided with a trainer plate, without electrodes, which was worn for increasing periods of time, including at least one 24-hour period prior to the first EPG recording session, so that he might become accustomed to the sensation of the plate in the mouth and allow the speech patterns to adapt to plate wear. Every effort was made to ensure the plates fitted exactly against the hard palate so that any potential interference with articulation due to the presence of the device was minimised.

Both boys recorded four repetitions of four word-lists, which consisted of 43 single-word

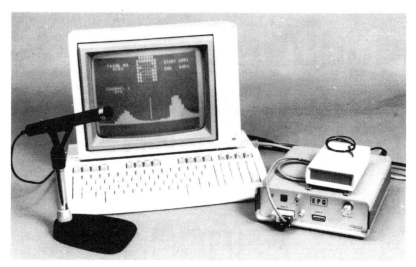

**Fig 6.3** The equipment used for electropalatography

**Fig 6.4** The electropalatography system being used by a therapist and child

items presented as flashcards containing both the written word and a pictorial representation. The words contained all the lingual consonants of English in a variety of vowel and consonant cluster environments (see Table 6.3). From the permanent EPG print-outs obtained, it was possible to describe the children's lingual articulations in various phonetic contexts. An audio-recording was taken simultaneously from which narrow phonetic transcriptions were made (Table 6.3), and these were then compared with the visual

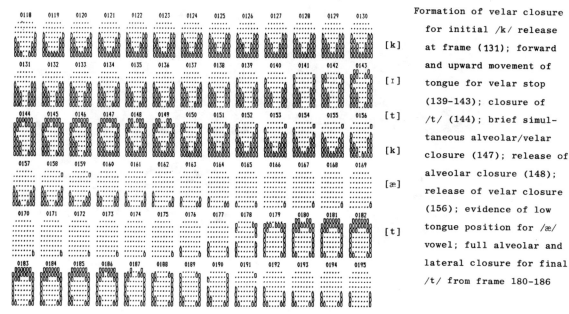

Formation of velar closure for initial /k/ release at frame (131); forward and upward movement of tongue for velar stop (139-143); closure of /t/ (144); brief simultaneous alveolar/velar closure (147); release of alveolar closure (148); release of velar closure (156); evidence of low tongue position for /æ/ vowel; full alveolar and lateral closure for final /t/ from frame 180-186

[k]
[ɪ]
[t]
[k]
[æ]
[t]

**Fig. 6.5** An EPG print-out showing tongue-palate contacts during a normal speaker's production of the word 'kitkat'. Sampling rate was 100 Hz

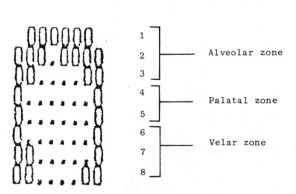

Row no.

1 ⎤
2 ⎥ Alveolar zone
3 ⎦
4 ⎤
5 ⎦ Palatal zone
6 ⎤
7 ⎥ Velar zone
8 ⎦

**Fig 6.6** An enlarged frame from an EPG print-out showing the arrangement of the electrodes into three articulatory zones

patterns provided by the EPG. For both the children, the visual data either:

a. Confirmed normal sounds
b. Confirmed the deviant sounds already subjectively noted
c. Partially explained deviant sounds noted
d. Provided additional information on sounds which were auditorily acceptable.

### Results of EPG investigation

#### EPG patterns for Carl

The *velars* /k, g, ŋ/ and *lateral* /l/ were confirmed by the EPG patterns to be within normal limits in that there was evidence of complete posterior closure for the velars and anterior closure with a partial lateral seal for the laterals. These patterns remained clearly defined when produced either as single consonants or as elements in clusters.

The *fricatives* /s, z, ʃ/ were perceived and transcribed as having a lateral fricative quality [ɬ]. For perceptual data of single consonant see Table 6.4. When compared with the normal, the EPG patterns for /s/ and /z/ showed no evidence of grooving in the alveolar zone, the tongue making complete contact with the palate across this zone, and there was extensive contact also in the velar and palatal zones (cf. Michi et al 1986). Figure 6.7 shows patterns produced for the fricative in 'zoo'. Similar patterns occurred for /s/. For /ʃ/ extensive contact occurred also but was generally more retracted (Fig. 6.8). Because of the lack of a grooved configuration for central

**Table 6.3** Transcriptions of final repetition of the EPG word-list

| Gloss | Carl | Tim |
|---|---|---|
| **List A** | | |
| a dart | ə daːtʰ | ə daːʔ |
| a lamb | ə læm | ə læm |
| a cot | ə k ʰɒtʰ | ə k ʰɒkt |
| a deer | ə dɪə | ə d̪ɪə |
| a leg | ə lɛgₒ | ə l̪ɛg |
| a chain | ə tjeɪn | ə kjeɪn |
| a shark | ə ɬaːk | ə ʃaːk |
| a key | ə kʰiː | ə k ʰiː |
| the dolls | də dɒuɣ | ə gdəuʒ |
| a leaf | ə liːf | ə liːf |
| a book | ə buːkʰ | ə buːkʰ |
| a well | ə wɛʊ | ə wɛʊ |
| a car | ə k ʰaː | ə k ʰaː |
| a girl | ə gɛːʊ | ə gɛːʊ |
| a beak | ə biːkʰ | ə biːkʰ |
| a knot | ə nɒt | ə ŋɒk |
| **List B** | | |
| a sun | ə ɬʌn | ə çɛn |
| a mouse | ə mauɬ | ə mauç |
| a fish | ə fɪɬ | ə fɪʃ |
| a zoo | ə ɬuː | ə çuː |
| a sheep | ə ɬiːp | ə ʃiːp |
| a brush | ə bɹʌç | ə bɹʌʃ |
| a seed | ə ɬiːd | ə çiːd |
| a shop | ə ɬɒp | ə çɒp |
| a bush | ə buɬ | ə buʃ |
| a shoe | ə ɬuː | ə ʃuː |
| a racer | ə ɹeɪɬə | ə ɹeɪçə |
| **List C** | | |
| the salt | ə ɬɒutʔ | ə çɒuʔ |
| a Kitkat | ə k ʰɪʔkæʔ | ə kʰɪʔkæʔ |
| a headlight | | ə hɛgəlaɪʔ |
| a clock | ə klɒkʰ | ə klɒkʰ |
| a tractor | ə tɹæktɔ | ə kɹæʔkɔ |
| the Hulk | də hʌuk | nə hʌuk |
| a catkin | ə kʰæʔkɪn | ə kʰæʔkɪn |
| a milking | ə mɪəkɪn | ə mɪukʰɪŋ |
| a weekday | ə wiːdeɪ | ə wːkd̪eɪ |
| a tickling | ə tlɪklɪn | ə tʰɪkəlɪn |
| a deckchair | ə dɛktlɛə | ə dgeçɛə |
| **List D** | | |
| a bookshop | ə buʔɬɒp | ə bukçɒp |
| a Welsh | ə wɛʊɬ | ə wɛʊʃ |
| a star | ə ɬtaː | ə k⁼aː |
| crashlanding | kɹæɬlændɪn | kɹæʃjændɪŋ |
| a box | ə bɒkɬ | ə bɒkç |
| a slide | ə ɬlaɪd | ə ɬlaɪd |
| a bikeshop | ə baɪʔɬɒp | ə baɪkçɒp |
| a fishcake | ə fɪɬkeɪkʰ | ə fɪʃkeɪkʰ |
| the hats | ðə hæʔɬ | və hæʔç |
| a squashkit | ə ɬkwɒɬkɪʔ | ə çkwɒçkɪtʰ |
| a skirt | ə ɬkɜːt | ə çkɜːtʰ |

**Table 6.4** Summary of EPG and perceptual data for single consonants

| Consonant target | Carl | Tim |
|---|---|---|
| Alveolar stop and nasal /t, d, n/ | Inconsistent patterns but generally area of contact more posterior than normal. Considerable movement during closure with change from palato-velar to alveolar zones (see Fig. 6.10 and Discussion below). Auditorily within normal limits | Inconsistent patterns with evidence of posterior involvement. Patterns include: complete closure over all or most of the palate; velar closure; or velar and palatal closure. Auditory impressions: [d, d̪, dg] [t, kt] [ŋ, n̪, n] There were no obvious phonetic environmental effects noted |
| Alveolar fricatives /s, z/ | Mostly complete anterior closure with generally more extensive contact in the palatal and velar zones than normal. Auditory impressions: most transcribed as [ɬ], one or two as [ɣ] | Patterns of contact very variable: few instances of anterior grooving, some full anterior closure. Mostly full palatal closure with varying amounts of velar involvement. Some examples of total palatal closure. Auditorily [ç] |
| Palato-alveolar fricatives /ʃ/ | Usually complete or almost complete palatal closure rather than a grooved configuration. More velar involvement than normal. Auditory impression: [ɬ] | Patterns very variable covering all zones of the palate (see Fig. 6.14). One or two examples of a normal palatal grooved configuration, perceived as normal. Auditory impression: most frequently [ʃ] occasionally [x] [tç] and [ʃ] (the latter in close vowel environments) |

*(Table 6.4 contd overleaf)*

**Table 6.4** (contd)

| Consonant target | Carl | Tim |
|---|---|---|
| Lateral /l/ | Patterns of contact were normal with bilateral release. Vowelised in post-vocalic word-final position. Auditorily normal | Anterior constriction rarely with full closure. Sometimes contact appeared on one side only. Auditorily normal |
| Velar stops /k, g/ and nasal /ŋ/ | Normal patterns and auditorily normal | Patterns usually within normal limits with velar constriction or full closure throughout but with much more extensive palatal involvement than normal in close vowel environments (see Fig. 6.11) |

passage of the airstream, the flow is presumably being forced out laterally between the teeth and cheek walls.

The *alveolar stops* /t, d/ and nasal /n/ were subjectively assessed as acceptable although the contact patterns showed some differences from the norm. For example in Figure 6.9 for 'dart', contact for the two alveolar stops was made not only in the expected alveolar region, but also across the other more posterior zones of the palate. A further noticeable feature revealed by the EPG data was that there is considerable forward movement of the tongue during the closure phase of the stop. The contact patterns for the alveolars showed considerable variability both for successive repetitions of the same word and in different environments (see schematic representation of contact patterns in Fig. 6.10 and in discussion below).

The *consonant clusters* were, with the exception of /kl/, found to be variable, with patterns that changed rapidly and continuously through the duration of the cluster elements. This was most apparent where the cluster occurred across a syllable boundary.

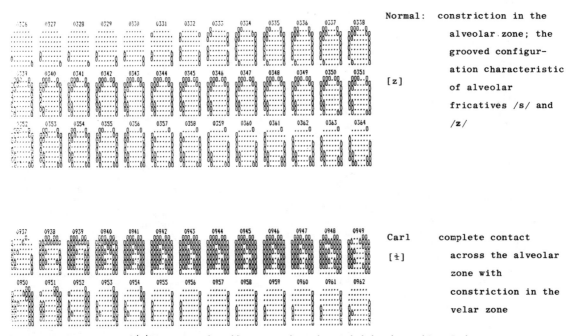

Normal: constriction in the alveolar zone; the grooved configuration characteristic

[z] of alveolar fricatives /s/ and /z/

Carl complete contact

[ɬ] across the alveolar zone with constriction in the velar zone

**Fig 6.7** An EPG print-out of /z/ in 'zoo' produced by a normal speaker and cleft palate subject Carl

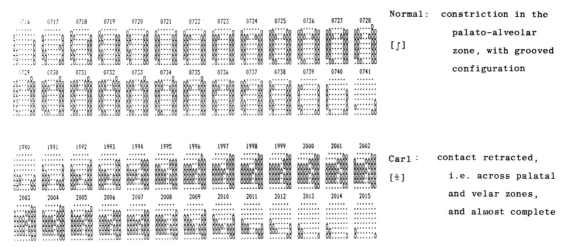

Normal: constriction in the
[ʃ] palato-alveolar
zone, with grooved
configuration

Carl: contact retracted,
[ǂ] i.e. across palatal
and velar zones,
and almost complete

**Fig 6.8** An EPG print-out of /ʃ/ in 'shop' produced by a normal speaker and by Carl

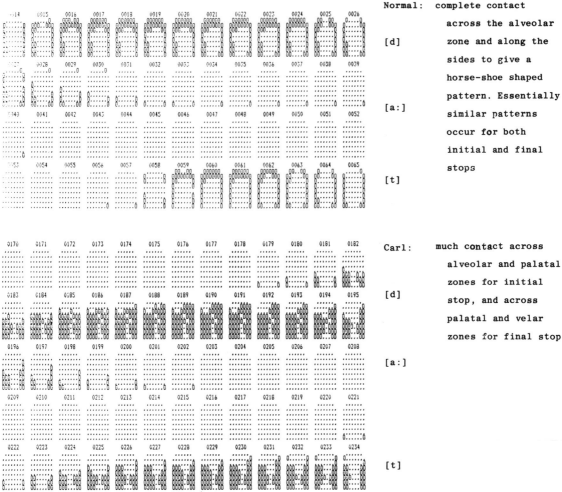

Normal: complete contact
across the alveolar
[d] zone and along the
sides to give a
horse-shoe shaped
pattern. Essentially
[a:] similar patterns
occur for both
initial and final
stops
[t]

Carl: much contact across
alveolar and palatal
zones for initial
[d] stop, and across
palatal and velar
zones for final stop

[a:]

[t]

**Fig 6.9** An EPG print-out of the alveolar stop at the beginning and end of 'dart' produced by a normal speaker and by Carl

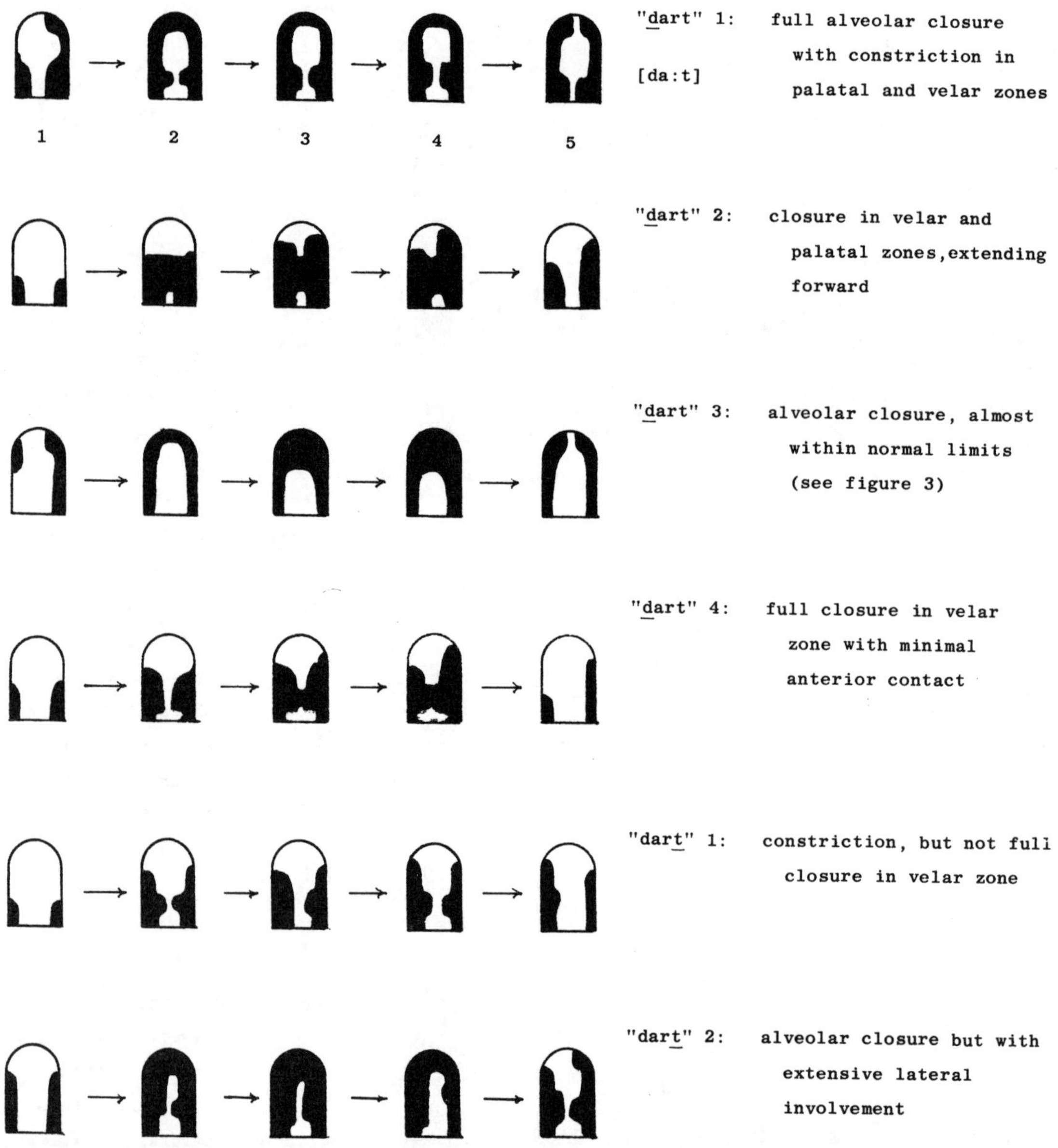

"d̲art" 1:    full alveolar closure
                   with constriction in

[da:t]              palatal and velar zones

"d̲art" 2:    closure in velar and
                   palatal zones, extending
                   forward

"d̲art" 3:    alveolar closure, almost
                   within normal limits
                   (see figure 3)

"d̲art" 4:    full closure in velar
                   zone with minimal
                   anterior contact

"dar̲t" 1:    constriction, but not full
                   closure in velar zone

"dar̲t" 2:    alveolar closure but with
                   extensive lateral
                   involvement

**Fig 6.10** Schematic representations based on the EPG print-outs of the alveolar stops in 'dart' produced by Carl. Four repetitions of initial /d/ and two repetitions of final /t/ are given. These schematic representations are normalised in time, to allow comparisons to be made between the different productions. For each sequence, diagrams 1 and 5 represent the onset and its release respectively; diagrams 2, 3 and 4 are at equal intervals between these two extremes. Each repetition was transcribed as [da:t]

There were some examples of perceived glottal substitutions, for example, 'weekday' [wi: ?deɪ] and 'bookshop' [bʊ: ?ʃɒp]. Generally, however, the elements of the cluster were found to be in accordance with the single consonant data. (For further details of the clusters see Table 6.5.)

*EPG patterns for Tim*

Tim's EPG patterns were characterised by much inconsistency and variability. As with Carl, the velar stops were auditorily acceptable with the EPG patterns mostly within normal limits (see comparison of the two chil-

**Table 6.5** Summary of EPG and perceptual data for consonant clusters

| Cluster-type | Carl | Tim |
|---|---|---|
| *Stop-stop*: 'kit<u>k</u>at' 'cat<u>k</u>in' 'tractor' 'wee<u>k</u>day' | Usually a glottal substitution was heard for first element with the exception of 'tractor'. Velar or palatal contact seen for remaining element. | In many cases glottal substitution heard for first element; velar or full palate contact seen for second element; 'tractor' in one example, was velar throughout the word. Some asymmetric patterns and evidence of metathesis of patterns in 2 repetitions of 'catkin'. |
| *Stop-lateral*: 'clock' 'headlight' 'tickling'; *Lateral-stop*: 'salt' 'hulk' 'milking' | Clearly defined within normal limits. /l/ vowelised with /k/ and /t/ as for singleton data. | Mostly within normal limits but abnormally long delay from [k] release to onset of [l] in 'tickling'. Some anomalies: metathesis of patterns with apical contact occurring <u>after</u> velar placement in 'hul<u>k</u>', 'mil<u>k</u>ing' (Fig. 6.17). Full palatal contact noted for 'salt'. |
| *Fricative-stop*: 'star' 'skirt' 'squashkit' 'fishcake' | Two elements heard but patterns similar so that demarcation was difficult. The stop element showed some undershoot and reduction in length. | 'star' showed full palate contact with velar release; 'skirt' was normal. The /ʃ k/ clusters showed much asymmetry and variability with extensive velar contact throughout. |
| *Stop-fricatives*: 'box' 'hats' 'bikeshop' 'bookshop' | Glottal substitution heard for stop element; abnormally long duration of palatal contacts as compared with normal subjects. | Variations across all repetitions with unusual and asymmetric patterns. |
| *Affricate*: 'chain' | Single full palatal contact pattern. | Slow transitions between elements with patterns not held for any length but changing continuously. 'chain' showed velar or palatal contacts. |
| *Fricative-lateral*: 'slide' 'crashlanding' | Two elements both seen and heard, but longer than normal transitions between them. | Variable and changing throughout closure; complete or alveolar and palatal contact. |
| *Lateral-fricative*: 'welsh' 'dolls' | /l/ vowelised: one element noted as for singleton data. | One example of 'welsh' showed apical followed by palatal contact; the remainder were reduced to one multi-variate contact element. |

dren in Table 6.4), although his patterns for /k/ in the /i/ vowel environment showed more extensive anterior contact than the normal (compare patterns for 'car' and 'key' in Fig. 6.11). The closure duration for the /k/ in 'key' was also abnormally long.

The *lateral* /l/, also auditorily acceptable, showed lack of full closure across the alveolar zone and was sometimes asymmetrical (see Fig. 6.12). This may have been due to apical contact being made between the tongue tip and the back of the front incisors anterior to the first row of contacts on the artificial plate. It should be noted, however, that incomplete closure in the alveolar region frequently occurs for normals in some environments (Hardcastle & Barry 1985).

Subjective auditory assessment of the *alveolar fricative* targets indicated some doubt as to the place of articulation. In most cases some friction was heard but the perceived place ranged from palatal to palatal-alveolar. The EPG patterns showed few instances of the normally expected grooving in the alveolar region, and extensive contact occurred across the palatal zone with varying amounts of velar involvement. There were also some examples of complete contact of the tongue with the whole palate (Fig. 6.13 for 'seed' and 'zoo').

The *palato-alveolar* fricative /ʃ/ was again

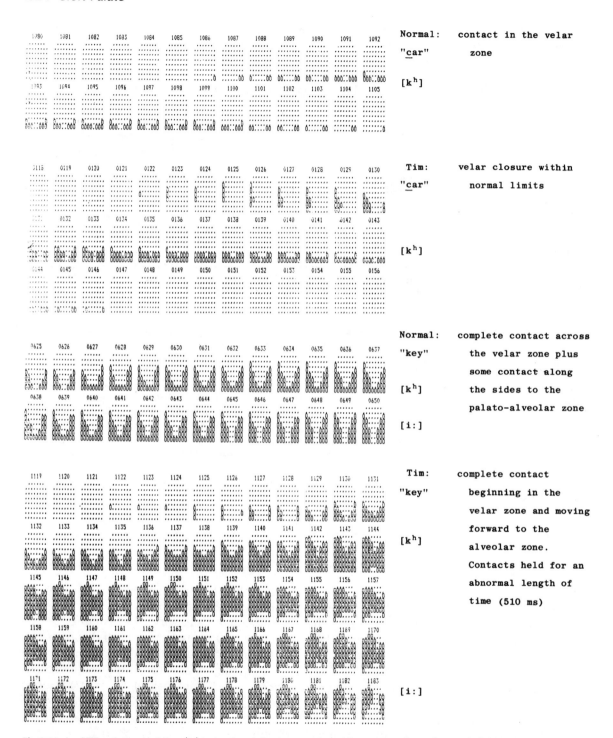

**Fig 6.11** An EPG print-out of the /k/ in 'car' and 'key' as produced by a normal speaker and cleft palate subject Tim

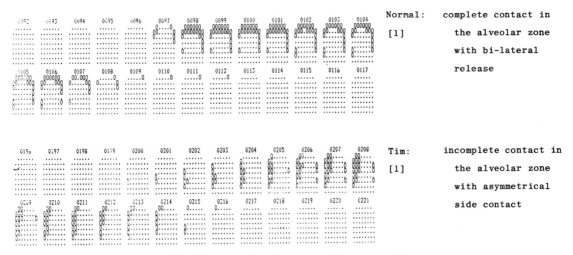

**Fig 6.12** An EPG print-out of the /l/ in 'lamb' produced by a normal speaker and by Tim

seen to be variable with maximum lingual contact being made either anteriorly, or posteriorly or both, and with the amount of contact varying. This inconsistency of tongue placement did not appear to be dependent on either the vowel environment or position in the word. Figure 6.14 shows schematic representations of the different patterns produced for two repetitions each of the words 'shoe', 'sheep', 'bush' and 'fish'. Contact patterns included: full anterior closure, full closure in the palatal zone, simultaneous alveolar/velar closure, almost complete contact throughout the hard palate.

The *alveolar stops* /t, d/ and the *nasal* /n/ can be seen from the phonetic transcription to be less acceptable auditorily, having in some instances a detectable velar element or substitution. This was verified by the EPG patterns, which showed either complete contact over all or most of the palate, or velar contact only, or velar plus palatal contact for alveolars in different environments (Fig. 6.15 for 'knot', 'sun' and 'deer') and for successive repetitions of the same word (Fig. 6.16 for three repetitions of 'dart' and for two repetitions of 'dart'). The retracted placement, noted for 'knot' and 'deer' and for most of the repetitions of 'dart', was observed also in some repetitions of Carl's tokens and has

frequently been mentioned in the literature as one of the articulatory features of cleft palate speech (e.g. Michi et al 1986, Edwards 1980).

The *consonant cluster data* (see summary in Table 6.5) showed one or two reductions, e.g. 'star' [k⁼a:], and some interesting anomalies such as metathesis seen in contact pattern, e.g. in two repetitions of 'catkin' and in 'hulk', 'milking' (see Fig. 6.17 for 'milking'), together with some examples which were almost within normal limits. It would appear that an increase in articulatory complexity led to an increase in variability and deviance.

The EPG data for both children are summarised in Tables 6.4 and 6.5.

## Discussion of EPG results

The general picture that emerges for the two cleft palate children is one of variability of tongue contact with the palate for both alveolar and palatal sounds. Figure 6.10 and 6.16 show schematic representations of the contact patterns for successive repetitions of the word 'dart' for both Carl and Tim, showing variability in both the location of contact across different zones of the palate (alveolar, palatal and velar) and also the amount of contact which ranged from partial constriction to full closure. Similar inconsistencies were

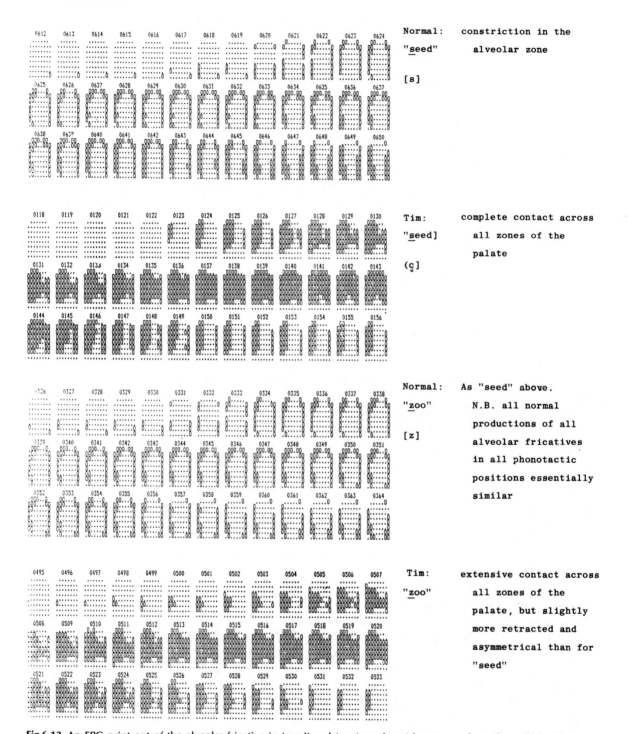

**Fig 6.13** An EPG print-out of the alveolar fricative in 'seed' and 'zoo' produced by a normal speaker and by Tim

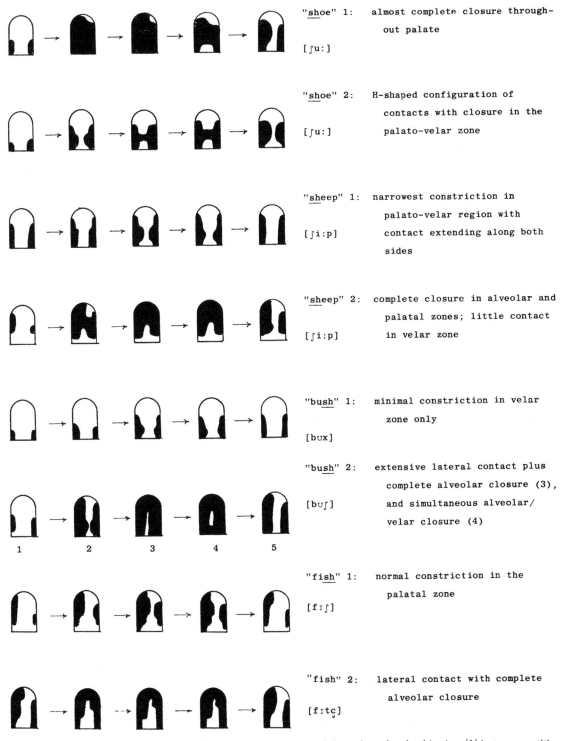

**Fig 6.14** Schematic representations based on the EPG print-outs of the palato-alveolar fricative /ʃ/ in two repetitions each of 'shoe', 'sheep', 'bush' and 'fish' produced by Tim. (For normal patterns see Figure 6.5.)

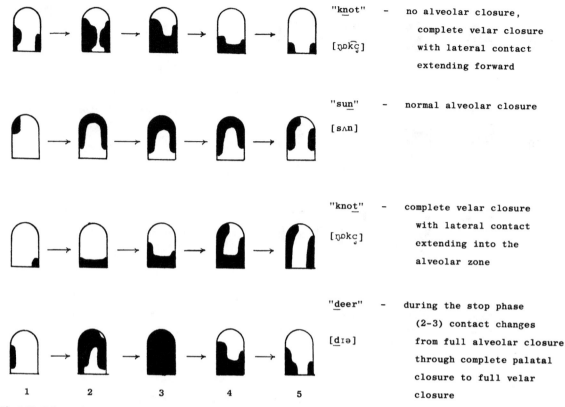

"kn<u>o</u>t"     –     no alveolar closure,
                      complete velar closure
[ŋɒk͡ç]           with lateral contact
                      extending forward

"su<u>n</u>"     –     normal alveolar closure
[sʌn]

"kno<u>t</u>"    –     complete velar closure
                      with lateral contact
[ŋɒkc̬]           extending into the
                      alveolar zone

"<u>d</u>eer"    –     during the stop phase
                      (2–3) contact changes
[dɪə]            from full alveolar closure
                      through complete palatal
                      closure to full velar
                      closure

1        2        3        4        5

**Fig 6.15** Schematic representation based on the EPG print-outs of the alveolar stops in 'knot', 'sun' and 'deer' produced by Tim

noted for the alveolar stops when they occurred in different vowel and consonant environments. Figure 6.15 illustrates, again schematically, the different patterns for Tim's production of the alveolars in 'knot' and 'sun' and 'deer' (see also Fig. 6.14 for the varying patterns Tim produced for the palato-alveolar fricative /ʃ/).

Although the patterns of contact were noticeably variable, nevertheless for both children some general tendencies emerged in the patterns they produced. Firstly, for these children there was generally more contact in the posterior zones of the palate than for a normal child's production. In some cases this was associated with a generally more retracted tongue position (e.g. Fig. 6.8 for Carl). In other cases there was no evidence of general tongue retraction, rather the back of the tongue seemed to be raised closer to the palate. This posterior involvement of the tongue has been frequently noted by other investigators as one of the main articulatory characteristics of cleft palate speech (Edwards 1980). A second general tendency was for both children to have relatively more extensive tongue palate contact than normal throughout the palate, frequently resulting in a full closure pattern (see Fig. 6.16 for Tim). This general tendency for increased contact area could perhaps be interpreted as inability to manipulate the tongue tip/blade system independently of the main body of the tongue, necessary, for example, in the production of alveolar and palato-alveolar fricatives. The tongue consequently appears almost to be moving around the oral region as a single undifferentiated mass, thus leading to more

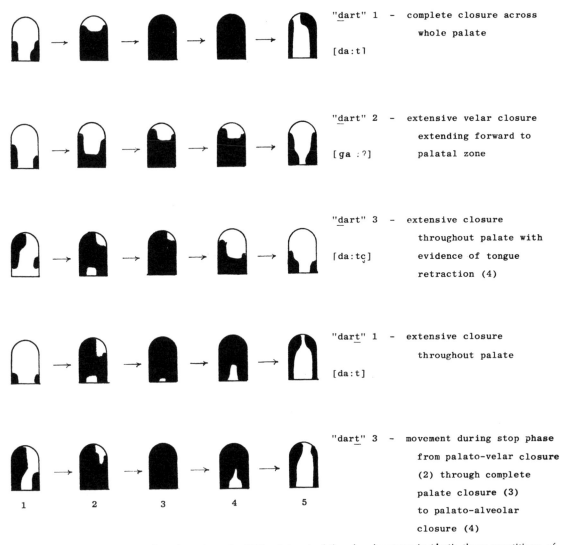

**Fig 6.16** Schematic representations based on the EPG print-out of the alveolar stops in 'dart': three repetitions of initial /d/ and two repetitions of final /t/; Tim's production

extensive contact and perhaps also to more posterior contact.

Thus it would seem that both boys had difficulty in achieving the accurate motions and configurations of the tongue required for obstruent sounds, even though the speech task required (production of isolated words) was relatively straightforward. In the test procedure each item was preceded by the indefinite or definite article in order to ensure

that the initial tongue position was relatively consistent. But even for these word-initial consonants, when the tongue was required to move from the relatively constant starting position, alveolar and palato-alveolar sounds caused difficulties. For Carl the alveolar stops remained auditorily acceptable, but the fricatives requiring particularly fine precision and accuracy varied in the placement and configuration of the tongue and were identified as

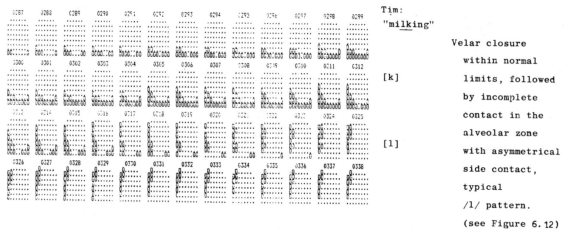

**Fig 6.17** An EPG print-out of the /lk/ cluster in 'milking', produced by Tim

'diffuse'. The failure to achieve precise target movements in the single word items became increasingly obvious in the more complex sequences with consonant clusters. For both Carl and Tim increased complexity of the text items led to increased deviance with unusual asymmetric and variable patterns emerging (Fig. 6.17 showing metathesis during /lk/).

### Possible reasons for persisting speech problems

A number of factors may be considered contributory to the articulatory difficulties of these children. First, both had a degree of hearing loss which had been fluctuating in severity during the speech acquisition years, and at the time of the EPG study may well have been a contributory factor to self-monitoring and self-awareness, particularly with Carl. This was confirmed during the therapy sessions.

Second, both boys had unrepaired hard palates, with fistulae remaining unrepaired until 7 years and 6 months (Carl) and 5 years and 5 months (Tim). This was accepted surgical procedure, but according to studies of speech of children with late hard palate repair (e.g. Cosman & Falk 1980) articulatory difficulties are found to continue in such cases. The unrepaired hard palates may have impaired the development of normal tongue

function, both by establishing abnormal sucking patterns during infancy, and by allowing the tongue tip to occlude the fistulae as compensatory action during speech movements. This may have given rise to impaired tongue activity and awareness, resulting in the abnormal and variable target positioning for the alveolar and palatal sounds. Another factor related to this aspect of speech production is that, for these children, surgical procedures to close the hard palate resulted in the presence of insensitive scar tissue at the alveolar and palatal zones, thus reducing tactile awareness further. The importance of tactile and proprioceptive awareness in the development of speech motor control and planning has been noted in Chapter 1. For further discussion see Kent (1976a and b) and Laver (1980).

The articulatory patterns reported in this study are frequently found in cleft palate cases. However, it is possible that a further factor, that of a concomitant oral and/or articulatory dyspraxia, may be present in these children, thus giving rise to the variability of tongue placement already noted. On the other hand, the factors mentioned above, which may have resulted in faulty feedback systems, could well lead to a dyspraxic-like disturbance with similar effects of inaccuracy of positioning to those of a 'true' dyspraxia.

In both cases, there is detriment to speech acceptability.

A further factor made clear by the use of EPG is that of the children's palate size and shape. In the present study both boys had flat, low-arched, narrow palates, such that the tongue would not need to be raised very high to make total contact across the palate in the mid-region, i.e. behind the alveolar ridge, thus making accurate tongue-tip placement for /t, d, s, z/ even more difficult. According to Laine (1986) there is a tendency for subjects with distortions of the /s/ sound, produced mainly too posteriorly, to have slightly narrower palates than subjects with correct /s/ sound (see also Lubit 1967). In Tim's case, there was a degree of maxillary hypoplasia, giving rise to a class III malocclusion and causing problems with the relationship of upper to lower teeth. This resulted in restricted intra-oral space with consequent retrogressive tongue-movement (see Edwards 1980 for a discussion on retro-placement of the tongue in these instances).

It is possible, therefore, that for these children, a combination of factors may be operating: inadequate hearing during the early years of speech development; the establishment of abnormal tongue movements due to the presence of a fistula; the presence of scar tissue and the size and shape of the palate after final surgery, some or all of which preclude the possibility of the tongue making the fine adjustments within the oral cavity for the production of accurate movements for acceptable speech sounds.

## THERAPEUTIC INTERVENTION

It may be useful at this point to outline the factors that can limit the achievements of therapy, and to note where EPG as a remediation technique may help to minimise these factors. It is becoming increasingly important to evaluate the efficacy of speech therapy; in judgemental terms, this means monitoring the patient's progress against the general and ultimate goal of clear, intelligible and acceptable speech. But this goal is not always readily achieved, and there are a number of reasons why therapy may have limited success.

### Reasons for limited success in therapy

It may be due to the *physical and/or physiological limitations* of the patient. This is obvious in terms of the severity of the disorder (dysarthria or dyspraxia for example), less obvious where other factors such as available energy levels, attentional ability or general health and well-being are uncertain.

### *Intellectual limitations*

Children with lower than average mental ability have more of a struggle (and their achievements are therefore greater).

### *Motivation*

Much of patient management is to do with demonstrating the need to use language, and to use it acceptably. If change is to be effected, it must be seen to be desirable. This links with the habit factor.

### *The habit factor*

Persistent speech 'errors' become part of the child's self-image—how he/she presents to the world. In some instances, the child may be aware of, and dislike this image, especially if listener feedback is negative; here the motivation to change may be high. In other cases, where the child *is* accepted by family, friends and the peer group, the habit factor persists and motivation may be low. This was felt to be a factor for Carl, one of the subjects described in this study. Examples have been quoted of cleft palate children who have been well aware of the 'correct' sounds, but have been heard to say they preferred their own (Morley 1979).

These first four factors are closely interlinked; they also overlap with a further three:

## Difficulty with metalinguistic awareness

However simply this is presented, at some point a patient needs to be able to appreciate speech at this level—in terms, for example, of understanding what speech consists of, its constituent elements (e.g. phonemes, syllables), and their structure, dynamics and usage. Therapists frequently encounter the problem of trying to elicit a sound that is not within the patient's sound system; where direct imitation is not possible, the task is a metalinguistic one.

## Irregular and intermittent attendance at clinic

This is a contributory factor due to a variety of reasons.

## Inadequate therapy

An essential part of the evaluative process is to weigh up all possible factors that may be preventing out-patients' progress and ask finally—how adequate is the treatment being provided? How can it be improved?

## THE USE OF VISUAL FEEDBACK IN THERAPY

What then can a visual feedback technique, such as EPG, offer to answer the last question, or to help to overcome some of the above difficulties and help the patient move nearer to an adequate speech goal?

With reference to the above factors: the physical and physiological limitations will remain, so too the intellectual ones, and, indeed, the use of an additional feedback technique may be contra-indicated in such cases, being more than the child can cope with. However, for improving motivation, assisting a child to overcome the habit factor and improve metalinguistic awareness, it can be very useful indeed. Failure to attend clinic affects overall patient management, and it was found that, to be of maximum value, therapy sessions with the EPG needed to be both regular and frequent. With reference to the

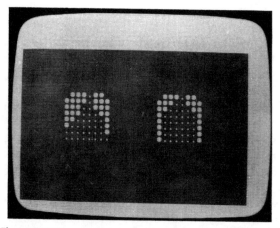

**Fig 6.18** VDU screen showing therapist's production of a normal /s/ (right) with child's attempt at replicating this (left)

last point, the questions it raises, it must be said that unless therapy is planned and based on the assessments, needs and abilities of the individual, and set within the framework of the patient as a whole person, then it cannot be adequate however many sophisticated instrumental techniques are used.

In the therapy programme described here, the electropalatograph was used as a feedback tool enabling the cleft palate children to monitor their own tongue contact patterns as they spoke. In the current system, two schematic palatal diagrams are displayed on the VDU: one diagram containing prescribed patterns of contact in real-time by the therapist, and the other the child's attempts at replicating these. Figure 6.18 shows the VDU screen during production of an /s/ by the therapist and child. Figure 6.4 shows a typical therapy situation with both child and therapist connected to the machine and patterns of contact displayed on the VDU.

### Therapy for Carl and Tim

The individual therapeutic programmes devised for Carl and Tim were based on both the diagnostic findings, and on the guidelines which had been formulated as a result of a pilot study on the use of EPG as a visual feedback device. The therapeutic guidelines are as follows:

1. Demonstrate the link between the speech sounds and the visual display for a normal speaker:
   a. in isolation
   b. in VCV syllables with different vowels
   c. in single-syllable words (VC, CVC, etc.)
   d. in two-syllable words (e.g. 'catkin')
   e. with consonant clusters (e.g. 'clock', 'skate')

2. Establish, for the subject, a link between:
   a. the visual display and random tongue movements
   b. visual display and specific targets (e.g. tongue-tip to alveolar ridge; back of tongue to back of palate)
   c. visual display and auditory target (e.g. /ata aka/ etc.)
   NB. emphasise proprioceptive/kinaesthetic sensation.

3. Focus subject's attention on normal patterns and sounds:
   a. begin with those the subject already achieves normally
   b. demonstrate those to be worked on.

4. Monitor the subject's production of normal target patterns and pattern movements:
   a. establish normal visual display
   b. add required sound
   c. add dynamic aspects, i.e. moving tongue up to and away from target (e.g. /asa/aka/)
   d. use monosyllabic words carrying no other EPG pattern than the one required (e.g. 'tar','art','pat','boat','top')
   NB. /p, b, m, a/ carry no tongue palate contact in normal speech.

5. Achieve target patterns in a number of articulatory environments in words and phrases from CV, VC, CCV, VCC etc.

6. Maintain target sounds without visual display—possibly practising this at each session.

Specific articulation work for both children concentrated on the following areas:
— more accurate and reliable placement for /t, d, n/

— elicitation of more acceptable fricatives /s, z, ʃ/
— improved auditory and kinaesthetic awareness, (particularly for Carl)
— incorporation of the improved sounds into spontaneous speech.

Although these guidelines are specifically designed for EPG use, many of the principles can be applied to conventional therapy.

### Intervention for Carl

Carl was given 15 1-hour sessions at the hospital at which the cleft palate team was based, for 2 weeks three times weekly, and thereafter on a once-weekly basis, with follow-up and practice being done at home.

Sessions 1 and 2 aimed at achieving *awareness of tongue-tip activity*, both visually and kinaesthetically. Work was done both with the artificial palate using visual feedback, and without it, concentrating on the tactile modality. It was found that he had poor kinaesthetic and proprioceptive awareness for tongue movements, and poor imitative ability, so that the therapist needed to manipulate the tongue with a cotton-bud to achieve changes in tip placement.

Sessions 3 and 4 concentrated on *accuracy of placement* for /t, d, n/, these first being modelled for visual accuracy by the therapist using the EPG. He achieved these quite quickly in CV, VC and CVC words, and work on achieving /ts/ and /dz/ followed. Auditory discrimination for these sounds was added to the sessions, as this was also found to be poor. Self-monitoring was not good, and although he appeared to enjoy the interaction with the computer, he seemed to have difficulty relating what he saw on the screen to his lingual activity. In these sessions, therefore, he was helped to link visual with auditory and tactile feedback.

Session 5 achieved a *separation of /s/ from /t/*, and practice of these sounds individually. An auditorily more acceptable /s/ was achieved when he was not wearing the artificial palate.

Session 6 was a *consolidating* session where

it was found that his auditory discrimination and self-monitoring skills, both with and without visual feedback, were improving.

Sessions 7–11 *worked on the improved sounds*, with special attention to /s, z/, in all phonotactic positions, and in words and phrases. The affricates /tʃ, dʒ/ were also elicited from the improved placing of /t, d/, together with a reasonable approximation of /ʃ/. The visual feedback was phased out after session 11, in an attempt to aid carry-over into everyday speech situations so that he was made to rely on auditory and kinaesthetic feedback for self-monitoring.

### Intervention for Tim

Tim received 5, 1-hour therapy sessions in 2 weeks, and related well to the computerised visual feedback. His auditory skills and kinaesthetic and proprioceptive awareness were good, and he quickly established a good correspondence between the visual patterns, tongue positions and auditory acceptability.

Session 1 introduced the *relationship between the three sensory modalities*, visual, tactile and auditory, and, aided by modelling from the therapist using the EPG, he practised improving his *accuracy of placement* for /t, d, h/.

This was followed by the /ts, dz/ configurations.

Session 2 *incorporated /s/ and /z/ into all phonotactic positions* (following separation from /t/ and /d/) and into short phrases. Improvement in *accuracy and acceptability* was effected, both with and without visual feedback.

Sessions 3 and 4 *elicited /tʃ, dʒ/ and /ʃ/*, and incorporated these into single words and phrases, while session 5 aimed to *consolidate* his improved speech skills. However, it was found that although there was a marked improvement, he continued to have some 'blurring' and lateralisation of velar stops and fricatives (/ks/sk/), especially in close vowel environments.

### Results of therapy for Carl and Tim

Previous therapy at their local speech therapy clinic had brought both children's speech intelligibility up to a reasonable level, in Tim's case by working on improvement of pace and rhythm, but for both Carl and Tim, particular sounds remained unacceptable. Both were aware of this, and keen to continue therapy and take part in the experimental use of visual feedback. As the results were different for each child, they will be given separately.

### Results of intervention with Carl

After 15 hours of therapy, initially given on an intensive basis, Carl was able to achieve reasonable alveolar and palato-alveolar fricatives, according to the assessment of the therapist, in all positions in single words and in careful speech and reading in the clinic situation. However, this was not maintained outside the clinic, and there was little carry-over into everyday speech. One reason for this may have been a psychological one: the 'new speech sounds' were not acceptable to him; he said he did not like the new patterns (Morley 1979). This may have been due to the fact that he was still having to speak rather carefully, deliberately and more slowly than usual to make the placements correctly, and this may have felt and sounded unnatural to him. Also, his previous speech pattern, although modified by therapy, had become part of how he presented himself to others, and assuming that he was acceptable to his family and peer group, a change in his self-image would need a corresponding change in his self-constructs. Further therapy, aiming at practising his new lingual skills until they could be achieved with ease, as well as changing his self-constructs to accommodate the new speech, would seem to be indicated.

### Results of intervention with Tim

Tim quickly established for himself new patterns of improved accuracy and quality for the alveolar stops, the fricatives /s, z, ʃ/ and the affricates in all word positions and carefully controlled speech situations. He continued to monitor pace and rhythm at the same time, but, again, carry-over into everyday speech was mitigated against by the habit of years. The remaining difficulty he had, that of producing a good /s/ when combined with a velar stop, may have been due to the anatomical limitations of a very shallow-arched palate.

## Conclusion

It would obviously have been advantageous to assess the children's articulations with the EPG after the therapeutic intervention, but due to a variety of factors such as availability of the children, changes in their oral growth and development, this was not possible. The accurate phonetic representation of disordered cleft palate speech is known to be difficult, given abnormal intra-oral structural relationships, and therefore abnormal oral acoustics. A visual display such as that provided by EPG can give reasonably accurate information about tongue placement and activity, and is therefore of special value with cleft palate children. It could also be of value in any case where poor tongue placement is identified. As we have shown from the work with these two children, auditory-based transcription will not provide such precise information. The therapeutic use of the visual feedback technique enabled these boys to monitor their tongue target positions more accurately, particularly in respect of tip and blade placements, although they differed in the amount of help and practice each needed to achieve this. Linking visual clues with kinaesthetic and auditory feedback proved more difficult for Carl than for Tim; nonetheless, speech improvement was effected for them both, and continued when the visual modality was phased out.

## ACKNOWLEDGEMENTS

Thanks are due to Chris Clark, Gavin Gregg and to the staff of the Speech Research Laboratory, University of Reading, for assistance in carrying out this project. The work was funded by a British Medical Research Council grant (Grant No. G8201596N) held by the senior author.

## REFERENCES

Bzoch K R 1965 Articulation proficiency and error patterns of pre-school cleft palate and normal children. Cleft Palate Journal 2: 340

Bzoch K R 1971 Introduction to Section B: Categorical aspects of cleft palate speech. In: Grabbe W O, Rosenstein S W and Bzoch K R (eds) Cleft lip and palate. Little Brown, Boston

Cosman B, Falk A S 1980 Delayed hard palate repair and speech deficiencies: a cautionary report. Cleft Palate Journal 17: 27

Edwards 1980 Assessment and remediation of speech. In: Edwards M, Watson A C H (eds) Advances in the management of cleft palate. Churchill Livingstone, Edinburgh

Green M C 1960 Speech analysis of 263 cleft palate cases. Journal of Speech and Hearing Disorders 25: 43

Hardcastle W J 1984 New methods of profiling lingual palatal contact patterns with electropalatography. Phonetics Laboratory University of Reading. Work in Progress. 4: 1

Hardcastle W J 1985 Instrumental articulatory phonetics. Linguistic Abstracts 1: 111

Hardcastle W J, Barry W J 1985 Articulatory and perceptual factors in /l/ vocalisation in English. Phonetics Laboratory University of Reading 5: 31

Hardcastle W J, Morgan Barry R A, Clark C J 1985 Articulatory and voicing characteristics of adult dysarthric and verbal dyspraxic speakers: and instrumental study. British Journal of Disorders of Communication 20: 249

Hardcastle W J, Morgan R A 1982 An instrumental investigation of articulation disorders in children. British Journal of Disorders of Communication 17: 47

Hardcastle W J, Morgan Barry R A, Clark C J 1987 An instrumental study of lingual activity in articulation-disordered children. Journal of Speech and Hearing Research 30: 171–184

Henningsson G E, Isberg A M 1986 Velopharyngeal movement patterns in patients alternating between oral and glottal articulation: a clinical and cineradiographical study. Cleft Palate Journal 23: 1

Jones W 1984 A micro-computer-controlled electro-palatograph. Phonetics Laboratory University of Reading. Work in Progress 4: 41

Kent R D 1976a Anatomical and neuromuscular maturation of the speech mechanism: evidence from acoustic studies. Journal of Speech and Hearing Disorders 19: 421

Kent R D 1976b Models of speech production. In:Lass N J (ed) Contemporary issues in experimental phonetics. Academic Press, New York

Kiritani S, Itoh K, Fujimura O 1975 Tongue-pellet tracking by a computer controlled X-ray microbeam system. Journal of the Acoustic Society of America 57(6): 1516

Laine T 1986 Articulatory disorders in speech as related to size of the alveolar arches. European Journal of Orthodontics 8: 192

Laver J 1980 Neurolinguistic control of speech production. In: Fromkin V A (ed) Errors in linguistic performance. Academic Press, London

Lawrence C W, Philips B J 1975 A telefluoroscopic study of lingual contact made by persons with palatal defects. Cleft Palate Journal 12: 85

Lubit E C 1967 The relationship of malocclusion and faulty speech articulation. Journal of Medicine 22: 47

Michi K I, Suzuki N, Yamashita Y, Imai S 1986 Visual training and correction of articulation disorders by use of dynamic palatography. Serial observation in a case of cleft palate. Journal of Speech and Hearing Disorders 51: 226

Morley M E 1979 Cleft palate and speech, 7th Edn. Churchill Livingstone, Edinburgh

Perkell J, Cohen M 1985 Design and construction of an alternating magnetic field system for transducing articulatory movements in the mid-sagittal plane. Paper presented at 109th meeting of the Acoustic Society of America, Austen, USA

Trost J E 1981 Articulatory additions to the classical description of the speech of persons with cleft palate. Cleft Palate Journal 18: 198

Van Demark D R 1974 Some results of speech therapy for children with cleft palate. Cleft Palate Journal 11: 41

Warren O W, Dalston R M, Trier W C, Holder M B 1985 A pressure-flow technique for quantifying temporal patterns of palatopharyngeal closure. Cleft Palate Journal 22: 11

*Introduction*
*The team working with the cleft palate child*
*Models of parent–professional relationships*
  *The expert model*
  *The transplant model*
  *The partnership model*

*The parents' views*
  *Collecting the information*
  *Anticipating a problem*
  *Finding out about the problem*
  *Reactions of society*
  *Feeding*
  *Coping with operations*
  *Coping in society; teenage and beyond*

*Summary from the parent group*
*How the speech therapist may foster parent/professional partnerships*
*List of useful addresses*

# 7

# Towards partnership with parents

*P. Phillips   J. Stengelhofen*

## INTRODUCTION

When this chapter was originally envisaged it was to be entitled 'Partnership with parents'; however, during its development it became evident that this was too ambitious a title. It is hoped that what follows will be viewed constructively and will help to establish ways in which more positive relationships might be fostered. The plan was that this chapter would consist mainly of parental views collected through one local branch of a parent support group in the U.K. This organisation is known as the Cleft Lip and Palate Association (CLAPA). It is a self-help parent group with charitable status. The chapter has been prepared by the Chairman of one local group, who provided the collated parental views, together with an introduction and commentary by the editor of this volume. Parent support groups, for many different handicapping conditions, are of value in providing mutual support to reduce feelings of isolation, as well to provide opportunities for joint discussion of problems (Hannon 1975, Irwin & McWilliams 1973). Professionals have a responsibility to listen to what parent groups have to say and to examine their own practices within the context of the insights provided. It is acknowledged that the views of one local group may not be representative of the experiences in other localities. Individual professionals and parents will be able to make these judgements. The views do, however, provide an opportunity to consider these parents' experiences in the broader context of ways professionals and parents relate to each other, while current practice for children with cleft palate can be compared to those practices reported in the literature.

Parent and professional partnership in working with children who have cleft lip and palate involves the interface of parents with a number of different professionals. It also requires the effective working together of the professionals themselves. In the first instance the professionals involved need to work together at the complex area of communication; if good communication has been set up between the professionals they will be more likely to effectively meet the needs of the parents and children coming into their care. Conflicting views from professionals can exacerbate parental anxiety and lead to lack of trust and disillusionment. The problems of a real partnership lie with every team member including the parents. Where professional members have not developed to a stage where they view each other as having equivalent expertise, they are not likely to see parents as possessing the ability to make an equal contribution (Wolfendale 1984). Lack of equal expertise recognition is often reported between the medical and so called 'paramedical' professions.

In a sociological model of interaction, all individuals have certain anticipated roles. In relation to medicine, parents, and children when they are old enough, traditionally expect to play a passive role. This parental expectation may put pressure on individual professionals to behave in expected ways. Consequently, if the professional does behave in an anticipated controlling way, the parent will behave passively and both sides are locked into roles based on prior experience (Tuckett 1976).

## THE TEAM WORKING WITH THE CLEFT PALATE CHILD

Most parents and professionals having their first experience of involvement with a baby or child with a cleft palate may not be fully aware of all the people who need to be involved. Team members may work in a number of different settings; these settings may in themselves be influential in colouring the parental view of the nature of the relationship. For example, professionals working in a hospital may be perceived as far more medical than the same professionals when working within the community. In addition to the parents, the initial team may include midwife, nurses, paediatrician, orthodontist and surgeon. Later the team may extend to include health visitor, speech therapist, ENT consultant, radiographer and audiologist and later still to include teachers and possibly psychologists. Some professionals may only be involved at birth, or in the post-natal period, while others may have input at different stages of the child's development. Surgery, orthodontics and speech therapy frequently need to continue into adolescence and adulthood. The view parents have of professionals will be influenced by the setting in which they work, by the kind of jobs they carry out and by the frequency and type of contact they have with them and their child. Before considering the particular instance of the child with cleft palate, it may be valuable to consider models of parent–professional relationships.

## MODELS OF PARENT–PROFESSIONAL RELATIONSHIPS

For professionals and parents to learn to work together effectively it is necessary to consider the various ways in which parent–professional relationships can be described. Cunningham & Davis (1985) describe three different ways. These three types of relationship are termed the expert, the transplant and the consumer.

## The expert model

The expert model has been traditionally used by medicine and those professionals termed 'helping'. In this model the professionals are viewed as expert because they are seen to take control and make decisions. The parents are seen purely as the receivers of the expert information and skills. Medical and paramedical professionals usually operate within this kind of model. The more technical a professional service becomes the more it is inclined to exclude parents, as they are peripheral to the techniques which can be used by the experts. Although there is no doubt that at times the adoption of an expert model is necessary, it should not be followed rigidly by a professional group throughout the management of an individual child. It is an approach which leads to deskilling of the parents, increases anxiety and inhibits dialogue. Furthermore, because the professional has set him/herself up to be all powerful with parents being dependent, parents' expectations are high, and there are some inevitable disappointments in relation to what the 'experts' are able to offer or achieve. Parents and professionals thus become trapped in a dysfunctional relationship (Cunningham & Davis 1985).

## The transplant model

In the second model, termed transplant, the relationship is one where the professional is viewed as a teacher. In this approach the professional decides on the assessments, sets the goals and defines the methods of intervention for the programme, but involves the parents in carrying this out. In this approach the professional remains the decision-maker. It is an approach used both by health and educational personnel. There may be dangers in it, if the roles taken by parents and professionals are not open to negotiation, as goals and procedures may be clear to the professionals but not clear to the parents. This lack of shared understanding leads to a superficial relationship and may precipitate ambivalent behaviour in parents, which swings from a passive type of co-operation to disagreement and sometimes a power struggle. Real dialogue between parents and professionals may be limited with the professional unaware of the confused state which parents may be in.

Hayhow (1987) poses a further danger in using this approach, believing that parents are best when 'teaching' their children through natural experiences. More formal teaching can result in power struggles and resentment. This can happen if the professional fails to capitalise on parents as informal 'teachers' and expects them to practise drills and exercises. This may interfere with the parent–child relationship and might put the child off set formal work. The situation is too emotionally laden for parents to remain patient with their children's efforts, especially if progress is slow.

The method of involving parents in a 'transplant' approach is now used considerably by health and education professionals, but not as much as one would expect in the context of recent legislation. Under-use of parents by speech therapists using an expert model has been noted (Stengelhofen, 1984).

There is a history in speech therapy of the therapist mainly using a child-centred approach within an expert-type model. This approach is now considered to be limited because it is in danger of ignoring the parent–child interaction, which is the main context in which children learn to communicate. If speech therapists are to change communicative behaviour it is essential that in the first place they take full account of the contextual factors (McDade 1981). McDade describes the use of a transplant model, first focussing on parent and child, then focussing on the child's linguistic needs.

It is recognised, however, that parents are not a homogenous group and therefore that their ability to participate in a programme may vary. Variations in ability may be related to such factors as poor health, housing, unemployment and marital problems, as well as other factors such as cultural and ethnic differences. The team of professionals, hopefully working together to meet a child's needs, should be well enough informed of the family circumstances so that the service offered can take into account the individual family situation.

Parents need to be helped to understand the possible long-term management needs of the child with cleft lip and palate. In the transplant model this has implications for parents' own long-term involvement. If this is not made clear early on, unfulfilled expectations will be inevitable.

## The partnership model

In the third model, the partnership or consumer model, the parents are seen as having the right to make decisions about what they consider is appropriate for their child. This model is based on the natural and legal responsibilities parents have for their children. These responsibilities include the right to 'monitor and evaluate the effectiveness of services provided for them' (Thomas 1982) leading to mutual accountability and progress.

The development of this chapter is within the spirit of the partnership model. Adoption of such a model requires that professionals acknowledge and are willing to attend to the expertise of parents who know most about their child and the total context in which the child functions. In this model the professional is required to become a 'catalyst', 'enabler' and 'supporter' (Pugh 1985). Ways towards achieving partnership in working with the parents of young children with communication problems have been given in Chapter 2 of this volume. The real adoption of such a model helps the professional to avoid the stereotyped views of parents which are all too easily adopted. If the professional has a stereotyped view of a parent there is no way forward in the relationship and the child may be deprived of effective help. The fact that there will be some parents who do not wish to be fully involved in a partnership is

accepted; professionals should always try to establish why this is so. As well as professionals having to change to adopt a partnership model, most parents when seeking health care provision will anticipate the 'expert' model and will need to adjust to a role where their opinions and decisions are sought. The development of altered roles on both sides takes time and effort. One way to foster a partnership is in the setting up of parent support groups and then seeking their views as part of the process of evaluation and monitoring of services. The editor therefore sought the views of a local CLAPA group. What follows is an account of how the information was collected, together with a report of the views expressed, followed by editorial comments on these views.

## THE PARENTS' VIEWS

### Collecting the information

The co-author of this chapter was, at the time of the investigation, chairman of a local CLAPA group. He is also the father of a girl with a unilateral cleft lip and palate. He describes CLAPA'S aims as follows:

1. To provide support and comfort to parents, especially during the early days, before developing an understanding of the professional help available and the ability to judge the seriousness of the defect compared to others.
2. To let doctors, nurses and the other professionals know how parents feel and what problems parents and children encounter in everyday life.

These aims fall clearly within the partnership model. The editor of this volume approached the CLAPA group, and was welcomed to a meeting. In this meeting the format of the present volume was outlined and participation of parents was sought to contribute to a chapter on parent views. There was a positive response and the group decided to go ahead and collect views on a number of identified topics. These topics were suggested and agreed during this initial meeting.

The first task was to mail all the 140 CLAPA members and, through the hospital secretariat, to contact all parents whose children attend the cleft clinic but are not registered as members of CLAPA. Although the main catchment is a mixed urban area there were only three Asian and one Afro-Caribbean family on the CLAPA mailing list.

The mailing explained what had been requested and included a 'memory jogger' to remind parents of various stages in their child's progress they might wish to comment on. It was suggested they recalled: their initial reaction; how they were treated at the birth; how they were told that their child had a defect; how they felt at that time; how they broke the news to relatives and friends; and how these people reacted. They were also invited to recall their own feelings towards the baby, how the medical staff handled the situation, and the help and advice that was made available in the early days. Information was also sought on the subjects of feeding; aftercare provided from clinics, health visitors, speech therapists and others; plus any contact with lay people, such as CLAPA. After the first months, how did the child cope: in developing communication; with the various stages at school; with the sequence of operations and with integrating into society.

10% of CLAPA members responded in writing, plus a welcome number of parents who were not and did not wish to become official members. Most respondents kept fairly rigidly to the format suggested in the 'memory jogger', although it had been emphasised that the less obvious could prove the most valuable.

In addition to asking for views in writing, all parents were invited to attend a forum where they could discuss their views; this gave them the chance to talk over what they had gone through and compare their experience with others. Twenty parents attended. The forum was taped and the Chairman subsequently collated the result of this and the written replies to record the views reported in this chapter.

Some parents chose to write at length rather than share their experiences face-to-face in the forum. The report which follows aims to give the flavour of how parents felt, how they coped and how they rated and related to the professional help offered to them.

In the main, the contributors were in fact active members of CLAPA, speaking from the experience of lay parents, some of whom were also professionals. The CLAPA chairman believes that membership of CLAPA may in fact consist of parents who have come to terms with their child's problem in a positive way. The absence of ethnic minority group families has already been noted. For them and for others whose first language may not be English, there may not be equal opportunity to express feelings and views. The group is aware of its narrow socio-economic and ethnic make-up.

This parent group also felt that there was a major gap in their understanding of problems following puberty. Because CLAPA gets its active membership from parents with a recent experience of having a child with cleft lip and palate, the problems of the adolescent child and the adult are perhaps not well covered by the organisation. However, it is encouraging to note that such is the advance in physical correction of the original defect, as well as a clearer understanding of its effect on the lifestyle of the child, that the experiences of those who are now adult serve mainly as a reminder of how different things were for parent and child not all that long ago.

In the following section the views expressed by parents on a range of topics will be reported first, and, where appropriate, editorial comment will follow. The following topics will be covered:
— Anticipating a problem
— Finding out about the problem
— Feeding problems
— Reaction to operations
— Reactions of society
— Coping in society
— Long-term treatment needs.

## Anticipating a problem, the parents' views

To begin at almost the beginning—with pregnancy — none of the 'panel parents' had the slightest inkling of any problem before the birth. Screening, where it took place, only served to make the final event more poignant. They felt that it is an unimaginative parent indeed who has not worried whether all will be well with the unborn child. The feeling gets more acute with each birth, as the odds of something going wrong appear to get worse. Mostly the unease is pushed to the back of parents' minds, sheltering behind the perpetual armour-plate, 'It only happens to other people'. This confidence-builder is all the stronger when tests are clear; the mother is in good health and there is no family history of cleft lip and palate—which was the case with most members.

### Comment

Parents obviously wish that they will have a perfect child, but it is usual to have fears that their baby may be damaged in some way (Solnit & Stark 1961). This may not be the same as parents having any 'inkling' of any problems before the birth.

When the expectation of a perfect child has to be measured against the reality of a child with some impairment, especially one which is immediately recognisable, such as cleft lip or other facial problem, parents need to build a whole new image of the baby. This is a painful process. It requires considerable adjustment time and may need much support, discussion and reflection. The way the parents are first told about the problem is extremely influential in fostering acceptance and establishing attitudes, both of the parents to the baby and to professionals involved in the baby's care.

## Finding out about the problem, the parents' views

The greatest period of crisis for all the parents was shortly after the baby was born: not necessarily at birth. The general tension, strain and fatigue of childbirth produced a sense of unreality in many cases: a detached belief that this cannot possibly be happening. Only when the mother and baby were tidied up and settled, often when father or mother found themselves alone for the first time, did the emotional dam burst. Unreality gave way to disbelief and then anger. 'Why *me*, what have I done to deserve this?' Paramount were a sense of failure, of isolation, of being the first ever to suffer this blow: above all, knowledge of an unwelcome and unacceptable departure from the conventional 'happy event'.

If parents have one message to convey to the medical profession, it is this—'please, please *tell* us what has happened and what can be done about it—and as quickly as you can'.

Reports were frequently received where unthinking delivery room staff or uncertain midwives whisked the baby away and left the parents unknowing but fearing the worst. Many parents acknowledged that perhaps the staff wanted to make absolutely sure there was nothing else wrong, rather than raise false hopes—but there was a great deal of insensitivity shown on occasions.

Parents reported that once a doctor or nurse had explained matters then optimism began to grow and most parents felt relief and an ability to come to terms with the facts, quickly and calmly. Parents felt that many nurses were unaware of the procedures for dealing with cleft problems. Indeed a number had never come across a case before, even those in specialist maternity units. Parents felt that this seemed strange in view of the relative frequency of the condition. It was explained to the CLAPA Chairman that turnover in staff, shift working and sheer statistics make this inevitable. Perhaps there is a strong case for training all nursing staff to react in a way that at least makes a difficult situation no worse, whatever the nature of the problem. Parents are in unfamiliar surroundings, in a stressful situation and desperately want someone to make the right noises.

Let some of the 'panel parents' recount their varied first experiences, in their own words:

They put him on my tummy to cuddle. I didn't know whether the midwife had noticed then. We did. I didn't know what it was at first. I just stared up and said 'is that a hare lip?' Straight away the midwife said 'they operate now and you can't tell the difference'. That really didn't help. I just thought of a boy at school and everyone took the mickey out of him. The doctor came in and said he also had a cleft palate. I didn't know what he meant by that, it meant nothing to me.

I was told very gently but in a matter-of-fact way that my daughter was fine but had a cleft lip. She was shown to me whilst I was still being stitched up. I held her and just felt stunned. Nursing staff were extremely reassuring. The (doctor) was very abrupt and rude. On the first morning of her life I asked if I could see the paediatrician because I wanted to know exactly what was going to happen to her. At that time she was breast-feeding beautifully. He told me he had no idea what he was going to do about her. He went on to say he was off on holiday for 4 weeks and would see me on his return. I asked for a little more information and he said, 'Well, if it is bothering you that much, you can always put a plaster over it'. He then left the room. Previous to this conversation I had been very calm, had got over the shock of my daughter's cleft lip but now felt very concerned for her future.

He was born about 11.00 and delivered by my own midwife who handed him to me face down. As she handed me the baby she kept telling me that he had a hare lip and although the words went in, it was not until I looked at my baby that I saw what she had been trying to tell me. I asked if he had a cleft palate as well and she said yes. My husband and I clutched each other and held tightly to this squirming baby with such a strange face and felt a curious mixture of calmness, numbness, horror and sadness. It was not until later that I could cry. (This mother is a doctor.)

## Comment

The views of this group of parents demonstrates that although some parents were told very sensitively about the problem, this unfortunately was not always so. They are not alone in experiencing 'midwives whisked baby away and left the parents unknowing but fearing the worst'. In instances where the survival of the baby is paramount, staff have to concentrate on the physical needs of the baby. This has the unfortunate result that the mother's psychological needs may be neglected. In some instances the preoccupation with the physical needs of the baby may be used to avoid disclosure to the parents. Harada & Pye (1981) describe the position of the midwife caught in this difficult communicative situation. They see disclosure as important in laying the foundations for satisfactory adjustment by the parents, and describe the reactions of midwives as being in 'varying bewildered ways'. The main problem Harada and Pye raise is that the midwife may not tell the parents about their baby without instructions from a doctor. In order to fill in time and avoid the mother's questions 75% of midwives they studied, in this situation, occupied themselves with the physical needs of the baby. They went so far as to keep the baby covered and out of sight. Further verbal avoiding tactics had to be used if the baby had to be taken to the intensive care unit. These research findings raise the problem of who should be allowed to disclose the problem, and how professionals should be prepared for this sensitive and difficult task.

Midwives and doctors themselves experience shock and stress, feeling emotionally vulnerable and ill-prepared for the task of telling the parents. This may make them behave in ways which appear insensitive and detached (Spriestersbach 1973).

The feelings described by this group of parents are well documented. Burden (1978) describes the most frequent reactions as: 'disbelief and denial; grief; isolation and inability to share feelings; need to blame someone or something, possibly leading to guilt; shame and embarrassment; over-compensation possibly leading to over-protection; lowering of self-esteem and uncertainty in handling the baby'.

MacKeith (1973) describes these feelings within a rather different but helpful framework. The framework, together with comments, is shown in Table 7.1.

It is reassuring for parents to know that they

**Table 7.1** Framework of parental responses

| Responses | Result | Comment |
|---|---|---|
| 1. Biological reactions: | a. protection of helplessness<br>b. revulsion at abnormal | a. child does need protection<br>b. normal reaction |
| 2. Feelings of inadequacy: | a. at reproduction<br>b. at rearing | a. strikes at self-respect and may produce depression<br>b. leads to loss of confidence |
| 3. Feelings of bereavement because of loss of normal child; leads to: | a. anger may cause aggressive behaviour<br>b. grief may cause depression<br>c. adjustment may appear to be achieved quickly | a. may be directed at those trying to help<br>b. a common experience<br>c. may not be stable |
| 4. Shock | may lead parents to seek other opinions | |
| 5. Guilt | keep baby away from relatives and friends | MacKeith feels this is less frequent than professionals tend to suggest |
| 6. Embarrassment | may lead to withdrawal | may make parents unable to join support group or respond to help offered |

are not unique in these feelings and parent support groups can be of great value in letting parents see that they are not alone in their experience or in their reaction to it.

Feelings of shock may result in a period of such profound distress and numbness that parents may not be able to grasp even basic information about the condition. This may be to the extent that they may even deny having been told. The mother who said 'she kept telling me' gives support to this (Thomas 1978). It may therefore be necessary for explanations to be given and gone over again, with plenty of time for parents to come back with questions. We are all bad at remembering what the doctor and other 'experts' have said to us. Unfortunately there is also evidence that professionals are inconsistent in what they expect parents* to know; consequently inadequate or inconsistent information may be provided (Walesky-Rainbow & Morris 1978). The practice of providing parents with back-up written information, as described in Chapter 2, is to be recommended.

There is evidence that parents retain negative feelings about the way they have been told many years later. Therefore professionals working with a cleft palate child after disclos- ure has taken place, should try to establish, ideally through another team member, or the records available, how and where parents were told and what their reactions were. Passing on this kind of information will save the parents from continually being asked the same questions. Knowledge about disclosure is particularly important to the speech thera- pist because it is central in the development of parental attitude and therefore will help the therapist to understand parent responses and parent/child interaction in which communi- cation develops. Delay in explaining to parents or delay in showing the baby to the mother can have adverse effects on the mother–baby bonding process (Clifford & Crocker 1971). These points have already been emphasised in Chapter 2.

The report above gives clear evidence of the not surprising lack of understanding parents have about cleft palate, prior to their own baby's birth. The mother who remem- bered a boy being teased at school shows how important it is to establish, as soon as pos- sible, what the parents understand and what their previous experience has taught them. Exploring parents' own understanding may be an almost insurmountable problem where the parents are not fluent English speakers, or when they come from different cultural backgrounds.

In the first parent–professional interface stage, where disclosure takes place, it is clear that the expert model is inappropriate. Indeed it can precipitate long-term resentment, distrust and unrealistic views. Clifford & Crocker (1971) say that often shock is quickly dissipated when parents are first told it will be all right because unlike some other problems treatment, including surgery, can be carried out. Although this positive view of provision is true to an extent, it needs to be presented realistically because, as Clifford and Crocker report, parents react as though the worst is over, which may not be so. Further evidence of this type of reaction is reported in the following section: parents describing how negative feelings 'dissolved once there was understanding of the repair process'.

Parents of children with cleft lip and palate are not alone in reporting dissatisfaction about the insensitive way they were told about their baby's problem. Other parents complain about what they perceive as confusing information and lack of practical guidance on how to cope with the baby on discharge from hospital (Chazan et al 1980, Walker et al 1971).

**Reactions of society, the parents' views**

The parent group commented that it is strange that because of the tremendous advances in surgery the general public have little or no first-hand knowledge of cleft lip and palate in everyday life. By the time the baby is big enough to sit up in its pram and greet the public, the first repair to the lip is usually complete. Prior to that, most parents confessed to tucking baby well in, so that the defect or the straps and wires were less obvious. So parents' initial reactions are mostly confused and based on half-remembered cases from childhood when repair was the exception and unskilled if done at all; parents recalled the 'village idiot' with the hare lip as a deformed

monster or the butt of cruel humour. Hence comments like: 'I recalled how, in the past, cleft lips were perhaps associated with outcasts and misfits.' 'When I looked at my daughter I kept remembering Dumb Ada in the village where I grew up and how cruel, how casually cruel, we kids were to her. Would this be my daughter's fate in a few years time?'

Whenever reassurance was quickly forthcoming, from the nursing or medical staff or from the follow-up teams, then many fears evaporated and parents felt happy to plan ahead.

Telling relatives and friends was often the biggest ordeal of the early days. Embarrassment, failure and guilt were frequently quoted descriptions of how parents felt. It was up to dads to spread the news, which they found extremely difficult. Fathers' initial ignorance of what had happened and what was involved was matched in most cases by family and friends waiting for the good news. One can only guess at the true feelings of grandparents, aunts and uncles and friends. Maybe parents should not be amazed at the ones who said: 'Get it adopted, it will grow up a freak.' Others blamed the mother for taking medicines, for smoking or trying to abort the child. Others were less blatantly heartless but simply turned their mental backs on the problem and frequently refused to have more than minimum contact.

Happily and consistently, the majority of families and close friends rallied round, sympathised, encouraged, said 'it's hardly noticeable' when it was *horribly* noticeable. They brought teddies, bootees and love to the bedside. Their support, then and afterwards, made so much difference. Little brothers or sisters took it in their stride as a rule. They were inquisitive, without sensing that mum or dad might be upset by the event, and once told what would happen, seldom made a fuss about it again. Once again the key to early acceptance was knowledge. If parents found it hard to get information, then those close to them were even more in the dark. Many phoned or asked medical staff on visits. Few were happy with the answers they got. Quick reaction and explanation would help a good deal, otherwise confusion and distress reinforces the problems of the parents and positive acceptance of the situation is delayed.

The following statements are typical of reactions from family and friends;

My husband's widowed mother was hostile and at first refused to see the baby. When she did eventually see her, she said she was very disappointed. It was a reaction I expected and I was not really concerned. Friends after seeing the baby had expected the cleft lip to be far worse than it was. One friend said she was unable to see me for some time as she did not know what to say to me. I felt I wanted to show her to people because then they could see her face was not as bad as they imagined.

The overwhelming reaction was one of great sadness.

Relatives and friends were shocked and didn't really want to visit me in hospital, but after making the effort, all said the lip was not as bad as they had imagined or expected.

The main reaction was shock and fear. We found people were frightened of the baby, i.e. would not feed her, did not hold her as much as a normal child. Children tended to react better than adults.

In general, though, initial shock, disappointment and embarrassment soon dissolved once there was understanding of the repair process; indeed parents and close friends soon got used to it. In fact some parents 'got a bit sick and tired' of well-meaning people, even complete strangers, reassuring them that it would be fine and that 'they' can do wonders these days. One mother said: 'I know they meant well but he wasn't a freak. In my eyes he was perfect already.'

The presence of friends, relatives and caring staff helped most mothers and quite a few fathers through the busy hospital day. But privacy when it finally came was a problem as well as a blessing. Parents found it helped to be alone on occasions, but quite a few mothers and babies were separated after birth and some considered that they were kept in hospital far longer than is current practice.

Mothers fed on imagination in the night. 'I imagined the hole in his face growing to monstrous size.' They cried for themselves, blamed themselves, felt that they had failed to give their husbands 'a good baby'. Above all they cried for the sad and deformed waif they felt they had brought into an intolerant world. Added to these night-thoughts was the sense of being different from the conventional happy mums and bouncing babies in the wards. Mothers often saw two or more 'generations' of mums come and go with babies blatant in their perfection. A lot of the cameraderie of mums in hospital passed them by. They were bruised emotionally by continually having to explain why baby was not with them on the ward and what was wrong. They had to brace themselves when other mothers compared their little darlings. They felt the hesitation and sensed the forced compliment, 'Oh—hasn't he got lovely eyes.'

The little rituals lost their savour: the joy of selecting and writing birth announcements, of buying first clothes. Some mothers fell into a kind of numbness and apathy which lasted beyond the discharge from hospital and added to the misery of post-natal depression. Certainly, all the mothers who talked in the forum came to terms eventually and said that they had been greatly helped in most cases by the support of the NHS after-care services. That help might not always have been consistent or up-to-date on the subject but was well-meant and readily available, with or without request.

Parents whose baby was in a special care unit until proper feeding was assured said that although this caused pangs, there was an unexpected side benefit. They were aware of the obvious contrast on parental visits between the large lump, in rude health as a rule, and other tiny scraps of humanity fighting for life rather than physical perfection. As with the first operation, it gave parents a chance to see how bravely other children cope with massive problems; that put the problem of cleft lip and palate in its rightful place.

## Comment

The points made by the group of parents raise a number of important issues, the majority of them fitting well with the parents' views and feelings already reported in the literature. The following are of note: the practice of not showing the baby with the unrepaired cleft lip is well documented. Spriestersbach (1973) in his study of 175 cleft lip and/or cleft palate children from 0 to 16 years found that 50% of the parents did not want their baby seen before the lip was repaired. Brantley & Clifford (1980) also reported that mothers of cleft palate babies had negative feelings about showing their babies to others. Furthermore, they had a tendency towards negative feelings about child care in general. These views have been taken into account by the surgeons who are attempting to bring the lip repair forward to as early as a few days.

It is evident that a number of different professionals need to consider more carefully the timing and the strategies used in telling parents about the problem, both for parents' own needs and in terms of passing on this information to family and friends. Butt (1977) recommends the use of audio tapes of the consultations; the tapes can then be taken home for further consideration by parents, family and friends. He found this most valuable in conveying information on diagnosis and treatment. This seems an excellent idea and one which could be used by a number of professionals. It is an approach that could be profitably used by speech therapists.

The classic feelings described, including that of mourning, are well documented in the literature; clearly this parent group had the same experiences. Such feelings are probably unavoidable in varying degrees. A supporting partnership type of approach from professionals, and acceptance and support from family and friends, is greatly needed.

It is not easy to anticipate how we ourselves would react to such a condition in our own families; our attitudes are deeply entrenched and developed over time. Attitudes have been shaped by the values and attitudes of those around us in the family context and in the community as a whole, as well as possibly being influenced by attitudinal traces which have been developed over centuries. Today Western culture views some impairments as of major consequence. The same impairments could be of little consequence elsewhere. Furthermore, present day society places very high value on physical attractiveness. This therefore puts great stress on families who have a baby with a facial deformity. It is the parents and family who are in the chief mediating position between the child and society. They are the medium through which societal attitudes are learnt and lead to the child's view of him/herself in society.

The last point in the parent report, that there may be benefits to the baby being in intensive care, is one of concern, because the longer the baby is in intensive care the more the early mother-baby bonding process is at risk. Perhaps ways can be found to protect parents from the pain of visiting time when their babies are compared to seemingly perfect infants.

Hayhow (1987) wonders if parents of babies with various problems could be encouraged to support each other, as they are all vulnerable, although for different reasons. In the short-term period in hospital, especially during a period of intensive care, this could be helpful. However contact with parents with 'normal' babies might reveal that other mothers also experience feelings of inadequacy and fearfulness.

### Feeding, the parents' views

The reported lack of direct experience amongst so many nursing staff on feeding problems, meant that most parents learned by trial and error. It is significant that most of the first contacts made by the new parents of a child with cleft with 'established' CLAPA parents seeking support, were concerned with feeding. Feeding is so central to the care of their baby that some parents will not admit to being a 'failure'. Certainly those that do 'fail' are not going to admit it in public, so the reported experiences all had a happy ending. The road to that ending was often rough and paved with more broken nights than were experienced with 'normal' brothers and sisters. Those who found the defect hardest to bear were the mothers who had hoped to breast-feed their child. One or two managed it with ease or with a struggle; most simply could not overcome the mechanical difficulties and their disappointment is obvious in the comments they made. Each cleft baby seemed different in the way he/she coped with feeding. Sometimes the answer was as simple as a large hole in a conventional teat. Even so, the rule of no naked flames on the ward caused many problems. Many were the undercover episodes with a piece of wire and a box of matches.

Some managed to get hold of special teats or persevered with a cup and spoon. It is disturbing to find how difficult it was for many to get hold of non-standard teats, even in a maternity unit. That is why CLAPA has produced a sample board displaying most teats known to man (and some to vets) that can be shown to parents. It is always a matter of trying different ways until the balance is right and the mother finds the combination of circumstances that gives her child nourishment in the minimum time with the least possible digestive upsets. Wind is definitely a problem. Problems also applied to weaning, and parents believed that far too many health visitors urged a change from liquid to solid when the baby couldn't cope. Then, of course, each operation on the child changes the circumstances. When the palate has been repaired, and functions to close off the nose, suction becomes easier and twin rivulets of Ribena that add so much colour to the early months, no longer appear.

Feeding seems to be a job for the parents alone at the beginning. There were few relatives or friends who felt confident enough to manoeuvre a teat past straps, wires and plastic plates.

Feeding problems tended to restrict parents' social lives, especially whilst night feeds were required. In the following quotations, some of the problems become sharper in focus. They certainly represent a fair cross-section of the members' experiences.

There were feeding problems. I think one reason was that the nurses didn't realise the problems cleft palate babies can have with feeding.

Another difficulty was wind. There were days when he took an hour and a half or 2 hours to take a good feed—even though I never admitted it to the doctor.

Feeding problems in hospital were the cause of the cleft palate being discovered, when she was 3 days old. I had difficulty getting the special teats and feeding still took an hour or more.

He had a plate straight away and that helped a great deal.

I wanted to breast-feed and she couldn't make a proper seal, so it became very painful. I had no help or advice and as it was the first time I had breast-fed a child, I accepted it as normal. I was very frustrated but persevered for 8 months. It became a little easier after the operation.

He never seemed satisfied after a feed. No sooner was one feed over than it was time for the next one.

In hospital, he wouldn't feed and lost weight all the time we were in. As soon as he came home, my mother suggested putting him onto Wysoy which he took to, and although we had some problems he did start to gain weight. He was a very slow feeder and very sick. He would get very tired during feeding, which initially took about 2 hours. There were many feelings of frustration throughout the first 8 weeks. The only advice we had on hand was my mother, who would phone every day.

In general parents received some advice but were often left to work out their own salvation. Special equipment was hard to come by and even then feeding took much longer than normal; the amounts taken at each feed were small and exhaustion and frustration were a major problem for parent and baby alike. Patience and flexibility of approach are the key.

## Comment

During normal feeding a baby's lower lip supports the nipple, while the upper lip closes over the top to form a seal. Pressure is exerted by the tongue thrusting forward to squeeze the nipple between the tongue and the alveolar process. Raising and lowering the tongue creates a negative air pressure within the mouth, allowing fluid to be drawn rhythmically into the mouth. In normal feeding the upper lip plays a fairly passive role, so babies with cleft of lip only do not usually experience a problem. Babies with a palatal cleft experience the greatest feeding difficulty, because in the absence of a properly functioning palate it is difficult to achieve and maintain negative pressure within the mouth. If lip and alveolus are also cleft the problems of negative pressure are complicated further by poor lip movement and the consequent ineffective seal over the nipple. In cases where a cleft of the alveolus (gum ridge) is present, milk can escape into the nose and may cause choking. The use of a feeding plate to occlude gaps in the lip and alveolus may be particularly helpful.

In babies with cleft of palate there are frequently problems of nasal regurgitation, as well as bouts of coughing and vomiting. Breast-feeding is noted to be particularly difficult in those babies where there is cleft of palate and underdevelopment of the mandible. These babies' problems are complicated further by respiratory difficulties; they usually require specialised nursing care in hospital until their feeding and respiratory problems are resolved.

A detailed account of the extent of feeding difficulties in different types of clefting is given in the classic study by Drillien et al (1966). The number of comments made on feeding by this parent group is clear evidence that it is still an area where much more help and specific advice is needed. Ideally, all new parents of a baby with a cleft palate should have immediate help and advice. This might come through experienced professionals, but could also be augmented by experienced parents, perhaps provided through a voluntary organisation. Campbell & Watson (1980) suggest that professional expertise may be from the paediatrician, the nurse or the speech therapist. Some centres have specialist paediatric nurses who provide a home care visiting service, starting as soon as possible after the baby goes home. These nurses can support both parents and health visitors in managing the very stressful problems of feeding. It is understandable that not all nurses and health visitors are experienced in feeding cleft palate babies, but presumably there are some principles related to feeding difficulties in general which could be applied. These may include the size of hole in a teat, consistency of feed and position of baby. Mothers who wish to do so should try breast-feeding, although this should not be continued if unsuccessful. The use of bottle-feeding with an appropriate teat may solve the problems. A long teat with a large hole or cross-slit is often best. In some cases feeding with a teaspoon will have to be resorted to. When the baby has a cleft palate a teat with a flange, which fills the hard palate cleft and acts as a temporary plate, may be successful.

There appears to be a need for an extension of opportunities for nurses working both in the hospital and the community to attend short courses on this topic. It should be possible to build up some expertise in one or two staff who can be called upon either in hospital or the community. Orthodontists may be able to provide special help; they will frequently be involved with the baby in fitting a feeding plate. It is evident that a number of babies described did have a plate fitted.

Feeding is of central importance not only as a life-maintaining activity but also because of its psychological implications. In usual circumstances feeding is a relaxed pleasurable time for both mother and baby. It involves close physical contact which establishes and maintains bonding and is a context in which early communication usually takes place. If feeding is difficult, takes a long time and is stressful, opportunity for early interaction will be lost.

85% of mothers of children with clefts report feeding problems (Spriesterbach 1973). Therefore, this group of parents is not unusual in their level of concern. The high incidence of feeding problems in babies with cleft palate is probably unavoidable because of the physical anomalies. What is of concern is that the group of parents still report considerable lack of satisfactory help. It is much the same as the dissatisfaction expressed by the parents in the Tisza & Gumpertz study over 25 years ago (1962). This situation is unfortunate because with appropriate support and guidance many feeding problems can be solved comparatively quickly, although some babies may experience continued problems.

## Coping with operations, the parents' views

It is not intended to dwell too much upon the attitudes expressed by parents on the operations involved in repair of lip or palate. It goes without saying that the child is not too keen, especially at the 15 to 18 month stage when they can express their concern, vocally and frequently. The operations are presumably less tricky than some and there is no doubt that most of the traumas are common to all infant surgery. Generally, the parents get more distressed than the child in the early days. Seeing their treasure lashed to the bars of the cot in arm splints, seeing the barbed lip guard and sometimes learning that the tongue has been stitched to the side of the mouth, is hard to take. Explanation and reassurance helped a great deal to calm fears and there was soon realisation that children are really much tougher than adults give them credit for.

Many babies seemed to bounce out of the palate operation with amazing speed, demanding cake and cornflakes for tea when they have just woken up from theatre. That does not stop parents from worrying about them and feeling for their discomfort. No operation, however minor, is totally without risk—so parents and children still need support, before, during and after. At least

each operation on a cleft child shows a real advance and this makes it easier for parents to feel less guilty about taking a 'well child' to hospital.

## Comment

For the parents of babies with a cleft lip the repair of the lip is an extremely important landmark, enabling them to show the baby to family and friends more easily. The more severe the facial deformity the more natural it will be for parents to try to shield the baby in a 'protective capsule' (Goffman 1974). With present-day techniques, in most countries it is possible to repair lips extremely early. However, the majority of surgeons still prefer to do this between 3 and 6 months. There will inevitably be a range of ages when it is undertaken according to the views of the surgeon and other factors such as the health of the baby. Repairs to the palate are usually undertaken between 6 and 18 months of age.

The baby being lashed to the bars of the cot as described here sounds drastic. It is simply a way of preventing the baby putting his fingers in his mouth and interfering with the operation after either lip or palate repair. Another method used today is putting the baby's arms into cardboard cylinders to prevent bending at the elbows and touching the mouth. Those babies who need to have their tongue fixed in some way, sometimes by the tongue 'being stitched to the side of the mouth', belong to a small group of babies where their cleft of palate is associated with a very small, posteriorly displaced mandible. The tongue is also small and not well developed, tending to fall back into the pharynx and block the air-way. These babies have a condition known as Pierre Robin syndrome (see outline of syndromes in Chapter 1). Obstruction of the airway by the tongue causes severe respiratory problems which must be helped by preventing the tongue from falling back into the pharynx. This is usually achieved by nursing the baby face downwards on a frame. Other procedures such as attaching the tongue in a forward position either to cheek or lip may occasionally be necessary.

As anxieties mount about forthcoming operations, parents who are at the other side of them may be particularly supportive. Seeing photographs of repaired lips can be helpful at this stage. Simple explanations on the role of the hard and soft palate in feeding and speech will help parents to understand more fully the need for the operation. Parents may feel concerned when in hospital they meet older children undergoing secondary palate repairs. Explanation of the possible reasons for surgery in later life should be provided.

It is easy for parents to appreciate the need for the lip repair, purely for appearance; however, it is much more difficult to grasp the necessity for palate repairs. In cases such as sub-mucous cleft or other velopharyngeal problems it may be particularly difficult for parents to appreciate the necessity. The speech therapist needs to be involved in explaining the functions of the palate to the parents. The study by Clifford & Crocker (1971) showed that immediately after the baby's birth parents are most concerned with: repair of the cleft; birth and general care; spouse's reactions; future adjustment of the child; appearance and survival. It is not until later that parents become concerned about other factors such as speech. The speech therapist needs to judge the parents' readiness to receive explanations about the implications of the cleft palate for speech. The use of simple diagrams to accompany explanations, with leaflets to study at home can be helpful.

In a model of partnership it is perhaps more possible for parents to refuse certain procedures, which may include surgery, considered to be essential by other team members.

### Coping in society: teenage and beyond, parents' views

Most of the panel and correspondents were parents of younger children, who usually form the bulk of CLAPA membership. The organis-ation appears to be largely focussed on initial support. However, a girl in her teens came to the forum and told of distressing experiences, involving over 20 operations with more to come. In a surprisingly dispassionate way she told of people who called her a 'dog' or a 'monster' to her face, who asked for a light in the street, then hurried away when they saw her face. Yet the defect, though obvious, was by no means extreme. Quite patently, we still live in a society where unhelpful attitudes will be encountered.

Another guest speaker to a CLAPA meeting, a woman in her forties, told of how she had overcome severe problems in her youth and young womanhood. She now holds a highly responsible job, yet as a young Cordon Bleu trainee in France was strictly forbidden to face the guests in her hotel. She recalls with gratitude that her grandfather was wealthy enough to pay for private operations. Parents are thankful for the standard and ready avail-ability of care today to smooth their children's passage through life.

So, by the time babies walk into the world, cleft children have the lip in fair repair, a palate that is mostly if not completely closed and quite a bit of speech therapy for those who need it. But they are still not totally like other children. The scar can show, the teeth are growing every which way, or not at all, their facial structure may not be totally symmetrical and speech for some may still be a severe problem. How do they cope? Adequate use of speech and language is of prime importance in social adjustment.

In cases where the child grew through the education system from nursery or infants with the same set of contemporaries, then few problems were reported. School friends tended to accept them, but that does not mean they escaped scot free. Childish bullying tends to be random, whoever the victim. Bully and butt often switch roles and different cliques form. But the child who *is* different naturally suffers more. In compen-sation, parents felt that children seem to have been given stronger personalities, brighter, quicker minds and a degree of in-built toughness that can shrug off a verbal attack with a counter-blast, or a punch on the nose. Sudden unkindness from close friends hurts more than the passing thoughtlessness of a stranger. But often that has little to do with the defect itself. Cleft lip or no, every parent is aware of how the intrusion of a 'new friend' and the desire to score cheap victories can cause a drama. It is necessary to be careful not to ascribe all the pains of growing up to the deformity. Parents also know that children do not tell them half of what happens. They sort it out, shrug it off or bottle it up. It is at worst an exaggeration of the agonies of growing up: the feeling that you are ugly or clumsy, that everyone is looking at you and laughing behind their hands at your big nose or teenage spots or mousy hair. Parents will be aware of this and supportive, but parents felt that the desperate desire they had for their children to be 'normal' must not make them over-react.

The real progress that is apparent at every stage encourages all parents. Surgery, dentistry and speech therapy helped the child take part to the full in most school activities, although star parts in plays eluded most of the infants and juniors. Dental problems were not seen as a major factor for parents in the early years. Many parents of older children remarked on the major change in their child's appearance that followed corrective dentistry: a change that was sometimes compared to the major improvement that lip closure produced. Children often sabotaged the efforts by making it difficult to fit and persevere with the orthodontic appliances, but the more mature they got, the more they could appreciate the changes taking place.

## Comment

The points made by parents on the long-term effects of having a cleft lip and palate are of central importance, because this is in the end what both parents and professionals are concerned about.

Parents held a balanced view about the role of the deformity in the context of the teen-agers' normal reactions. The evidence does seem to be that in the long-term cleft palate individuals generally become well-adjusted adults. The definitive study by Spriesterbach (1973) does, however, give some indications of differences in behaviours during their development. This includes a tendency to choose more solitary activities, have more temper tantrums and generally be less happy than their peers. There is some reported reluctance to talk to people outside the family, to have less confidence and engage in fewer outside school activities than their peers. There are reports of greater passivity, less gregariousness, less maturity and less independence. Peter et al (1975 a & b) in a study of 196 cleft palate individuals found that the cleft palate group had substantially lower incomes than the control group, and showed certain social limitations. It is understandable that as teenagers these youngsters have a high level of concern about their appearance. This may over-ride concerns about other factors such as speech and school progress. Richman (1983) found social introversion to be more related to concerns about appearance than to speech. The team should carefully consider the priority of concerns a child has at any one time.

Parents and teachers will be aware of these children's vulnerability in relation to teasing, especially for those who have poor appearance and/or poor communication. Teachers may indeed be in a position to help to prevent teasing. The report of the teenager is particularly telling. Teachers will be concerned to know that research findings indicate that as a group fewer cleft lip and palate children liked school than their normal peers. All professionals need to keep in mind that we tend to rate individuals with poor appearance as less able than their peers. A study by Clifford & Walster (1973) asked teachers to rate childrens' academic ability on the basis of looking at photographic studies of the children. The results showed that the teachers viewed physically attractive children as more popular, more socially desirable and more intelligent and as therefore more likely to make successful academic progress. We all tend to judge individuals positively if they are physically attractive and negatively if they are not. In a study by Richman (1978) it was found that teachers were inaccurate in their judgement of children with obvious facial disfigurement, underestimating the ability of brighter children and overestimating the ability of less bright children.

Children with physical disfigurement do not perceive themselves as different until 4 or 5 years of age. At the same time they may begin to be aware of differences in their communicative abilities. This stage of growing awareness will be of great consequence in the context of entry to school, a time when children with cleft palate may be especially vulnerable.

## SUMMARY FROM THE PARENT GROUP

Parents felt that their most vulnerable time was immediately following the birth, through the introduction of the baby into the circle of family and friends up to closure of the lip. There is therefore a need throughout this period for rapid explanation that is honest and positive and for shared experience. CLAPA and other parent support groups can satisfy that need for many parents. Parents considered that there are gaps in the experience and competence of medical staff that appear surprising to the layman. The health visitor plays an important role in after-care. Many respondents were full of praise but others felt that appropriate understanding and support was lacking. By the time baby becomes infant, the need for mutual support grows less and most parents have come to terms with the defect and face the remaining stage of treatment with confidence.

Parents considered that cleft lip and palate was not the worst card fate could deal but that did not lessen the desire to get the best for their children. The majority appreciated the care and concern received. The comment that this was the NHS at its very best came from many parents, but not all. Some parents had

not received what they considered to be a high standard of care and support, reporting insensitivity and lack of co-operation and co-ordination between hospital and support staff. Many parents experienced almost total isolation at home.

As a group they asked for continued and wider understanding from all levels and types of provision, stressing that as parents they are anxious to co-operate and participate, in the knowledge that every stage marks an improvement in the quality of life for their children. They appreciated that as a regional group their own experiences may not be universal, nevertheless there is evidence that they reflect the literature on many issues. They felt concern for other parents, because as a group their mutual support had enabled them to express their views, even though these views might sound naive to the professional ear. They felt that there were other parents who were not able to take this opportunity to talk about the problem or even acknowledge its existence in an open way. They believed that their experience was common to all parents whose child is born with an impairment or develops some disability early on. They felt lucky as a group because the methods of remediating the problem became apparent quite quickly. They expressed deep concern for parents with children with what they viewed as more disabling conditions.

## HOW THE SPEECH THERAPIST MAY FOSTER PARENT/PROFESSIONAL PARTNERSHIPS

Because of the nature of a speech therapist's work in dealing with bringing about changes in communicative behaviour there is often the need for frequent and extended client contact. This provides greater opportunity than with some other professionals for building up a sharing relationship with children and their parents. Changes in speech and language cannot be brought about purely by the application of techniques, but require the therapist to work within a personal interactional framework with clients and relatives. These opportunities may place the speech therapist in a unique position, as a member of the professional team, for enhancing the relationship with parents. The chapter has primarily focussed on the parent/medical and 'para-medical' personnel team relationships. However, for the child with a cleft palate there are other people meeting them in their daily life who will be of particular importance. Teachers are of major significance and need to be included in management. For some children, especially those with special needs, others may be involved, for example educational psychologists, main-stream and special needs teachers and teachers of the deaf etc.

The following guidelines are suggested with all team members in mind. However, they have a particular focus on the work role in speech therapy and how the speech therapist may act in fostering team partnership with parents. The speech therapist should:

1. Establish his/her involvement in the team early on in a child's life (see Ch. 2).
2. Provide opportunity, in a less formal clinical setting, for parents to rehearse, or reiterate questions which they may not have felt able to ask, did not think to ask, or did not understand answers to, in some other setting.
3. When necessary take any problems raised by the parents back to team members. Never try to handle areas out of your field of competence.
4. Answer parents' questions honestly but ensure that the answers given tie in with the views of other team members. If in doubt discuss with relevant colleagues first.
5. Take information back from colleagues to the parents. The speech therapist's relative frequency of contact can provide an excellent link in the communication system.
6. Provide ongoing support to parents regarding the relationship between various management procedures, e.g. orthodon-

tics and secondary surgery and the possible influences on speech.
7. Refer to professional colleagues for diagnostic opinions where there is any doubt about progress. Do not continue with intervention for too long when there is uncertainty about the status of the vocal tract.
8. Encourage parents to attend appointments with other medical and educational personnel.
9. Provide careful and simple explanations to parents about the need, aims and techniques of diagnostic procedures, e.g. nasendoscopy. This is more likely to ensure parental agreement.
10. Help parents to gain more understanding of the surgical and remedial processes involved by explanation, discussion and provision of literature. (Many cleft palate units have their own leaflets.)
11. By working with other medical personnel, especially by setting up joint clinics if you work in a specialist unit, or at least being present at 'unilateral' clinical sessions, deepen your own understanding of the various specialists' contributions to management. An understanding of the role of other personnel will help the speech therapist not to make unreasonable requests, and to make appropriate requests in an informed way.
12. Through participation provide opportunities for other members to gain a greater knowledge of speech therapy contributions, thus helping others to reach a deeper understanding of the problems they are dealing with and the speech and language outcomes, e.g. the orthodontists' work with malocclusions and whether treatment is likely to hinder speech or facilitate speech change.
13. Encourage the team to be alert to those conditions which may co-occur but may not be in a direct causal relationship to the communication problems resulting from the cleft palate, for example speech problems, e.g. phonological delay, unrelated to the cleft condition.

14. Provide (a) high level skills to be used in the description and analysis of the presenting speech and language patterns, and (b) information on normal speech and language development processes.

15. General practitioners in speech therapy should try to establish and maintain links with the speech therapist in the cleft palate unit. Additionally they should occasionally attend consultations especially for diagnostic investigations and when decisions are going to be made about the need for further management, e.g. surgery. This is more likely to ensure that all relevant factors are brought to bear and informed management decisions are reached. This use of the speech therapist's time can be supported in cost effectiveness. If management is precisely targeted to a child's needs the period of treatment is likely to be shortened. The classic example would be where a plastic surgeon has recommended that speech therapy should continue for another year, but where the speech therapist working with the child is certain that the status of the velopharyngeal mechanism does not allow further speech progress.

16. Where the general speech therapy practitioner is unable to attend an appointment make sure that a written report is available for the consultation. This helps the speech therapist in the 'cleft palate team' to support the 'home' speech therapist's views. The report should include a review of progress and views about the need for further diagnostic, surgical or medical procedures.

17. The speech therapist can provide a link between medical and educational services through explanation to the nursery, play-group or school about the child's problem and the possible relationship with educational progress. This will be particularly important when children have hearing impairment and/or delayed language.

18. Establish what parents understand about their child's difficulties and how these relate to speech and language.

19. Provide simple explanations, helped by illustrations of the functions of the vocal tract, in particular the velopharyngeal mechanism.

20. Provide simple explanations of normal speech production as a basis for the understanding of speech problems.

21. Provide a positive but realistic view of the possible speech and language outcomes, especially in instances where there are known conditions which will be a handicap to the development of good communication.

22. When a child's speech and language is not developing normally foster a shared understanding of the remedial processes through explanation, discussion and literature provision. Remember to include an explanation of the possible length of involvement and the likely outcomes.

23. Encourage parents to use natural everyday experiences to encourage language development, including opportunities for the child to talk. Encouragement needs to be maintained, especially when a child is not easily intelligible.

24. Enable parents to participate in the process of assessment and evaluation, firstly by being present during any sessions undertaken with the child and by collecting and 'recording' speech and language samples at home. This involvement helps to ensure the recognition of problems present and a greater understanding of their nature. Furthermore it ensures that the speech therapist and other team members have a realistic view of the child's behaviour and attainments outside the clinical setting.

25. Tape-record sessions, so that they can be used as a model for continued work, or if the session has included explanations, these can then be more easily relayed to other family members.

26. Lead parents to an understanding that the development of communication is affected not only by the original condition but by such factors as hearing impairment, psychological and social factors.

27. Where secondary procedures are under-taken, e.g. pharyngoplasties, ensure that the parents have a realistic view about the immediate results in relation to speech changes. Too many parents believe that the operation itself will bring about dramatic speech change. The general clinician should check this out with the speech therapist in the cleft palate team.

28. Explore and try to establish what the best way will be for parents to participate in changing the speech and language. Should it be only through general language stimulus as natural teachers, or would it be appropriate for them to undertake specific speech and language work with agreed goals and methods? The type of involvement will vary according to age and individual needs.

29. Provide clear guidelines to parents through demonstrations, written or audio instruc-tions for tasks they are required to carry out.

30. Provide opportunity for parents to demon-strate how they got on, as well as to bring new ideas to the intervention programme.

31. Help parents to understand the exact stage which a child is at so that they have realistic expectations and do not, for example, over correct.

32. Support parents in reaching an acceptance of the child's limitations where, even after maximum provision, the child is not going to become a normal communicator.

33. Be alert to other problems, for example reaction to appearance, dental problems (broken plates etc.), upper respiratory infection, broken hearing aids. Arrange appointments or help and encourage parents to seek appropriate advice.

34. Continuously review your own remedial programme to consider how it relates to all health and educational provisions for the child. Take into account the parents' and child's views, if old enough, on the relative importance of various aspects of the problem at any given time, and plan your programme, as far as possible, in response to these priorities.

## USEFUL ADDRESSES

Association for All Speech Impaired Children
347 Central Markets
Smithfield
London EC1

The Cleft Lip and Palate Association
c/o The Dental Department
The Hospital for Sick Children
Great Ormond Street
London WC1N 3JH

The College of Speech Therapists
Harold Poster House
6 Lechmere Road
London NW2 5BU

The Cranio-Facial Society
c/o A G Huddart
Consultant Orthodontist
The Corbett Hospital
Stourbridge
West Midlands

King's Fund Publishing Office (for PRDS)
126 Albert Street
London NW1 7NF

National Association for Welfare of Children in Hospital
Argyle House
29–31 Euston Road
London NW1 2SD

National Children's Bureau
8 Wakley Street
London EC1V 7QE

Royal National Institute for the Deaf
105 Gower Street
London WC1 6AH

Voluntary Organisations Communication and Language
336 Brixton Road
London SW9 7AA

# REFERENCES

Brantley H, Clifford E 1979 Maternal and child locus of control and field dependence in cleft palate children. Cleft Palate Journal 16: 183

Burden R L, 1978 An approach to the evaluation of early intervention projects with mothers of severely handicapped children. Child Care, Health and Development 4: 171

Butt H R 1977 A method for better physician-patient communication. Annals of Internal Medicine 86: 478

Campbell M L, Watson A C H 1980 Management of the neonate. In Edwards M, Watson A C H (eds) Advances in the management of cleft palate. Churchill Livingstone, Edinburgh

Chazan M, Laing A F, Shackleton, Bailey M, Jones G 1980 Some of our children. Open Books, London

Clifford D E, Crocker E 1971 Maternal responses: the birth of a normal child as compared to the child with a defect. Cleft Palate Journal 8: 298

Clifford E, Walster T 1973 The effect of physical attractiveness on teacher expectation. Sociology of Education 46: 248

Cunningham C, Davis H 1985 Working with parents. Framework for collaboration. Open University Press, Milton Keynes

Drillien C M, Ingram T T S, Wilkinson E M 1966 The causes and natural history of cleft lip and palate. E & S Livingstone, Edinburgh

Goffman E 1974 Stigma and social identity in Boswell. David M, Wingrove J J (eds). The handicapped person in the community. Tavistock publications in association with the Open University Press, Milton Keynes

Hannon C 1975 Parents and mentally handicapped children. Penguin Books. Harmondsworth

Harada A E, Pye P J 1981 Handicapped babies: How midwives cope. Child Care, Health and Development 7, 4: 211

Hayhow R 1987 Personal communication

Irwin E, Mc Williams B J 1973 Parents working with parents: The cleft palate program. Cleft Palate Journal 10: 360

McDade H L 1981 A parent child interaction model for assessing and remediating language disabilities. British Journal of Disorders of Communication 16, 3: 175

MacKeith R 1973 The feelings and behaviour of parents of handicapped children. Developmental Medicine and Child neurology 15: 524

Peter J P, Chinsky R R, Fisher M J 1975a Sociological aspects of cleft palate adults. III Vocational and economic aspects. Cleft Palate Journal 12: 193

Peter J P, Chinsky R R, Fisher M J 1975b Sociological aspects of cleft palate adults. IV Social integration. Cleft Palate Journal 12: 304

Pugh G 1985 Parents and professionals in partnership. Issues and implications in parent involvement. Partnership Paper 2. National Children's Bureau, London

Richman L 1978 Effect of facial disfigurement on teachers' perceptions of ability of cleft palate children. Cleft Palate Journal 15: 155

Richman L 1983 Self-reported social, speech and facial concerns and personality adjustment of adolescents with cleft lip and palate. Cleft Palate Journal 20: 108

Solnit A S, Stark M J 1961 Mourning the birth of a defective child. Psychoanalytic Study of the Child 16: 523

Spriestersbach D C 1973 Psychological aspects of the 'cleft palate problem', Vol I. University of Iowa Press, Iowa

Stengelhofen J 1984 Curricula for professional education: an investigation into theory and practice in the work of speech therapists. MEd unpublished dissertation, the University of Birmingham

Tisza V B, Gumpertz E 1962 The parents' reaction to the birth and early care of children with cleft palate. Paediatrics 30: 86

Thomas D 1978 The social psychology of childhood disability. Methuen, London

Thomas D 1982 The experience of handicap. Methuen, London

Thompson K 1984 The speech therapist and language disorders. In: Lindsay G (ed) Screening for children with special needs. Croom Helm, London

Tuckett D (ed) 1976 An introduction to medical sociology. Tavistock Publications, London

Walesky-Rainbow P A, Morris H 1978 An assessment of informative-counselling procedures for cleft palate children. Cleft Palate Journal 15: 20

Wolfendale S 1984 A framework for action: professionals and parents as partners. In: Working together: Partnership paper I. National Children's Bureau, London

# Index

Accent affecting intelligibility, 20
Acceptance of cleft palate baby, 140
Accident RTA, 116
Acoustic, *see also* Coupling
  signal trace, 143
Adam's cribs, 126, 129
Adenoid, 6, 7, 11, 23
Adenoidectomy, 6, 7, 11, 121
Adolescent, 28, 166, 169
Adult, 18, 166, 169
  system, 43
  target phones, 50
Affricates 23, 25, 84, 123, 140, 141
  lateralised 123, 139
Afro-Caribbean, 169
Aid, *see also* Appliance PTA, VSA
  hearing, 85
  palate, 112
  tongue, 112
Air flow, 7, 92
  intra-oral, 13, 23, 24, 34, 67
  nasal, 7, 10, 69, 113, 126, 141
  oral, 69, 141
  pressure, 83, 93, 100
Air stream mechanisms, 8
Allergy to acrylic material, 117, 126,
  128
Alveolar
  arch, or ridge, 2, 15, 108, 109, 115
  placement, 126
  processes in feeding, 177
  stops, 146
  tongue grooving, 146, 151
Alveolus, 53, 177
Anaesthetic, 23, 79, 112
Anatomy in VPI, 9
Anemometer, 44, 50, 67, 69, 81, 86,
  98, 107, 118, 129, 131
  Exeter nasal, 69, 107
  training models, 132
Appearance, 2, 27, 180, *see also*
  Facial
  effects on communication, 18, 27,
  183

Appliance
  intra-oral, 36
  orthodontic, 84, 129
  palate, 129
  tongue, 129
Approximants, 48
Articulation, 5, 6, 17, 42
  ability, 41, 42
  compensatory, 44, 80, 99, 137
  complexity, 129
  development, 33
  diffuse, 158
  double, 26, 128
  environments, 161
  glottal, 33, 101
  imprecise, 17
  instrumentation for analysis,
    137–138
  lingual, 137, *see also* Tongue
  manner, 8, 24, 26
  patterns, 94, 136
  placements, 2, 8, 15, 17, 45, 46,
    101, 128, 161
  problems, 27, 234, 236
  secondary, 8, 26
  tense, 102
  velopharyngeal function and
    articulation, 83
  *see also* Therapy
Asian, 169
Assessment
  eighteen months, 39
  hearing, 38
  language, 65, 66
  objective of vocal tract, 67–81
  phonetic, 66
  phonological, 53, 57, 66
  speech, 39, 41, 65, 88, 89, 139
  subjective of speech and vocal
    tract, 65–67
  two years, 39
Association for all speech impaired
  children, 183
Attitudes, 37, 170, 175

  *see also* Social and Family
Attractiveness, 175, 180, 181
Audiologist, 66
Audiometry, 11, 82, 85
Auditory
  attention, 46
  discrimination, 11, 46, 98, 102, 106
  impairment 35, *see also* Hearing
  memory, 129
  perception, 22, 67
  recognition, 102, 106
  skills, 32
  stimulation, 34


Babble, 33, 43, 45, 83, 121
  patterns, 48
  practice, 83
  repertoire, 34
Backing, 33, 42, 50, 53, 57
Barium coating, 72, 73, 74, 88, 91
Behaviour, 180
  parent reaction to, 32
  teenager, 180
Bilingual, 84
Birth, 65, 166, 170, 172, 174, 179,
  181
Biofeedback, 71, 94, 98, 131
Bonding
  mother-baby, 26, 172, 175, 177
Bottles, *see* Feeding
Breast, *see* Feeding
Breath, 25
  direction, 25, 88, 91
  support, 25


Caries, 123
Case history, 39, 65–66
Cervical spine deformities, 74
Chewing, 65
Children
  pre-school, 44

CLAPA Cleft Lip & Palate
    Association, 36, 165, 168–169,
    170, 175, 179, 181, 184
Cleft range and nature, 1–4
    alveolus, 15, 36, 140
    bilateral, 2, 48
    extent, 40
    hard palate, 3, 119
        with soft palate, 121, 123
    lip, 2, 26
        with palate, 108, 138, 140
    primary, 47
    secondary, 47, 81
    severity, 35
    size, 40
    soft palate, 119
    sub-mucous, 4, 65, 67, 101, 102
    unilateral, 53
Cluster reduction, 42, *see also*
    Consonant clusters
Clinic speech therapy
    attendance, 160
    screening, 38
Cognition, 9
College of Speech Therapists, 38,
    384
Communication, 7–9, 27–28
    adequacy, 42
    competence checklist, 40
    development, 7, 9, 35, 39, 169,
        172
    disorders, 7–9
    monitoring of progress, 38
    prerequisites for development, 32
    skills, 37
Congenital velopharyngeal
    incompetence, *see*
    Velopharyngeal incompetence
Consonants
    elicitation, 103–104
    environment, 145
    failure to achieve in isolation, 104
    manner
        affricate, 53
        approximant, 104
        fricative, 50, 53, 93
        nasal, 50, 81, 86, 104, 132
        plosive, 50, 53, 93
    place
        alveolar, 50, 83
        bilabial, 50, 128
        lateral, 109
        palatal, 109
Consonant clusters, 148, 151, 153
    environments, 148, 151, 153
    fricative-lateral, 151
    fricative-stop, 151
    lateral-stop, 151
    nasal-stop sequences, 43, 142
    stop-fricative, 151
    stop-lateral, 151
    stop-stop, 151
Consultations audio-recorded, 175
Consumer model of

parent/professional
    relationship, *see* Models
Contrasts
    oral/nasal, 43
    system, 43
Coupling
    acoustic, 136
    oral/nasal cavities, 22
Correlates
    acoustic, 23
    physiological, 23
Counselling, 35, 37, 53
    parent support, 35, 47
Cranial nerves, 6
Cultural background, 172, 168

Deficits, *see* Hearing, Intelligence,
    Neurological
Dental
    arch, 2
    extractions, 116
    impressions, 116, 126
    management, 4
    plate, 104, *see also* Orthodontic
        PTA, VSA
    problems, 13, 15, 180, 183
Dentist, 104, 112
Dentition, 67
    second, 2
Derbyshire Language Scheme, 41
Development, 35
    checklists, 38
    monitoring, 38
    of cleft palate child, 35
    phonetic, 40, 50, 65, 98
    phonological, 40, 53, 65, 98
    pragmatic, 40
    social, 35
Delivery room, 170
Depression, post-natal, 174
Diagnosis, 66, 92, 182, 183
    by EPG, 141
    differential, 5, 6
    procedures, 3
Dialogue, mother-baby, 34
Diplopia, 92
Doctor, 168, 170
Drooling, 6, 65, 118
Dysarthria, 81, 130, 136
Dysphonia, 7, 65, 89, 136
Dyspraxia, 8, 130, 158
    Nuffield programme, 131

ENT consultant/surgeon, 7, 38, 53,
    92, 94, 121
Ear
    drum scarring, 106
    middle ear effusions, 10, 105
    function, 4
Eating, 65

Edinburgh Articulation Test, 66
Education, 66, 183, 140, 141
Electrodes, 142, 144, 146
Electrolaryngography, 93, 98
Electromyography, 138
Electropalatography, 136–164
    plate, 142, 144
    printout of contacts, 144
Emotional factors affecting
    communication, 9
Endoscope, 76
    flexible, 76, 84
    rigid, 76
Endoscopy, 23, 81, 82, 84, 89, 93
    studies, 67
Environmental factors, 9
Ethnic differences, 168
    minority groups, 169
Eustachian tube, 10, 11
    cushions, 86
    malfunction, 32
Evaluation, *see* Assessment and
    Examination
Examination
    audiological, 65
    ENT, 11, 22, 105
    intra-oral, 40, 42, 68
    otolaryngological, 65
    otological, 38
    palate, 4, 75
Eye
    contact, 28
    lids drooping, 91

Facial
    deformity, 28, 170, 175, 178, 181
    expression, 91
Family, 18–19, 35, 37
    attitudes to the cleft palate baby,
        175
    circumstances, 168
    reactions, 19
    stress, 19
Fatigue as a sign of myasthenia
    gravis, 91
Feedback
    auditory, 11, 98, 112, 118, 128,
        131, 161
    kinaesthetic, 11, 112, 161
    listener, 159
    proprioceptive, 112, 158, 161
    sensory, 2, 118, 128, 131
    tactile, 98, 104, 112, 118, 130, 158
    via EPG, 160
    visual, 98, 104, 118, 128, 131, 160
Feeding, 33, 38, 46, 53, 65, 126, 169,
    175–178
    bottle, 18, 40, 47, 65, 177
    breast, 18, 65, 171, 176
    cup and spoon, 176
    patterns, 38
    plates, 108, 176, 177

Feeding (*cont'd*)
  problems, 4, 18–19, 169, 175–178
  routine, 38
  spoon, 65, 84
  teats, 34, 40, 47, 176, 177
Feelings of parents, 171–176
  anxiety, 167
  apathy, 175
  disappointment, 174
  disbelief, 171
  embarrassment, 171, 173, 174
  failure, 173, 176
  fear, 175
  grief, 171
  guilt, 171, 173
  inadequacy, 175
  negative, 172, 175
  numbness, 174
  shock, 171, 172, 173, 174
  stress, 174
Feelings of professionals, 171
Fistula, 13–15, 23, 25, 40, 57, 70,
    106, 115, 123, 129, 133, 139,
    140, 158
  naso-labial, 15
  tongue tip occlusion, 15
Fluency, 66
Fricatives, 3, 15, 22, 23, 25, 26, 43,
    84, 86, 121, 136, 140, 141, 142,
    146
  alveolar, 3, 41, 42, 53, 123, 151
  bilabial, 17
  labio-dental, 17
  nasal, 108
  palatal, 41, 42, 53
  palato-alveolar, 151
  pharyngeal, 106
  weakened, 25
Fronting, 17, 53

Gag reflex, 87, 130
Generalisation of improved speech,
    104–105
Gesture with vocalisation, 34
Glide, 33
Glottal, 33, 48
  substitutions, 33
Glottis (vocal folds), 8
Goldman Fristoe Test of
    Articulation, 66
Grommets, 11, 40, 105, 106, 121,
    139, 141
Growth
  centres, 10
  cranio-facial, 11
  maxillo-facial, 98, 128
  outcomes, 10
Habits, speech, 159, 163
Head
  injury, 6
  position, 107
Health, 167

Health visitor, 166, 169, 177, 181
Hearing, 10–11, 35, 67, 105, 108, 132
  aids, 184
  assessment/tests, 38, 121
  causes of loss, 10–11
    dynamic, 10
    infective, 10
    mechanical, 10
  conductive loss, 11, 32, 42, 53,
    106
  loss/problems, 4, 24, 26, 27, 39,
    41, 81, 106, 123, 132, 137, 139,
    141, 158, 183
  sensori-neural loss, 11
Home care visiting service, 177
Hospital staff, 33, 181
Hospitalisation, 27, 33, 53, 173
Housing, 167
Hypernasality, 5, 6, 7, 21, 22, 43, 65,
    67, 71, 80, 88, 89, 90, 91, 94,
    98, 99, 114, 115, 118, 123, 130,
    136
Hyponasality, 22, 23, 106

Image
  of baby, 170
  of self, 28, 159, 162
Imitation, 42, 50, 57
  consonants, 42, 104
  games, 46
  lip movement, 45
  non-verbal, 42
  tongue movement, 45
  verbal, 42
  vocal, 45
Incidence
  hearing loss in cleft palate, 10
  palate clefts, 3
  sub-mucous cleft, 4
  voice problems in children, 21
Incisive foramen, 3, 13
Incisors, 15, 142
Infections
  viral, 6
Income, 180
Intelligence, 19–20, 27, 67, 105, 159,
    160, 180
  deficit, 81
  speech and language
    development, 19–20
Intensive care unit, 171, 175
Intra-oral
  air pressure assessment, 142
  examination, 40, 68, 69
  film, 74
  movement, 74
  space, 125
  structures, 42, 67
Intelligibility, 20–21, 66
Interpreter, 37
Intervention strategies, 44
Intonation, 34, 48

Japanese cleft palate cases, 138

King's Fund, 138

Language, 26–27, 98, 179
  comprehension, 40
  delay, 26–27, 44, 105, 182
  development, 20, 32, 34, 40, 106,
    119–120, 182
    comprehension, 57
    pre-linguistic, 40
  expressive, 27, 34, 35, 40, 41
  facilitation, 44
  first, 37, 169
  problems, 26, 39
  receptive, 27, 35, 41
  skills, 66
  structures, 57
LARSP 41
Larynx, 9, 21–22
  pathology, 21
  structures, 22
    supra-laryngeal, 22, 23
Laryngoscope, 64
Lateralisation, 17
Laterals, 146, 151
Linguistic needs, 167
Lip
  cleft, 108
  lower, in feeding, 177
  movement, 9, 42, 91
  placement, 88
  repair, 48, 53, 178
  scars, 42
Liquids (sounds), 25
Loop, wire, 119, 121, 130

Magnetometers, 138
Malocclusion, 15–17, 25, 108
  Class II, 16, 25, 84
  Class III, 16, 17, 25, 108–109, 128,
    159
Management,
  long term needs, 168, 169
  young children, 35
Mandible, 16, 22
  retrusion, 84, 178
  space, 128
  under-development, 177
Marital problems, 168
Mask, face, 132, 141
Maternity unit, 140
Maturation, 109
Maxilla, 15, 16, 17, 22, 25, 108, 128
  hypoplasia, 159
Meaning, 42
Measles encephalitis, 6

Measurement
  air flow, 141
  pressure, 141
Metalinguistic awareness, 160
Midwives, 167, 169, 171
Milestones
  motor, 65
Minimal pairs, 46
Mirror work, 83
Misarticulations, *see* Substitutions
Models, parent/professional
    relationships, 166
  consumer, 166
  expert, 166–167, 173
  transplant, 166, 167, 168
Monitoring self, 119
Mother–child interaction, 32, 34
Motivation, 67, 98, 105, 159
Motor impairment
  movement, 66
  of oral structures, 32
Motor neurone disease, 116
Mouth
  breathing, 23
  degree of opening, 22, 107
  open posture, 23, 107
Mucosa, nasal, 36
Mucus, 24
Multiple sclerosis, 116
Muscles
  levator, 4, 83, 89, 113
  musculus uvuli, 3, 6
  oral, 112
  palato-glossus, 113
  pharynx, 123
  superior constrictor, 89
  synergism, 119, 131
  tensor, palati, 10
  tensor tympani, 10
Musculature lax, oro-facial, 23
Myasthenia gravis, 90, 92

'N' indicator on anemometer, 119,
    128, 132
Nasal, 153
  bilabial, 85
  emission (escape), 9, 14, 23, 25,
    43, 65, 70, 76, 84, 86, 87, 88,
    94, 98, 106, 107, 113, 115, 118,
    128, 130, 134, 136
  grimace, 7, 23, 28, 42, 81, 89
  passages, 22
  polyps, 89
  post-nasal space, 89
  septum, 23, 24
    deflected, 24
  snort, 24
  sounds, 25, 48
  turbulence, 23, 24
Nasalisation of vowels, 9, 132
Nasality phoneme specific, 101, 107
Nasendoscopy, 67, 75–80, 83, 89,

91, 92, 93, 100, 106, 107, 108,
    121, 129
Nasopharyngoscopy, 64, 94
Nasopharynx, 7, 74
National Association for the Welfare
    of Children in Hospital, 184
NHS after care service, 174, 181
Neonates, 118
Neurological
  acquired disorders, 5
  assessment, 89
  disease/deficit, 66, 81, 89
  factors, 9
  maturation, 6
Neurologist, 5, 87, 92
Neuromotor patterns, 32, 41, 43
Neuromuscular
  co-ordination, 67
  disorders, 89, 115
Newborn cleft lip and palate, 38
Nose holding in therapy, 100
Nostril, 23
Nursery, 66, 185
Nurses, 166, 168, 170, *see also* Staff

Obstruents, 14
Obturator, 13, 22, 125, 126
  of fistula, 128–129
  oral hygiene, 116, 130
  to help feeding, 126
  use in unrepaired cleft of hard
    palate, 125, 126
Occlusion, *see* Malocclusion
  relationships, 67
Operations, *see also* Pharyngoplasty
  age, 9, 40, 178
  delayed hard palate repair, 14
  nose, 19
  parents coping with, 177
  primary palate repair, 98
  secondary repairs, 19, 43, 48, 81,
    97, 179, 182
Operative procedures, *see also*
    Pharyngoplasty
  Gillies-Fry, 123
  Pharyngeal flap, 74, 81, 84, 85, 86,
    87, 100
  Schweckendiek, 128
  V–Y procedure, 138, 140
Oral
  communication problems, 20–27
  form discrimination, 17
  sensation and perception, 17–18
Oral surgeon, 24
Oro-pharynx, 112
Oro-sensory
  development, 32
Orthodontics, 10, 19, 47, 53, 67, 84,
    112, 182, *see also* Appliances
  in adolescence, 108
  pre-surgical, 15, 38, 40, 65, 108,
    125, 126

Orthodontist, 24, 36, 42, 88, 104,
    115, 116, 123, 130, 166
Orthopaedic pre-surgical
    intervention, *see*
    Orthodontics
Oscillogram, 142
Otitis media, 32, 40, 53, *see also*
    Hearing loss
Otolaryngologist, *see* ENT

Paediatric, 37
  nurses, 177
Paediatrician, 39, 65, 92, 166, 171
PTA Palatal training appliance,
    88–89, 91, 98, 107, 113,
    115–118, 119, 121, 122, 123,
    125, 129
  design, 129
  fitting, 121
  patient selection, 130
  procedure for use, 115, 116, 129
  results of use, 117
  therapy guidelines, 130, 131
Palate, *see also* Cleft
  artificial for EPG, 144
  elevation, 86
  examination, 68
  exercises, 88
  hard, 3
    notch in hard palate, 4, 83
    length of soft palate, 128, 130
    movement, 91
  repair, *see* Operations
  size and shape, 159, 163
  soft, 81, 89, 115
    palate oscillation, 142
Palato-pharyngeal incompetence,
    *see* Velopharyngeal
    incompetence
Panendoscope, 94
Parents, 19, 98, 180, 181–184, *see
    also* Feelings
  anxiety, 45, 167
  attitudes to professionals, 172
  child relationship, 172
  co-operative working, 44
  disclosure of cleft condition,
    171–173
  expectations, 33, 166
  guidelines on development and
    speech, 39, 183
  participation, 45
  partnership, 165–185, *see also*
    Model
  reactions, effect on language
    development, 33
  support, 35
    groups, 168
  views, 168–185
Patient, stroke, 118, 130
Perception, *see* Oral sensation

Personality characteristics of cleft
　　palate individuals, 19
Pharyngeal *see also* Velopharyngeal
　　disproportion, 99–100
　　flap, *see* Operations
　　wall, 6, 24, 74, 89, 91, 92, 93, 113,
　　　　126
Pharyngoplasty, 80–81, 82, 83, 97,
　　115
　　Honig, 100, 106
　　Hynes, 123
　　Orticochea, 81, 82, 83
　　Riechart, 89
Pharynx, 9, 74, 178
Phonation, 5, 6, 43, 93
　　problems/disorders, 21–22
Phonemic distinction, 26
Phonetic
　　ability, 41
　　analysis, 41, 42, 43, 136
　　context, 22
　　delay, 41
　　development, 32, 34, 98
　　deviance (difficulties/problems),
　　　　2, 6, 13, 24–26, 41, 66, 102,
　　　　111, 113
　　environment, 145
　　inventory, 42, 43, 53, 57
　　place description, 25, 144
　　transcription, 145, 147
Phonology
　　analysis of, 41, 42, 43, 57, 66
　　development, 26, 98, 102
　　disorder
　　　　(difficulties/problems/delay),
　　　　26, 42, 102, 111, 182
　　normal processes, 42
　　mismatch, 57
　　phonotactic positions, 162
Phonetically balanced speech
　　sample, 76
Phonetician, 69
Physical, *see also* Attractiveness
　　limitations, 159
Physiological problems in speech
　　mechanism, 9, 65
Pierre Robin, *see* Syndrome,
Placement, *see* Articulation,
Plastic surgeon, 5, 22, 24, 65, 116,
　　121, 183
Plate, *see also* Appliance, Obturator
　　dental, 47
　　oral hygiene, 116, 126, 128, 130
　　retention 117, 121, 126, 130
　　ridges, 130
　　withdrawal, 132
Play, 40
　　group, 183
　　leaders, 19
　　vocal, 50
Plosives, 3, 15, 23, 25, 48, 132
　　alveolar, 3, 42, 86
　　bilabial, 42, 43, 81
　　glottal, 43, 45

oral, 25
velar, 42
voiced, 24
voiceless, 24, 43
Pneumotach system, 141
Pragmatic development, 33, 34, 40
Pressure
　　transducing system, 141
Problem
　　identification, 35
　　prevention, 35
Professionals, 165, 166, 167
Prognosis, indicators for, 26
Prosody, 20, 137
Prosthetics, 64, *see also*
　　Orthodontics
Protective capsule, 178
Psychological, 119
　　factors affecting communication,
　　　　7, 67, 81, 183
　　overlay, 89
Psychologist, 81, 166, 182
Puberty, 169


Radiographer, 74, 166
Radiographs, 74, 84, 86, 89, 91
　　antero-posterior views, 74
　　basal, 74
　　images, 74
　　intra-oral, 14, 81
　　lateral, 74, 82
　　speech, 67, 72–73, 76, 85, 88, 92
Radiologist, 74
Rate of utterance, 141
Reactions to birth of cleft palate
　　baby, 170–175
　　of society, 169, 173–175
REEL Receptive Expressive Emergent
　　Language Scales, 40
Reflector mirrored surface, 114, 118,
　　128, 131, 133, 134
Regurgitation, 4, 57, 65, 88, 177
Re-inforcement, 18, 27, 98, 131
Relationships
　　dysfunctional, 167
　　parent/child, 33, 167
Repair, *see* Operations
Repetitions, 131
Resonance, 5, 6, 43, 50, 65, 66, 111,
　　*see also* Hypernasality,
　　Hyponasality
　　Cul-de-sac, 22
Respiration
　　difficulties, 32, 183
　　in feeding, 176
　　effort, 14
Retrognathia, 12, 32, 84, 86
RDLS Reynell Developmental
　　Language Scales, 41, 66, 81
Rhythm 141
Royal National Institute for the Deaf,
　　184

Saliva, stringing across PTA
　　contacts, 134
Scan, EMI, 89
Scar tissue, 158
School, 66, 81, 169, 171, 180, 181,
　　183
Schweckendiek technique, *see*
　　Operations
Screening, 170
Sea-Scape, 107
Self, *see* Image
Sensation
　　oral, 17–18
Sensory, 13
　　awareness, 15, 25
　　impairment, 9
　　modalities, 162
Sentence length reduced by
　　articulation ability, 27
Servo-system, 17, 112
Situation avoidance, 19, 28
Sound, *see also* Consonants
　　alveolar, 119
　　nasal, 22
　　production, 8
　　sequencing, 115
　　system, 34
　　voiced/unvoiced, 129
Social
　　adjustment, 18
　　desirability, 180
　　development, 32
　　factors affecting communication,
　　　　18, 67, 81, 183
　　limitations, 180
　　problems, 39, 66
　　reactions to individuals with cleft
　　　　palate, 173, 175, 179
Socio-economic factor, 169
Sociological model of parent
　　professional relationships,
　　*see* Model
Special care unit, 174
Speech
　　accuracy, 131
　　adaptive behaviour, 8
　　adequate use, in individual, 179
　　assimilating new patterns, 131,
　　　　161, 162
　　clinician, *see* Therapist
　　development, 6, 17, 19, 20,
　　　　119–120, 183
　　in VPI, 121
　　facilitation, 44
　　phonetic aspects, 42
　　phonological aspects, 42
　　rate, 131
Speech therapist, 5, 13, 22, 69, 70,
　　76, 116, 166, 169
　　intervention, 19, 35, 44
　　member of a team and role, 35,
　　　　37, 130, 172, 176, 179,
　　　　181–185
　　training, 29

Speech therapy, 67, 83, 84, 85, 86, 87, 89, 92, 123, 139, 179, *see also* Therapy
articulation, 97, 98, 102–106
diagnostic, 43, 99
frequency, 100–102
in malocclusion, 108
intensive, 83, 84, 101, 107
timing, 98–99
with PTA, 118
Staff
delivery room, 170
medical, 169, 173, 181
nursing, 170, 171, 175
Stimulation
auditory, 34
oro-sensory, 34
tactile, 45
visual, 45
Stopping, 25, 42
Stops, 22, 136, 139, 142
alveolar, 141, 148, 153
glottal, 25, 26, 98, 106, 123
velar, 150
Substitutions
glottal, 81, 150
lateral, 138
palatalised, 138
pharyngeal, 81
velar, 85
Sucking, 6, 32, 158
Supra-bulbar palsy, 6
Surgeon, 35, 42, 53, 67, 75, 166, 175
Surgery, 6, 36, 64 *see also* Operations, pharyngoplasty
cosmetic, 10
in infancy, 4, 10
in submucous cleft, 4
secondary palate, 10
Swallow, 65, 72, 74, 99
difficulties, 6, 88, 91, 118
Symbolic representation, 46
Syndromes, 12–13
Apert's, 12
Klippel Feil, 12
Pierre Robin, 12, 32, 84, 123, 124–125, 178
Treacher Collins (mandibulo-facial dysostosis), 10, 13
Van der Woude, 13

Teacher, 19, 104, 166, 167, 180, 181, 182
of the deaf, 182
Team, 116, 168
cleft palate, 5, 80
interdisciplinary co-operation, 112, 166
professional, 35, 36
Tensilon test, 92
Therapy, *see also* Speech therapy
adequacy of, 160

group, 44
guidelines, 128, 160
in unrepaired cleft palate, 128
hypernasality, 106, 132, 134
nasal emission, 106–107, 132
phoneme specific nasality, 106, 108
results with EPG, 162
Thymectomy, 92
Tomography, 93
Tongue, 14, 15, 34, 48, 74, 80, 82, 85, 112
alveolar placement, 128
blade, 25, 26, 113
configuration, 157
co-ordination with velopharyngeal mechanism, 142
contacts with hard palate, 138, 142, 153
fixing in Pierre Robin syndrome, 178
function, 14, 128
grooving, 146, 159
habits, 80
height, 107
movement, 42, 46, 85, 89, 91, 126, 131
patterns, 85
placement, 67, 85, 86, 88, 115, 119
position, 15, 21, 23
retracted, 156
tapping exercises, 102, 106
targets, 113, 126
thrusting, 123
tie, 119
tip, 9, 15, 25, 112, 113, 123, 159
awareness, 161
Tonsillectomy, 7, 123
Treacher Collins, *see* Syndromes
Treatment, *see* Therapy
Tumour, causing VPI, 116

Ultra-sound, 92–93, 138
Unemployment, 167
Upper motor neurone, 6
Uvula, bifid, 3, 4

Veau flaps, *see* Operations
Vegetative
activities, 67
functions, 3
patterns, 118
Velar, 141, 146
Velarisation, 9
Velopharyngeal, 9, 10, 67, 85
assessment of function, 43
aperture, 91
closure, 11, 48, 57, 87, 113, 130, 132

competence, 45
disproportion, 6, 65, 99–100, 114
functions, 89
gap, 89, 106
incompetence (inadequacy, insufficiency), 4, 34, 43, 46, 75, 80, 81, 89, 94, 98, 99, 106, 136, 175
acquired, 88–90
developmental, 5–7, 121, 123
post-adenoidectomy, 6–8
mechanism, 21, 22, 185
orifice, 91
palsy, 87
valve, 70, 74, 75, 93, 94
Velum, 23
friction, 24
functions in speech, 8
Verbal ability, 20
Video-fluoroscopy, 93, 105, 113, 121, 123, 129
Video radiographic report, 78–79
VDU of electropalatography contacts, 141, 161
VSA, Visual speech aid, 98, 107, 113, 133
Vocabulary, 53
Vocal fold nodules, 21
techniques, 94
Vocal tract, 6, 9, 11, 13, 14, 21, 64, 66, 72, 81, 87, 182
anomalies, 67, 115
assessment/examination, 65–96
function, 67
misuse, 7
tension, 22
Vocalisation
early, 33
in unoperated clefts, 33
pre-speech, 33, 34, 42
speech like, 45
Voice, 45, 66
disorders, 21, 93
hoarseness, 21
measurement, 142
pitch changes, 21, 22
therapy, 94
weakness, 21
VOT, voice onset time, 142
Volume, 20
Voluntary organisations, communication and language, 184
Vowels, 9, 22, 23, 48
duration, 142
environments, 145, 153
nasal, 123

Weaning, 176
Western culture, 175
Word
articulation in, 131

Word (*cont'd*)
   single word utterances, 34
   two word utterances, 34, 50
Wysoy feed, 176

Xero-radiography, 93–94
X-ray, 72, 99, 100, 106
   conventional techniques, 138
   computerised, 138

Zona pellucida, 4